Henry White Bellows, James Freeman Clarke

Christianity and Modern Thought

Henry White Bellows, James Freeman Clarke

Christianity and Modern Thought

ISBN/EAN: 9783744660006

Printed in Europe, USA, Canada, Australia, Japan

Cover: Foto ©Lupo / pixelio.de

More available books at **www.hansebooks.com**

CHRISTIANITY

AND

MODERN THOUGHT.

CHRISTIANITY

AND

MODERN THOUGHT.

BOSTON:
AMERICAN UNITARIAN ASSOCIATION.
1873.

Entered according to Act of Congress, in the year 1872, by
THE AMERICAN UNITARIAN ASSOCIATION,
In the Office of the Librarian of Congress at Washington.

CAMBRIDGE:
PRESS OF JOHN WILSON AND SON.

INTRODUCTION.

THE following discourses were delivered in Boston, at Hollis-Street Church, on successive Sunday evenings, and repeated at King's Chapel on Monday afternoons, during the winter of 1871-72, in response to an invitation of the Executive Committee of the AMERICAN UNITARIAN ASSOCIATION, whose purpose was thus declared in the letter of invitation: —

"It is not proposed that the course shall be a merely popular one, to awaken the indifferent and interest them in familiar religious truths; but rather to meet the need of thoughtful people perplexed amid materialistic and sceptical tendencies of the time. Nor is it desired simply to retrace in controversial method the beaten paths of sectarian or theological debate; but rather, in the interest of a free and enlightened Christianity, to present freshly the positive affirmations of faith."

The several discourses were prepared independently, without conference or concerted plan; and for their statements and opinions the responsibility rests solely with their respective authors.

CONTENTS.

	PAGE
INTRODUCTION	v

BREAK BETWEEN MODERN THOUGHT AND ANCIENT FAITH AND WORSHIP 3
By *Henry W. Bellows.*

A TRUE THEOLOGY THE BASIS OF HUMAN PROGRESS . . . 35
By *James Freeman Clarke.*

THE RISE AND DECLINE OF THE ROMISH CHURCH 61
By *Athanase Coquerel, Fils.*

SELFHOOD AND SACRIFICE 101
By *Orville Dewey.*

THE RELATION OF JESUS TO THE PRESENT AGE 129
By *Charles Carroll Everett.*

THE MYTHICAL ELEMENT IN THE NEW TESTAMENT 157
By *Frederic Henry Hedge.*

THE PLACE OF MIND IN NATURE AND INTUITION IN MAN . 179
By *James Martineau.*

THE RELATIONS OF ETHICS AND THEOLOGY 209
By *Andrew P. Peabody.*

CHRISTIANITY: WHAT IT IS NOT, AND WHAT IT IS . . . 231
By *G. Vance Smith.*

THE AIM AND HOPE OF JESUS 273
By *Oliver Stearns.*

THE BREAK BETWEEN MODERN THOUGHT

AND

ANCIENT FAITH AND WORSHIP.

By HENRY W. BELLOWS.

THE BREAK BETWEEN MODERN THOUGHT

AND

ANCIENT FAITH AND WORSHIP.

THERE is evidently a growing disrelish, in an important portion of the people of our time, for professional religion, technical piety, and theological faith. These were always unpopular with youth, and people in the flush of life and spirits; but this was because they called attention to grave and serious things; and youth, as a rule, does not like even the shadow of truth and duty to fall too early or too steadily upon it. Restraint, care, thoughtfulness, it resists as long as it can; and none who recall their own eager love of pleasure and gayety, in the spring-time of life, can find much difficulty in understanding or excusing it. Of course, too, careless, self-indulgent, sensual, and frivolous people have always disliked the gravity, and the faith and customs, of people professing religion, and exhibiting special seriousness. They were a reproach and a painful reminder to them, and must be partially stripped of their reproving sanctity, by ridicule, charges of hypocrisy, and hints of contempt. But, all the while this was going on, the youth and frivolity of previous generations expected the time to come when they must surrender their carelessness, and be converted; and even the worldly and scoffing shook in their secret hearts at the very doctrines and the very piety they caricatured. The old relations of master and pupil describe almost exactly the feeling which youth and levity held toward instituted faith and piety, a generation or two since. The schoolboy, indeed, still thinks himself at liberty to call his master nick-names, to play tricks upon him, and to treat with great levity, among his fellow-pupils, all the teaching and all the rules of the school. But he nevertheless sincerely respects his teacher; believes in him and in his teachings, and expects to derive an indispensable benefit from them, in preparing himself for his coming career. So it was with the religion and piety of our fathers. The people profoundly respected the creed, the elders in piety, and the eminent saints in profession and practice, although the young had their jibes and jests, their resistance to church-going, their laugh at sanctimony; and the majority of people then, as now, were not fond of the restraints of piety, or the exercises of devotion.

But the alienation to which I wish to draw your attention now is something quite different from the natural opposition of the young to serious thoughts; or the gay, to grave matters; or those absorbed in the present, to what belongs to the future; or of those charmed with the use of their lower or more superficial faculties and feelings, to the suggestions and demands of their deeper and nobler nature. That the body should not readily and without a struggle submit to the mind; that thoughtlessness should not easily be turned into thoughtfulness; that youth should not readily consent to wear the moral costume of maturity, or the feelings and habits of riper years; that the active, fresh, curious creature, who has just got this world with its gay colors in his eye, should not be much attracted by spiritual visions, and should find his earthly loves and companions more fascinating than the communion of saints or the sacred intercourse of prayer,—all this, to say the least of it, is very explicable, and belongs to all generations, and hardly discourages the experienced mind, more than the faults and follies of the nursery the wise mother who has successfully carried many older children through them all.

It is quite another kind of antipathy and disrelish which marks our time. It is not confined to youth, nor traceable to levity and thoughtlessness. The Church and its creed on one side, the world and its practical faith on the other, seem now no longer to stand in the relation of revered teachers and dull or reluctant pupils; of seriousness, avoided by levity; of authoritative truth, questioned by bold error; of established and instituted faith, provoking the criticisms of impatience, caprice, ignorance, or folly. An antagonism has arisen between them as of oil and water,— a separation which is neither due to period of life, nor stage of intelligence, nor even to worth of character; which does not separate youth from maturity, the thoughtless from the thinking, the bad from the good, but divides the creeds, observances, and professions of Christians, from a large body of people who insist that after a certain fashion they are Christians too, and yet will have little or nothing to do with professions of faith, or pious pretensions, or religious ways of feeling, talking, or acting.

Clearly, it would not do any longer to say that the worth and virtue and influence of society, in this country, could be estimated by the number of communicants in the churches, by the degree of credit still given to any of the long-believed theological dogmas, deemed in the last generation the sheet-anchors of the State. We all know hundreds of people, who could sign no creed, and give no theological account of their faith, whom we do not count as necessarily less worthy in the sight of God or man than many who have no difficulty in saying the whole Athanasian Creed. Nay, there are some millions of people in this country, not the least intelligent or useful citizens in all cases, who never enter a church-door. A generation or two back, you would safely have pronounced all these absentees to be worldly, careless people, infidels, atheists, scoffers. Do you expect to find them so now? Some, of course, but not the majority. Indeed, you would find a great many of these people supporting churches, to which their families go, and not themselves; or to which others go, for whom they are glad to provide the opportunity. They would tell you, if they could discriminate their own thoughts, something like this: "Public worship and church organizations, and creeds and catechisms, and sermons and ceremonies, and public prayers and praises, are doubtless very good things, and very useful up to a certain stage of intelligence, and for a certain kind of character. But we have discovered that the real truth and the real virtue of what people have been misnaming religion is a much larger, freer, and more interesting thing than churches, creeds, ministers, and saints seem to think it. Here is this present life, full of occupations and earnest struggles and great instructions. Here is this planet, not a thousandth part known, and yet intensely provoking to intelligent curiosity; and science is now every day taking a fresh and an ever bolder look into it; and we want our Sundays to follow these things up. That is our idea of worship. Then, again, the greatest philosophers are now writing out their freest, finest thoughts about our nature; and, if we go to church, we are likely to find some fanatical and narrow-minded minister warning us against reading or heeding what these great men say; and it is a thousand times fresher and grander and more credible than what he says himself! Why, the very newspapers, the earnest and well-edited ones, contain more instruction, more warning, more to interest the thoughtful mind, than the best sermons; and why should a thinking man, who needs to keep up with the times, and means to have his own thoughts free, go where duty or custom makes it common to frown upon inquiry, doubt, and speculation, — to shut out knowledge and testimony, and stamp a man with a special type of thinking or professing?"

For there are, you observe, — in justice to these thoughts, — these two instructors to choose between in our generation. Here is the Church, with its ecclesiastical usages and its pious exhortations; its Sunday school for the children; its devotional meeting in the week, and its Sunday teaching and worship, — all acknowledged as good for those that like them, and are willing to accept what people thought or believed was true a hundred or five hundred years ago; and here is the modern press, with the wonderful profusion of earnest and able books, cheap and attractive, and treating boldly all subjects of immediate and of permanent interest; and here are the reviews, quarterly and monthly, that now compress into themselves and popularize all that these books contain, and furnish critical notices of them; and then, again, here are the newspapers, wonderful in variety and ability, that hint at, suggest, and bring home all the new and fresh thoughts of the time. And the marvel is, that most of these books, reviews, papers, are in the interest of, and seem inspired by, something larger, freer, fresher, truer, than what the churches and the creeds are urging. Thus church religion and general culture do not play any longer into each other's hands. If you believe what the men of science, the philosophers, the poets and critics, believe, you cannot believe, except in a very general way, in what the creeds and churches commonly profess. Accordingly, the professors in college, the physicians, the teachers, the scientists, the reformers, the politicians, the newspaper men, the reviewers, the authors, are seldom professing Christians, or even churchgoers; and if they do go to church from motives of interest or example, they are free enough to confess in private that they do not much believe what they hear.

Assuming that this is a tolerably correct account — although doubtless exaggerated for pictorial effect — of the existing state of things among the reading and thinking class of this country, what is the real significance of it? Is it as new as it seems? Is it as threatening to the cause of religious faith as it seems? Reduced to its most general terms, is it any thing more or other than this? The faith and worship of this generation, and the experience and culture of a portion of this generation, have temporarily fallen out; and, as in all similar quarrels, there is, for the time, helpless misunderstanding, mutual jealousy and misrepresentation. The faith and piety of the time pronounce the culture, the science, the progressive philanthropy, the politics, the higher education and advanced literature, to be godless and Christless; and the culture of the age retaliates, perhaps, with still greater sincerity, in pronouncing the faith and worship of the time to be superstitious, antiquated, sentimental, and specially fitted only to people willing to be led by priests and hireling ministers.

Now, if this were a quarrel between experience and inexperience, between good and bad, between truth and falsehood, it would be easy to take sides. But faith and knowledge have both equal rights in humanity. People who are sincerely in love with knowledge and science and philosophy are not thereby made enemies of God or man; certainly are not to be discouraged and abused for their devotion to practical and scientific truth, their search for facts, their interest in the works of the Creator, even if they are not possessed of what the church properly calls faith and piety. And, on the other hand, however shocked established faith and piety may naturally be by the handling which religion and its creeds and worship receive from modern inquisitors, ought the deeper believers to be seriously alarmed for the safety of its root or its healing leaves, on account of the shaking which the tree of life is now receiving? However slow science and culture may often show themselves to be in recognizing the fact, can any reasonable and impartial mind, acquainted with history or human nature, believe that faith itself is an inconstant or perishable factor in our nature? prayer a childish impulse, which clear-seeing manhood must put away? the conscience, not the representative of a holiness enthroned over the moral universe, but an artificial organ, which social convenience has developed, much like the overgrown liver in the Strasburg goose? In short, who that considers the part that faith and worship have played in the history of the race, can doubt their essential and permanent place in human fortunes? The question of *some* religion, of *some* worship, for the people, does not seem debatable. The only alternative among nations has been a religion in which mystery, awe, and fear prevailed, clothing themselves in dread and bloody sacrifices, or else a religion in which more knowledge, more reason, more love, embodied themselves in a simpler and gentler ritual. The nations have had only a choice — not always a wholly voluntary one — between terrific superstitions and more or less reasonable religions. Christianity has prevailed in civilized nations, since Constantine, by accommodating its theological dogmas and external ritual to the needs of successive eras; beginning with coarser and more heathenish symbols, and running itself clearer and more clear, as the mind and taste and experience of the race have developed "sweetness and light." But does this make Christianity only a human growth, and so predict a coming decay, which many seem to think has already begun? On the contrary, the decisive fact about Christianity is, that, while its intellectual history is changing, its early records are in form fixed and permanent, and that its real progress has been uniformly a return towards its original simplicity. Other faiths develop. It is *we* who develop under Christianity, and are slowly changed unto the original likeness of Christ. Christ's statements, Christ's character, Christ's words, do not become antiquated. We are not called upon to explain away, as superstitions of the time, any of the *certain* words he said, or thoughts he had, or commandments he left. True, there are critical embarrassments about the record, and room enough to question how it was made up; and we cannot always trust the reporters of that age, or our own. But when we get, as we certainly do get in hundreds of cases, at Christ's own words; or when we really see — as by a hundred vistas, through all the *débris* and rubbish of the age, we may see — the true person and bearing and spirit of Jesus, we behold, we recognize, we know, a Being who, transferred to this age, and placed in the centre of the choicest circle of saints and sages whom culture and science and wisdom could collect, would bear just the same exalted relation of superiority to them that he did to the fishermen and publicans and kings and high-priests and noble women and learned rabbis of his own day. We should not hesitate, any more than they did, to call him Master and Lord; to say, "To whom else shall we go? Thou hast the words of eternal life."

Those, then, who fear that true culture, that science or philosophy boldly pushed, that learning and logic impartially applied, — whether in studying God's method in creation, or his method in revelation, — can injure permanently faith and piety, or endanger Christianity, as a whole, must either think the religious wants of man very shallow or very artificial, or the providence of God very easily baffled, and the harmony of his word and works very badly matched. If there be in nature or in man, in earth or in our dust, in chemistry, astronomy, anthropology; in geology, the language of dead eras; or in language, the geology of buried races, any thing that disproves the existence and providence of a living God, the holiness and goodness and trustworthiness of his character; the moral and religious nature of man, his accountableness, his immortality; the divine beauty and sinless superiority of Jesus Christ, and the essential truth of his religion, — by all means let us know it! Why should we allow ourselves to be beguiled by fables and false hopes and make-believes? But the faith of religious experience, the confidence of those who know and love and have become spiritually intimate with the gospel of Jesus Christ, is usually such that they would sooner mistrust their senses than their souls. They have found a moral and spiritual guidance, a food and medicine in their Christian faith, which enables them calmly to say to criticism, to science, to culture, "We do not hold our faith, or practise our worship, by your leave, or at your mercy." Faith leans first on the spiritual nature of man, and not on demonstrable science. It would not be faith, if it were only a sharper sight. It is insight, not sight. It springs from its own root, not primarily from the intellect. As we love our wives and children with something besides the judgment, or the logical faculty, so we love God with the heart, and not with the understanding. We stand erect, with open eyes, when we are seeking truth; we fall on our knees with closed eyelids, when we are seeking God! Religion is not the rule of three, but the golden rule; it is not the major and minor premises and copula of logic, but the sacred instinct of the soul, which Jesus Christ has satisfied, and guided, and owned, and directed, in an inestimable way.

But when faith and worship have taken this true and independent tone, let them not join the foolish bigots, who think that because faith rests on other foundations than science, therefore it owes nothing to science and culture, and can wholly separate its fortunes and future from them. True, *faith* and *culture*, religion and science, in spite of their general and permanent agreement and connection, when they cannot get on honestly together, had better for the time separate; for they embarrass each other, and it is in their insulation that they sometimes ripen and prepare in separate crucible elements that are ultimately to blend in a finer compound than either ever knew before. Thus faith, driving science and culture out of her cell, and closing the doors on fact and observation, wrapt in devotion, has sometimes caught visions of God through her purely spiritual atmosphere, which sages in their laboratories have never seen. The great religious inspirations have not come from scholars, but from seers; from men of soul, not men of sense. "How knoweth this man letters, having never learned?" said his contemporaries of Christ. Well, he knew no letters, but he had what letters never teach, — divine wisdom! He knew God, that end of knowledge; he knew man, that last of philosophy. Faith therefore often recruits itself in a temporary divorce from science, just as Romanism profitably drives her priests into periodical retreats for prayer and exclusive meditations on God and Christ. It is beautiful to study even those humble and uninstructed Christian sects, whose simple and implicit faith is protected, yes, and exalted, by their providential indifference to science or unacquaintance with speculative difficulties. It is not their ignorance that kindles their devotion, but it is faith's vitality, which in certain exceptional natures and times beams and glows most purely, fed only on its own sacred substance. When you have reached the inner kernel of a true Moravian, or even a true Catholic heart, and found a solid core of faith, unsupported by any other evidence than that which the Scripture described in the words, "Faith is the substance of things hoped for, the evidence of things not seen," you have gone far towards fathoming the holiest secret in our nature, the well of living water. And, on the other hand, how much better, both for faith and science, that science should, at a time like this, go without religious ends into physical or metaphysical pursuits, investigate, inquire, test, question, in absolute independence of theological or spiritual results. It is only when thus free and bold and uncommitted that her testimony is worth any thing. Think of Newton, meditating and exploring the solar system, in the simple love of truth, without let or hindrance from ecclesiastical intermeddlers, and compare him with Galileo, lifting his telescope under the malediction of the priesthood of Rome.

No: let science be as free as light, as brave as sunbeams, as honest as photography! Encourage her to chronicle her conclusions with fearless and unreproached fidelity. She will doubtless make many things which have been long associated with religion look foolish and incredible. But it is only so religion can shed some husks, and get rid of some embarrassments. It is, in short, only just such assaults and criticisms from science and experience that ever induces religion to strain out the flies from her honey; to dissociate what is accidental in faith from what is essential and permanent. And, when science and culture have gathered in the full harvest of this wonderful season of discovery and speculation, we may expect to find faith stripped of many garments, now worshipped, which ignorance and fear put upon her for protection and defence; but really strengthened in substance, by the free movements allowed her lungs, and the dropping of the useless load upon her back. Then, too, science and philosophy will again resume their places at the feet of the master-principle in our nature, until again driven away, by new disagreements, to return again by the discovery of a finer harmony.

Self-culture will never supersede worship, more than golden lamps burning fragrant oils will ever supersede the sun; more than digging and hoeing and planting will supersede sunshine and rain from heaven. Self-culture? Yes: by all means, and in any amount, but not as an end. When people look to ornamental gardening for the crops that are to feed the famine-smitten world, and not to the pastures and prairies, as they lie in the light of the common sun, they will look to self-culture for the characters, the hearts, the souls that glorify God and lift and bless the world. "Thou shalt love the Lord thy God with all thy heart, and thy neighbor as thyself." That is the irrepealable law of growth. "Seek first the kingdom of God and his righteousness, and all other things shall be added unto you." Worship, faith, duty, devotion to God, Christ, humanity, to justice, freedom, truth, — these, and not self-culture, have lifted the race and the world. Learn, acquire, cultivate, improve, develop yourselves, by art, music, reading, languages, study, science, experience, but do it all in seeking to know and love and serve God and man. Seek to know Christ, and you will learn more, indirectly, than though you sought all knowledge without this thirst. Seek to know God, and you shall find all science and culture healthful, sacred, harmonious, satisfying, and devout.

The break between modern thought and ancient creeds and worship, thus considered, though serious, and worth the utmost pains to heal, by all arts that do not conceal or salve over, without curing the wound, is not permanently discouraging to earnest and well-considered Christian faith. Nor are all the signs of the times one way. For — after all that has been said about the restless and dissatisfied condition of the critical and conscious thought of the time, and the scepticism of the learned, or the speculative class, or of the new thinkers born of the physical progress of the age, and the decay of worship in the literary and artistic, the editorial and poetical circles — it remains to be said, that, leaving this important and valuable body of people aside, — not badly employed, and not without personal warrant for their doubts and withdrawal from positive institutions, — there remains a mighty majority, on whom the Christian religion and historical faith and the external church have a vigorous and unyielding hold; whose practical instincts and grand common-sense and hereditary experience anchor them safely in positive faith, while the scepticism raves without and blows itself clear, and passes over. Christianity first addressed itself to common people, not to avoid criticism, but to secure the attention of the moral affections and the spiritual powers, instead of the meaner understanding. It has lived on the heart and conscience and needs and yearnings of the masses, from and to whom practical wisdom and fixed institutions and simple faith always come and always return. Common sense is not the sense that is common, but the sense that is *in* common. And popular faith is not the faith of private ignorance massed, but of that wisdom which alone enables ignorant people to find a basis for feelings and actions that all feel to be beyond and above their private ignorance or self-will. The common people were the first to hear Christ gladly: they will be the last to hear any who deny him.

It is easy to exaggerate the decline of modern faith, and to misread the tendencies of the time on which we have been dwelling. Thus, paradox though it seem, it were just as true to say that more people are deliberately interested in Christian faith and worship to-day than at any previous era in the history of our religion, as to asseverate that more people doubt and regret it than ever before. Both statements are true; and they are reconciled only by the fact that it is only in this century that the claims of faith and worship have been popularly debated, or that the people were expected or allowed to have any independent opinion about them. The general soil of our humanity is for the first time surveyed and sown; and it is found that, with more *wheat* than ever, there are also more *tares*. With more intelligent and convinced worshippers, there are more wilful or logical neglecters of worship; with more genuine believers, more sceptics; with more religious activity, more worldliness. Without an army in the field, there will be no deserters; without a common currency of genuine coin, no counterfeits; without a formidable body of affirmers, few deniers.

The positive institutions of Christianity decline in one form, to spring into new life in other and better forms. Doubtless, fourfold more money is expended to-day upon temples of worship than in what have been falsely called the ages of faith, — rather the ages of acquiescence. Religion does not decline as a costly interest of humanity, with the progress of doubt, freedom, intelligence, science, and economic development. It is a permanent and eternal want of man, and is always present, either as a vast, overshadowing superstition, or as a more or less intelligent faith Nowhere has it a stronger hold on society than in free America, which false prophets, with their faces to the past, muttered was about to become its grave. This busy, delving, utilitarian country, without a past, denied the influence of ruins and the memory of mythic founders, a land without mystery or poetry, — how could so tender and venerable a sentiment as reverence live in its garish day? how so sweet a nymph as Piety kneel in its muddy marts of trade, or chant her prayers in its monotonous wilderness, ringing with the woodman's axe or the screeching saw? But now delegates of all the great religious bodies in the Old World are visiting America, for religious instruction and inspiration. Nowhere, it is confessed, is there to be found a people so generally interested in religion, ready to make so great sacrifices for it, or so deeply convinced that its principles and inspirations are at the root of all national prosperity. Nowhere do churches and chapels spring up with such rapidity, and in such numbers; nowhere is the ministry as well supported, or its ministers as influential members of society; nowhere do plain men of business and intelligence, I do not say of science and philosophy, participate so freely in religious worship. And since all political compulsion has been taken off from the support of religion, and it has been made purely voluntary, its interests have received even more care. There is little doubt that the decline of religious establishments, the decay of priestly authority, the complete withdrawal of governmental patronage, the discrediting of the principle of irrational fear, the dispersion of false dogmas, the clearing up of superstition, the growth of toleration and charity, instead of weakening true faith or lessening public worship, will greatly increase and strengthen both. For it is not man's ignorance, weakness, and fears, that lead him most certainly to Christian worship and faith. There is a worship and a faith of blindness and dread; but they have no tendency to develop a moral and spiritual sense of the character of God, or the character becoming man, or to survive the spread of general intelligence and mental courage. If thought, if courage of mind, if inquiry and investigation, if experience and learning and comprehensive grasp, if light and sound reason, and acquaintance with human nature, tended to abolish a living God from the heart and faith of man, to disprove the essential truths of Christianity, or to make life and the human soul less sacred, aspiring, and religious, the world would be on its rapid way to atheism. But I maintain that science itself, philosophy and free inquiry, however divorced from religious institutions and dogmas, were never so humble, reverential, and Christian as since they partly emancipated themselves from theological or ecclesiastical censure and suspicion. For ages science knelt to religion as she went to her crucible or laboratory, like the sexton passing the altar in a Catholic cathedral, and with as little thought or feeling as he, simply to avert censure, while she pursued inquiries she knew would banish the superstition she pretended to honor. Faith and knowledge were at opposite poles; religious truth and scientific truth, finally and permanently amenable to different standards. How dishonoring to religion was this distrust of light and knowledge! how faithless in God, this faith in him which could not bear investigation! how compromising to Christianity, the sort of trust which refuses as blasphemous the application of all the tests and proofs which are required in the certification of every other important conviction! Religious faith rests on the spiritual nature; but its basis is not less real for being undemonstrable, like the axioms of mathematics. That is not real faith which dares not investigate the grounds of its own being. It is irreverent to God, to affirm that he does not allow us to try his ways; to demand proofs of his existence and righteous government; to ask for the credentials of his alleged messengers; to doubt until we are rationally convinced. If the artificial feeling that faith is opposed to reason; religious truth to universal truth; that belief in unseen things is less rational or less capable of verification than the radical beliefs of the senses, — if these prejudices were sound, or not the reverse of true, the world would be on its inevitable way to universal infidelity and godless materialism. But is that the tendency of things? Is it that religion is growing *less* mystic? or only science more so? Have not real and affecting mysteries been very much transferred for the time from theology to philosophy, from the priest to the professor? I doubt very much whether men of science are not more truly on their knees than men of superstition, in our days. Never did such candor, such confessions of baffled insight, such a sense of inscrutable wisdom and power, such a feeling of awe and dependence, seem to prevail in science as now, when so many theologians are raising the eyebrow, and seeking to alarm the world at what they call the atheism of the most truth-loving, earnest, and noble men. I would sooner have the scepticism — reverent and honest and fearless — of these solemn and awed inquisitors in the inner shrines of nature, than the faith of self-bandaged priests, who are thinking to light the way to heaven with candles on the mid-day altar, or to keep faith in God alive only by processions in vestments of purple and gold

Nor has Christianity any thing permanently to fear from the disposition which now so largely prevails, to separate it from its accidents, its accretions, and its misrepresentations. The days have not long gone by when men were counted as entitled to little respect, if they did not wear side-swords and bag-wigs. You recollect how our Benjamin Franklin surprised, shocked, and then delighted all Europe, by appearing at the court of France in plain citizen's clothes? Religion, too, has had her court-dress, and her sounding court-titles, and official robes, and circuitous ceremonies. The world has felt horror-stricken whenever any brave and more believing spirit has ventured to ask the meaning of one of these theological tags and titles. But how much less wholesome is living water, if drunk out of a leaf, or the palm of one's hand, than if presented on a salver, in a curiously jewelled flagon, by a priest in livery? How much has theological ingenuity of statement and systematic divinity, which it takes the study of a life to understand, added to the power of the simplicity of Christ as he unfolds himself in the Sermon on the Mount? Yet, if any one has dared to be as simple as Christ himself was in his own faith, he has been said to deny the Lord that bought him. It has been called infidelity, to think Christ meant only just what he said, and was understood to say, in his simple parables. You must believe something not less incredible and abstruse than the church Trinity; something not less contrary to natural justice and common sense than the church vicarious atonement; something not less cruel and vindictive than the eternal misery of all who through ignorance, birth, or accident, or even perversity and pride, do not hear of, or do not accept, the blood of Christ as their only hope of God's mercy and forgiveness, or you are no Christian. Now I hold these dogmas themselves to be unchristian in origin and influence, although held by many excellent Christian men. I believe that they are the main obstacles with many honest, brave, and enlightened men in our day, to their interest in public worship; and that millions repudiate the Church, and Christianity, which is a different thing, simply because they suppose her to be responsible for these barnacles upon the sacred ship. It would be just as reasonable to hold the Hudson River responsible for the filth the sewers of the city empty into it; or to hold the sun answerable for the changes in its beams, caused by the colored glass in church-windows.

Christianity, the Christianity of Christ, is simple, rational, intelligible, independent of, yet in perfect harmony, — if it be often an unknown harmony, — with philosophy, ethics, science; true, because from God, the God of nature as well as grace; true, because the transcript of self-evident and self-proving principles; true, because guaranteed by our nature; true, because of universal application, unimpeached by time or experience. It affirms the being and authority of a righteous, holy, and all-loving God, whom man can serve and love and worship because he is made in his image; can know, by studying himself; and to whom man is directly related by reason, conscience, and affections. It affirms divine science and worship to consist in obedience to God's laws, written on man's heart, and for ever urged by God's Spirit. It affirms the present and persistent penalty, the inevitable consequences, of all moral and spiritual wrong-doing and disobedience; the present and future blessedness of well-doing and holiness. It sets forth Jesus Christ as the Son of God and Son of Man, — appellations that, deeply considered, really mean the same thing,— the direct messenger, representative, and plenipotentiary of God,— his perfect moral image. It insists upon men's putting themselves to school to Christ, honoring, loving, and following him; forming themselves into classes,— another name for churches,— and by prayer, meditation, and study of his life, informing their minds and hearts, and shaping their wills in his likeness, which is the ideal of humanity. Its clear object is to dignify and ennoble man, by presenting God as his father; to show him what his nature is capable of, by exhibiting Christ in the loveliness, sanctity, and power of his awful yet winning beauty; to make him ashamed of his own sins, and afraid of sin, by arousing moral sensibility in his heart; safely to fence in his path by beautiful and sacred customs,— the tender, simple rites of baptism and communion; the duty of daily prayer, the use of the Scriptures, and respect for the Lord's Day.

Here is a Christianity without dogmatic entanglement; plain, direct, earnest, simple, defensible, intelligible to a child, yet deep enough to exhaust a life's study. For it is the simplicities of religion that are the permanent and glorious mysteries that never tire. They draw our childhood's wonder, our manly reverence, and age's unquenched curiosity and awe. Do we ever tire of the stars, or the horizon, or the blue sky, or the dawn, or the sunset, or running water, or natural gems? Do we ever tire of the thought of a holy, all-wise, all-good Spirit of spirits, our God and our Father, or of hearing of the reverence and trust, the obedience and the love, due to him? Do we ever tire of Jesus Christ, considered as the sinless image, within human limitations, of God's love and truth and mercy and purity? Do we ever tire of hearing the wondrous story of his obedient, disinterested, and exalted life and sacrifice? or of the call to follow his graces and copy his perfections into our own hearts and lives? Are we ever weary of hearing of the blessed hope of immortality, with the comfortable expectation of throwing off the burden of our flesh, and winging our way in spiritual freedom nearer to God and the light of our Master's face? Who can exhaust, who can add to, the real force and attraction and fulness of those truths and promises? Truly received, they grow with every day's contemplation and use; they fill the soul with an increasing awe and joy; they prove only less common-place as they are more nearly approached, more copious as they are more drawn upon, and more sacred as they are more familiar.

It is the common, simple, universal truths that are the great, inexhaustible, powerful, and never-wearying truths. But doubtless it requires courage, personal conviction, and self-watchfulness, to maintain personal piety or religious institutions under free and enlightened conditions, when they are just beginning. When sacramental mysteries are exploded, when the official sanctity of the ministry is disowned, when the technical and dogmatic conditions of acceptance with God are abandoned, when every man's right of private judgment is confessed, when common sense is invited into the inner court of faith, when every man is confessed to be a king and a priest in that temple of God which he finds in his own body and soul, when real, genuine goodness is owned as the equivalent of religion, then it is evident that the support of religious institutions, of public worship, of the church and the ordinances, must appeal to something besides the ignorance, the fears, the superstitions, the traditions of the Christian world. They must fall back on the practical convictions men entertain of their intrinsic importance. They must commend themselves to the sober, plain, and rational judgment of men of courage, reflection, and observation. They fall into the same category with a government based not on the divine right of kings, or the usages of past generations, the artificial distinctions of ranks and classes, owing fealty each to that which is socially above itself, but resting on the consent of the governed, and deriving its authority and its support from the sense of its usefulness and necessity. We have not yet achieved fully, in this country, the passage of the people over from the Old World status of *subjects* to the New World status of *citizens*. We are in the midst of the glorious struggle for a State, a national government, which rests securely on the love and service of hearts that have created it, and maintain and defend it on purely rational and intelligible grounds. It is so new, so advanced, so sublime an undertaking, that we often falter and faint, as if man were not good enough, nor reasonable enough, to be entitled to such a government. We often doubt if we can bear the dilution which the public virtue and good sense in our native community suffers from the flood of ignorance and political superstition coming with emigrants from other and coarser states of society and civil organizations. We are not half alive to the glory and grandeur of the experiment of free political institutions, and do not press with the zeal we ought the general education, the political training, the moral discipline, which can alone save the State, when it has no foundation but the good-will, the respect, and the practical valuation of the people. But is the State or the nation ever so truly divine as when it is owned as the voice of God, calling all the people to maintain equal justice, to recognize universal interests, to embody Christian ethics in public law? And despite our local mortifications and occasional misgivings, what nation is now so strong and firm, what government so confident and so promising, as our own? What but freedom, fidelity to rational principles and ideal justice, give it this strength? What is it, on the other hand, but traditions that represent the ignorance and accidents and injustice of former ages, — what is it but authority usurped and then consecrated, social superstitions hardened into political creeds, — that is now proving the weakness and peril of European nationalities, and imperial or monarchical governments? Knowledge, science, literature, progress, truth, liberty, become sooner or later the enemies of all governments, and all social institutions, not founded in abstract justice and equal rights. Yet how fearful the transition! Who can contemplate the downfall of the French empire, and then look at the architects of the new republic, working in the crude material of a priest-ridden or unschooled populace, without dismay? Yet the process is inevitable. Democratic ideas are abroad: they are in the air. They corrode all the base metal they touch; and thrones and titles, and legalized classes, and exceptional prerogatives, are predestined to a rapid disintegration. How blessed the nation that has transferred its political homage from traditions to principles; from men or families, to rights and duties; from a compromise with ancient inequality and wrong, to an affirmation of universal justice and right! Yet never had a people so grave and so constant and so serious duties as we have. And there is nothing in our principles or government that *must* save our country, in spite of the failure of political virtue, intelligence, and devotion, in our private citizens. God has buried many republics, because the people were unworthy of them. Their failure was no disproof of the principle involved, but only an evidence that the people fell wholly below their privileges and ideas. America may add another to this list of failures, but can do nothing to discredit the truth and glory and final triumph of the democratic idea. I do not believe we shall fail; on the contrary, I have an increasing faith in the sense and virtue and ability of the people of this country. But the success of American political institutions depends very much on the success of the Christian and religious institutions that match them, and are alone adapted to them. We cannot long guarantee religious institutions, in a country of free schools, public lyceums, unlicensed newspapers, unimpeded inquiry, and absolute religious equality, if they do not rest on grounds of reason and experience and sober truth. Mere authority, mere ecclesiasticism, mere sacred usages, mere mystery, or mere dogmatism, will not long protect the creeds and formularies of the church. They are undergoing a species of dry-rot, like to that which the rafters of my own church lately suffered from the confinement and unventilated bondage in iron boxes in which their ends had been placed for greater security. They wanted air and light, and more confidence in their inherent soundness; and, if they had been permitted it, they would have lasted a hundred years. It is precisely so with the Christian religion, boxed up in creeds. It grows musty, worm-eaten, and finally loses its life and hold. A certain timid and constitutionally religious portion of the community will cherish any creed or usage which is time-honored; and the less robust and decisive minds of the time will rally about what is established and venerable, however out of date, incredible, or irrational. But it is what is going on in the independent and free mind of the common people, that should have our most serious regard. What is the faith of the fairly educated young men and women who are now springing up in America? Certainly, it is not, in the more gifted or the most thoughtful part of it, in sympathy with any form of sacramental or dogmatic Christianity. It is not Trinitarian; it is not biblical; it is not technical. It is hardly Christian! It is bold, independent, inquisitive, questioning every thing, and resolute in its rights of opinion. It is alienated from church and worship to a great degree. It suspects the importance of religious institutions, and reads and thinks and worships in books of poetry and philosophy. A timid heart might easily grow alarmed at the symptoms, and think that irreligion, and decay of worship and fellowship in the Christian Church, were upon us. But sad and discouraging as the present symptoms are to many, I see more to hope than fear in these tendencies. They are a rebuke to formal and technical theology, — to mere ecclesiasticism, to outworn ways. They are bringing a violent assault upon the hard crust of a stifling belief, of which the world must get rid before the gospel of Christ can emerge, and be received in its primitive simplicity. It is the only way in which faith is ever purified, — by doubt and denial. The gospel requires a new statement. It must come out of its ecclesiastical bulwarks. It must abandon its claim to any other kind of judgment than all other truth claims and allows. It must place itself by the side of science, experience, and philosophy, and defy their tests. It must invite the most rigid investigation. It must claim its foundations in eternal truth. It must prove its efficiency, not with the weak, but the strong; not with the ignorant, but the learned; not with the bound, but the free. And then it will recover its lost ground, and take a stronger and diviner position than it ever had before.

This is the work that Liberal Christianity has in hand; a difficult, slow, and often discouraging work, but one that is intensely patriotic, intensely practical, intensely necessary. That which was the mere fortress into which the enlightened and free-minded people of Massachusetts fled for refuge from ecclesiastical tyranny, a half-century ago, — Unitarianism, — is now become a recognized crusade for religious liberty for the American people. The liberty is coming fast enough, and surely enough; but will the worship, will the Christian seriousness, will the fellowship of faith, will the piety that gives aromatic beauty as well as health to the soul, come with it? If it were not to come, liberty would be only license and secularity and worldliness. Every firm, well-ordered, earnest and religious congregation of the liberal faith; exhibiting stableness, order, solemnity; doing religious work among the poor, and cultivating piety in its own youth; making sacrifices to its own ideas, and upholding its own worship, — is an argument of the most solid kind, an example of contagious power, an encouragement of priceless cheer, for those who think that Christian liberty necessarily leads to license and decay of worship; or that Christ is less revered and loved and trusted when he is accepted in the derived and dependent character he claimed, — the only tenable, rational, possible character in which a century hence he can be received by any unsuperstitious persons. We have a sacred privilege, a glorious opportunity. We only need to show ourselves warm, earnest, united, attached to worship, fruitful in piety, devoted to good works, zealous for God's glory and man's redemption, sincere, humble, yet rational and free followers of Christ, to win an immense victory for the gospel in this inquiring and doubting age. I have no great *immediate* hopes, but hopes beyond expression in the gracious development of another generation. I bate not a jot of heart or hope that absolute liberty in religion will favor the growth of piety, as much as political freedom has favored the growth of order and peace and prosperity. Oh! not a thousandth part the power of Christian truth and righteousness has yet been shown in the world. The love of God, the love of man, have only begun their glorious mission. Christ yet waits for his true throne. Humanity is just come of age, and, with some wild festivity, is claiming its heritage. But God is with and over it; and Jesus Christ is its inspirer and guide. He will not lose his headship. He will be more followed when less worshipped; more truly loved when less idolized; more triumphant when more clearly understood! Darkness, wrath, threats, enchantments, sacraments, prostrations, humiliations of reason, emotional transports, affectations of belief, belief for its own sake, — none of these things are truly favorable to Christ's kingdom or the glory of his gospel. God is light, and in him is no darkness at all. Christ is the Sun of righteousness. When reason, conscience, affection, rule the world; when love and justice, and mild and tender views of life and humanity, of

God and Christ, displace the cruel terrors and superstitions that have survived the social and political meliorations of the age, we shall begin to see that love is the fulfilling of the law, and liberty of thought the greatest friend of worship, the finest result of Christ's coming, and the throne from which he commands the whole human heart and history.

A TRUE THEOLOGY THE BASIS

OF

HUMAN PROGRESS.

By JAMES FREEMAN CLARKE.

2*

A TRUE THEOLOGY THE BASIS

OF

HUMAN PROGRESS.

THE subject of the present lecture is "A True Theology the Basis of Human Progress." And, in order to strike the key-note, and to indicate the object at which I aim, I will read four or five passages from the New Testament, which describe such a Theology in its spirit and root.

The Apostle Paul says:[1] "I count not myself to have apprehended: but this one thing I do, forgetting those things which are behind, and reaching forth unto those things which are before, I press toward the mark." So he declares himself a Progressive Christian.

Again he says:[2] "We know in part, and we prophesy [or teach] in part. But when that which is perfect is come, then that which is in part shall be done away." So he declares that all intellectual statements, his own included, are relative and provisional. He is here speaking, doubtless, not of rational insights, but of the insight when elaborated by the intellect into a statement; not of intuitional knowledge, but that which comes from reflection. In regard to all such propositions, he would accept the

[1] Phil. iii. 13.   [2] 1 Cor. xiii. 9, 10.

modern doctrine of the Relativity of Knowledge; thus cutting up by the roots the poisonous weed of Bigotry.

Again: "Brethren, be not children in understanding: howbeit, in malice be ye children, but in understanding be men."[1] He thus requires and authorizes a manly, intelligent Theology.

Again: "Who also hath made us able ministers of the New Testament; not of the letter, but of the spirit: for the letter killeth, but the spirit giveth life."[2] He here rejects the Theology of the letter, including the doctrine of Literal Inspiration.

Again: "God hath not given us the spirit of fear; but of power, and of love, and of a sound mind."[3]

My Thesis to-night is not a truism; my argument is not unnecessary or uncalled for. Nothing is more common than to undervalue the importance of Theology; to regard it as having no bearing on life, no influence on human progress, no causative power in regard to civilization. Mr. Buckle, one of the most recent English philosophical historians, contends that Theology is the result rather than the cause of national character; that it is merely symptomatic of the condition of a people. If they are in a good condition, they have a good Theology; if in a bad condition, a bad one. He even thinks it owing to a mistaken zeal that Christians try to propagate their religion, because he believes that savages cannot become Christians. Civilization, Mr. Buckle supposes, depends greatly upon soil, upon climate, upon food, upon the trade-winds; but not much upon religious ideas. He says that, in England, "theological interests have long ceased to be supreme." "The time for these things has passed by."

[1] 1 Cor. xiv. 20. [2] 2 Cor. iii. 6. [3] 2 Tim. i. 7.

And this is also a very common opinion among ourselves. Many reformers have a notion that we have done with Theology, that we can do without it. Some men of science tell us that Theology has nothing to do with the advance of civilization, but that this comes from discovery in the sphere of physical science. But I believe that the one thing which retards the progress of reform is a false philosophy concerning God and man, a false view of God's ideas concerning this world; and that the one thing needful for Human Progress is a deeper, higher, broader view of God and his ways. And I hope to be able to show some grounds for this opinion.

The religious instinct in man is universal. Some individuals and some races possess more of it, and others less; but the history of mankind shows that religion in some form is one of the most indestructible elements of human nature. But whether this religious instinct shall appear as faith or as fanaticism; whether it shall be a blind enthusiasm or an intelligent conviction; whether it shall be a tormenting superstition or a consoling peace; whether it shall lead to cruel persecutions or to heavenly benevolence; all this, and more, depends on Theology. Religion is a blind instinct: the ideas of God, man, duty, destiny, which determine its development, constitute Theology.

The same law holds concerning Conscience and Ethics. Conscience in the form of a moral instinct is universal in man. In every human breast there is a conviction that something is right and something wrong; but what that right and wrong is depends on Ethics. In every language of man, there are words which imply ought and ought not, duty, responsibility, merit, and guilt. But what men believe they ought to do, or ought not to do, — that depends on the education of their conscience; that is, on their Ethics.

Conscience, like religion, is man's strength, and his weakness. Conscience makes cowards of us all; but it is the strong-siding champion which makes heroes of us all. Savages are cruel, pirates are cruel; but they cannot be as cruel as a good man, with a misguided conscience. The most savage heart has some touch of human kindness left in it, which nothing can quite conquer, — nothing but conscience. That can make man as hard as Alpine rock, as cold as Greenland ice. The torture-rooms and *autos da fe* of the Inquisition surpass the cruelties of the North American Indian. The cruelties of instinct are faint compared with the cruelties of conscience. Now what guides conscience to good or to evil? Theology, in the form of Ethics, is the guide of conscience. For, as soon as man believes in a God, he believes in the authority of his God to direct and control his actions. Whatever his God tells him to do must be right for him to do. Therefore religion in its inward form is either a debasing and tormenting superstition or a glad faith, according to the Theology with which it is associated. And religion, in its outward form, is either an impure and cruel despotism or an elevating morality, according to the idea of God and Duty which guide it; that is, according to its associated Theology.

Some persons, like Lucretius, seeing the evils of Superstition, Bigotry, and Fanaticism, and perceiving that these have their root in religion, have endeavored to uproot religion itself. But could this be effected, which is impossible, it would be like wishing to get rid of the atmosphere, because it is sometimes subject to tempests, and sometimes infected with malaria. Religion is the atmosphere of the soul, necessary to the healthful action of its life, to be purified, but not renounced.

Every one has a Theology, who has even a vague idea of a God; and every one has this who has an idea of something higher and better than himself, higher and better than any of his fellow-men. The Atheist therefore may have a God, though he does not call him so. For God is not a word, not a sound: he is the Infinite Reality which we see, more or less dimly, more or less truly, rising above us, and above all our race. The nature of this ideal determines for each of us what we believe to be right or wrong; and so it is that our Theology rules our conscience, and that our conscience determines with more or less supremacy the tendency and stress of our life.

No one can look at the History of the Human Race without seeing what an immense influence religion has had in human affairs. Every race or nation which has left its mark on Human Progress has itself been under the commanding control of some great religion. The ancient civilization of India was penetrated to the core by the institutions of Brahmanism; the grand development of Egyptian knowledge was guided by its priesthood; the culture of China has been the meek disciple of Confucius for two thousand years. Whenever any nation emerges out of darkness into light, — Assyria, Persia, Greece, or Rome, — it comes guided and inspired by some mighty religion. The testimony of History is that religion is the most potent of all the powers which move and govern human action.

Such is the story of the past. How is it at the present time? Has mankind outgrown the influence of religion to-day? Has the spread of knowledge, the advance of science, the development of literature, art, culture, weakened its power in Christendom? Never was there so much of time, thought, effort, wealth, consecrated to the Christian Church as there is now. Both branches of that Church, the Catholic and Protestant, are probably stronger to-day than they ever were before. Some few persons can live apart from religious institutions; but mankind cannot dispense with religion, and they need it organized into a Church or Churches.

Religion is a great power, and will remain so. But what is to determine the character of this power? It may impede progress or advance it; it may encourage thought or repress it; it may diffuse knowledge or limit it; it may make men free or hold them as slaves; it may be a generous, manly, free, and moral religion or a narrow, bigoted, intolerant, fanatical, sectarian, persecuting superstition. It has been both: it is both to-day. What is to decide which it shall be? I answer, its Theology; the views it holds concerning God, man, duty, immortality, the way and the means of salvation. Religion is an immense power: how that power is to be directed depends on Theology.

Proceeding then with my theme, I shall endeavor to show how false ideas in Theology tend to check the progress of humanity, and afterward how true ideas always carry mankind onward along an ascending path of improvement.

But first let me say that my criticism is of ideas, not of sects, churches, nor individuals. By a true Theology, I mean neither a Unitarian nor a Trinitarian Theology, neither a Catholic nor a Protestant Theology. I do not mean Calvinism nor Arminianism. I have nothing to say concerning these distinctions, however important they may be; and I, for one, consider them important. But I refer to a distinction more important still, lying back of these distinctions, lying beneath them; a difference not of opinions so much as of ideas and spirit.

By a true Theology, I mean a manly Theology, as opposed to a childish one; a free, as opposed to a servile one; a generous, as opposed to a selfish one; a reasonable and intelligent Theology, as opposed to a superstitious one.

By a true Theology, I mean one which regards God as a father, and man as a brother; which looks upon this life as a preparation for a higher; which believes that God gives us freedom, inspires our reason, and is the author of whatever is generous, self-forgetting, and noble. I find something of this Theology in all sects and churches; from the Roman Catholic at one extreme, to the Universalists and Unitarians, the Spiritualists and Come-outers, at the other. And the opposite, the false Theology, dishonorable to God, degrading to man, I find in all sects, and accompanying all creeds. And if I shall show, as truth compels me to show, that certain parties and persons are specially exposed to danger in one or another direction, I wish distinctly to state my belief that sincere and earnest men continually rise above the contagion of their position, and live untainted in an atmosphere which may have in it some special tendency to disease.

One false idea in Theology, which opposes human progress, is that Pantheistic view of the Deity, which loses sight of his personality, and conceives of him as a blind, infinite force, pervading all Nature, and carrying on the universe, but without intelligence and without love.

I know indeed that many views have been accused of being Pantheism which are not. I do not believe in a God outside of the universe. I believe that he is one "in whom we live, and move, and have our being," one "from whom, and through whom, and to whom are all things,"— a perpetual Creator, immanent in his world. But this view is quite consistent with a belief in his personal being, in his intelligent, conscious, loving purpose. Without such a belief, hope dies out of the heart; and without hope mankind loses the energy which creates progress. Unless we have an intelligent Friend who governs the universe, it will seem to be moving blindly on toward no divine end; and this thought eats out the courage of the soul.

In some poetical natures, as in the case of Shelley, this Pantheism takes the form of faith in a spirit of beauty, or love, or intellectual power, pervading all things. In more prosaic minds it becomes a belief in law, divorced from love. It turns the universe into a machine, worked by forces whose mutual action unfolds and carries on the magnificent Cosmos. Often this view comes, by way of a reaction, against an excessive Personality of Will. When the Christian Church speaks of the Deity as an Infinite Power outside of the world, who creates it and carries it on according to some contrivance, of which his own glory is the end, it is perhaps natural that men should go to the other extreme and omit person, will, and design from their conception of Deity. But thus they encounter other and opposite dangers.

A gospel of mere law is no sufficient gospel. It teaches prudence, but omits Providence. This utilitarian doctrine, which reduces every thing to law,— which makes the Deity only a Great Order, not a Father or

Friend, — would soon put a stop to the deepest spring of human progress. It takes faith and hope out of our life, and substitutes observation, calculation, and prudence. But the case of Ecclesiastes and of Faust teaches us what comes from knowledge emptied of faith. He who increases such knowledge increases sorrow. The unknown, wonderful Father; the divine, mysterious Infinite; the great supernatural power and beauty above Nature, and above all, — these alone make life tolerable. Without this brooding sense of a Divine love, of a Heaven beyond this world, of a Providence guiding human affairs, men would not long have the heart to study, because all things would seem to be going nowhere. Without such a Heavenly Friend to trust, such an immortal progress to hope, all things would seem to revolve in a circle. Not to believe in something more than a God of Law is to be without God in the world, is to be without hope. And hope is the spring of all progress, intellectual progress as well as all other. Intellect, divorced from faith, at last kills intellect itself, by destroying its inner motive. It ends in a doctrine of despair, which cries continually, "What is the use?" and finds no answer. And so the soul dies the only death the soul can die, — the death of torpor and inaction.

Another false idea in Theology, which interferes with human progress, is that of ecclesiastical authority in matters of faith and practice. When the Church comes between the soul and God, and seeks to be its master rather than its servant, it takes from it that direct responsibility to God, which is one of the strongest motives for human effort. I know that this has always been done from a sincere desire, at any rate in the beginning, to save men from apparent dangers. The Church has assumed authority, in order to do good with it. It has commanded men not to think for themselves, lest they should err. But God has meant that we should be liable to error, in order that we should learn to avoid it by increased strength. Therefore Christ said, "Be not called Rabbi; be not called Masters, and call no man father on earth." His church, and his apostles, and he himself are here, not to be masters of the soul, but to be its servants.

The Roman Catholic Church is a great organization, which has gradually grown up, during a thousand years, the object of which has been to educate men in Christian faith and Christian conduct. It has sincerely endeavored to do this. But, unfortunately, it took a narrow view of Christian education; supposing that it meant instruction and guidance, restraint and tuition, but not development. It has magnified its own authority, in order to produce docility in its pupils. It has not allowed them freedom of inquiry nor liberty of conscience. It has not said, like Paul, "Be not children in understanding;" on the contrary, it has preferred to keep them children, so as to guide them more easily. It has not said, with Paul, "Stand fast in the liberty wherewith Christ has made you free;" for it has come to hate the very name of liberty. What is the result? You may read it to-day in France, where, as Mr. Coquerel tells us, that Church has prevented the steady development of free institutions. It has always supported the principle of authority in the State, as the natural ally of authority in the Church. There are so few republicans in France to-day, because the people have been educated by the Church to blind submission. The priests are not to blame, the people are not: it is the Roman Catholic Theology which is to blame. That Theology teaches that the soul is saved by the reception of external sacraments, and not by vital, independent convictions of truth.[1]

Or, if you wish another illustration of the same thing, look at New York. Why have republican institutions in New York almost proved a failure? Why were a few robbers able to take possession of the city, and plunder the citizens? Because they could control the votes of the Irish Catholics in a mass; because this vast body of voters were unable to vote independently, or to understand the first duties of a free citizen. And why was this? Not because the Irish are naturally less intelligent than the New-Englanders, the English, the Germans. No; but the Roman Catholic Church, which has had the supreme control over the Irish conscience and intellect for a thousand years, has chosen to leave them uneducated. Of course, the Roman Church, if it had pleased to do so, might long ago have made the Irish nation as enlightened as any in Europe. But its Theology taught that education might lead them into heresy, and so take them out of the true Church, and that ignorance *in* the Church was infinitely better than any amount of intellectual and moral

[1] The proof of this may be amply found in the famous Encyclical and Syllabus of Pius IX., Dec. 8th, 1864. In the Syllabus he denounces as errors such propositions as the following: —

That "every man is free to embrace and profess that religion which guided by the light of reason, he holds to be true." § 15.

That "one may well hope, at least, for the eternal salvation of those who are in no wise in the true Church of Christ." § 17.

That " the Church has no power to employ force." § 24.

That "men emigrating to Catholic countries should be permitted the public exercise of their own several forms of worship." § 78.

That "the Roman Pontiff can and ought to reconcile and harmonize himself with progress, with liberalism, and with modern civilization." § 80

culture *out* of it. The fatal principle of Roman Catholic Theology — "Out of the true Church there is no salvation" — has been the ruin of the Irish nation for hundreds of years, and has very nearly entailed ruin on our own.

Do you wonder that the priests oppose our school system? If I were a Roman Catholic priest, I should oppose it too. Should I run the risk of poisoning my child's body by accepting as a gift a little better food than that I am able to buy? And shall I risk the vastly greater evil of poisoning its soul, by allowing it to be tainted with heretical books and teachers in free schools? The Roman Catholic priest is consistent: it is the Theology which teaches salvation by sacraments that is to blame. It is a theology which naturally, logically, necessarily, stands opposed to human progress. It says, "In order to be children in malice, you must also be children in understanding."

When the Protestant Reformation came, it brought with it a manly Theology. It put the Bible into all men's hands, and asserted for each the right of private judgment and liberty of conscience. Therefore the Reformation was the cause of a great forward movement in human affairs. It awakened the intellect of mankind. Science, literature, invention, — all were stimulated by it. It ran well, but something hindered. Its reverence for the Bible was its life; but, unfortunately, it soon fell into a worship of *the letter*. It taught a doctrine of verbal inspiration. It forgot the great saying of Paul, "not of the letter, but the spirit; for the letter killeth." Very soon that saying was fulfilled. Reverence for the letter of the Bible killed the spirit of the Bible. That spirit is as free as air. It teaches no creed, it demands no blind acceptance of any dogma. It declares that where the spirit of the Lord is, there is liberty. But the letter-theology has opposed nearly all the discoveries of science and all moral reforms with the words of the Bible. It has set Genesis against geology, and the book of Psalms against the Copernican system. Because the Book of Genesis says the heavens and earth were made in six days, the letter-theology declared that the fossil shells were made in the rocks just as they are, or were dropped by pilgrims returning from the Holy Land. Because the book of Psalms said that "God hath established the earth so that it shall not be moved for ever," the letter-theology denied its daily and yearly revolution. Because Noah said, "Cursed be Canaan," the letter-theology defended the slavery of the negro. Because Noah also said, "He who sheddeth man's blood, by man shall his blood be shed," the letter-theology has defended capital punishment as a religious duty. Because the Jews were commanded to rest on the seventh day, the letter-theology forbids the Boston Public Library to be open on the first. Becoming ever more timid and more narrow, it clings to the letter of the common English translation, and the received text. It even shrinks from alterations which would give us the true letter of the Bible, instead of the false one.

Some years ago the American Bible Society appointed a committee of the most learned scholars, from all Orthodox denominations, to correct the text and the translation of our common English Bible, so as to make it conform to the true Hebrew and Greek text. They were not to make a new translation, but merely to correct palpable, undoubted errors in the old one. They did their work;

printed their corrected Bible; laid it before the Bible Society, — *and that Society refused to adopt it.* They had not the slightest doubt of its superior correctness; but they feared to make any change, lest others might be called for, and lest the faith of the community might be disturbed in the integrity of the Scriptures. Jesus had promised them the Holy Spirit to lead them into all truth, to take of his truth and show it to them; but they did not believe him. They preferred to anchor themselves to the words chosen by King James's translators than to be led by the Spirit into any new truth. So it is that "the letter killeth." It stands in the way of progress. It keeps us from trusting in that ever-present Spirit which is ready to inspire us all to-day, as it inspired prophets and apostles of old. It is an evidence not of faith, but of unbelief.

Thus, this false idea in Theology, that inspiration rests in the letter of a book or a creed rather than in its spirit, is seen to be opposed to human progress.

And then there is another Theology which is opposed to human progress. It is the Theology of Fear. It speaks of hell rather than of heaven; it seeks to terrify rather than to encourage; it drives men by dread of danger rather than leads them by hope. Its ruling idea is of stern, implacable justice; its God is a God of vengeance, who cannot pardon unless the full penalty of sin has been borne by some victim; whose mercy ceases at death; who can only forgive sin during our short human life, not after we have passed into the other world. To assuage his anger, or appease his justice, there must be devised some scheme of salvation, or plan of redemption. He cannot forgive of pure, free grace, and out of his boundless love.

Now those who hold such a Theology as this will apply its spirit in human affairs. It will go into penal legislation, into the treatment of criminals. It will make punishment the chief idea, not reformation. Jesus taught a boundless compassion, an infinite tenderness toward the sinful, the weak, the forlorn people of the world. He taught that the strong are to bear the burdens of the weak, the righteous to help the wicked, and that we are to overcome evil with good. When this principle is applied in human affairs, the great plague spots of society will disappear: intemperance, licentiousness, pauperism, crime, will be cured radically. Society, purified from these poisons, will go forward to nobler achievements than have ever yet been dreamed of. But this principle will not be applied while the fear-theology prevails, and is thought more of than that of love. The progress of human society depends on the radical cure of these social evils, not their mere restraint. And they can only be cured by such a view of the divine holiness and the divine compassion as is taught by Jesus in the Sermon on the Mount and the Parable of the Prodigal Son; showing the root of crime in sin, and inspiring a profound faith in God's saving love.

It may seem to some persons that I go too far in asserting that a true Theology is at the basis of human progress. They may ascribe human progress to other causes,—to the advance of knowledge, to scientific discovery, to such inventions as printing, the steam-engine, the railroad, and the like. But I believe that spiritual ideas are at the root of all others. That which one thinks of God, duty, and immortality,—in short, his Theology,—quickens or deadens his interest in every thing else. Whatever arouses conscience, faith, and love, also awakens intellect, invention, science, and art. If there is nothing above this world or beyond this life; if we came from nothing and are going nowhere, what interest is there in the world? "Let us eat and drink, for to-morrow we die." But if the world is full of God, — if we come from him and are going to him, — then it becomes everywhere intensely interesting, and we wish to know all about it. Science has followed always in the steps of religion, and not the reverse. The Vedas went before Hindoo civilization; the Zend-Avesta led the way to that of Persia; the oldest monuments of Egypt attest the presence of religious ideas; the Laws of Moses preceded the reign of Solomon; and that civilization which joined Greeks, Romans, Goths, Vandals, Franks, and Saxons in a common civilization, derived its cohesive power from the life of Him whose idea was that love to man was another form of love to God. "The very word *humanity,*" says Max Müller, "dates from Christianity." No such idea, and therefore no such term, was found among men before Christ came.

But it may be said that these instances are from such obscure epochs that it is uncertain how far it was religion which acted on civilization. Let us, then, take one or two instances, concerning which there is less uncertainty.

In the deserts, and among the vast plains of the Arabian Peninsula, a race had slumbered inactive for twenty centuries. Those nomad-Semitic tribes had wandered to and fro, engaged in perpetual internecine warfare, fulfilling the prediction concerning Ishmael, "He will be a wild man; his hand will be against every man, and every man's hand against him." No history, no civilization, no progress, no nationality, no unity, could be said to exist during that long period among these tribes. At length a man comes with a religious idea, a living, powerful conviction. He utters it, whether man will bear or forbear. He proclaims the unity and spirituality of God in spite of all opposition and persecution. At last his idea takes hold of the soul of this people. What is the result? They flame up into a mighty power; they are united into an irresistible force; they sweep over the world in a few decades of years; they develop a civilization superior to any other then extant. Suddenly there springs up in their midst a new art, literature, and science. Christendom, emasculated by an ecclesiastical and monastic Theology, went to Islam for freedom of thought, and found its best culture in the Mohammedan universities of Spain. Bagdad, Cairo, Damascus, Seville, Cordova, became centres of light to the world. The German conquerors darkened the regions they overran: the Mohammedans enlightened them. The caliphs and viziers patronized learning and endowed colleges, and some of their donations amounted to millions of dollars. Libraries were collected. That of a single doctor was a load for four hundred camels. That of Cairo contained a hundred thousand manuscripts, which were lent as freely as those in the Boston Public Library. The College Library of Cordova had four hundred thousand. In these places grammar, logic, jurisprudence, the natural sciences, the philosophy of Aristotle, were taught to students who flocked to them from all parts of Christendom. Many of the professors taught from memory: one man is reported to have been able to repeat three thousand poems. The Saracens wrote treatises on geography, numismatics, medicine, chemistry, astronomy, mathematics. Some, like Avicenna, went through the whole circle of the sciences. The Saracens invented pharmacy, surgery, chemistry.

Geber, in the eighth century, could prepare alcohol, sulphuric acid, nitric acid, corrosive sublimate, potash, and soda. Their astronomers measured a degree of the earth's meridian near Bagdad, and determined its circumference as twenty-four thousand miles. They found the length of the year, and calculated the obliquity of the ecliptic. Roger Bacon quotes their treatises on optics. Trigonometry retains the form given it by the Arabs, and they greatly improved Algebra. We received from them our numerical characters. We all know the beauty and permanence of their architecture, and much of our musical knowledge is derived from them. They also made great progress in scientific agriculture and horticulture, in mining and the working of metals, in tanning and dying leather. Damascus blades, morocco, enamelled steel, the manufacture and use of paper, the use of the pendulum, the manufacture of cotton, public libraries, a national police, rhyme in verse, and our arithmetic, all came to us from the Arabs.

All this fruitful intellectual life must be traced directly back to the theological impulse given by Mohammed to the Arab mind; for it can be derived from no other source.

It is not quite so easy to define the precise influence on human progress given by the doctrines of the Reformation; for, before Luther, these were in the air. But no one can reasonably doubt that the demand for freedom of conscience and the right of private judgment in religion has led to liberty of thought, speech, action, in all other directions. To the war against papal and ecclesiastical authority in concerns of the soul we owe, how much no one can say, of civil freedom, popular sovereignty, the emancipation of man, the progress of the human mind. The theses of Luther were the source of the Declaration of Independence. And modern science, with the great names of Bacon and Newton, Descartes and Leibnitz, Goethe and Humboldt, is the legitimate child of Protestant Theology.

It is true that printing and maritime discoveries preceded Luther. But these inventions came from the same ideas which took form in the Lutheran Reformation. The discovery of printing was a result, no less than a cause. It came because it was wanted; because men were wishing to communicate their thoughts more freely and widely than could be done by writing. If it had been discovered five hundred years before, it would have fallen dead, a sterile invention, leading to nothing. And so the steam-engine and the railroad did not come before, because they were not wanted: as soon as they were wanted they came. That which lies at the root of all these inventions is the wish of man to communicate easily and rapidly and widely with his brother-man; in other words, the sense of human brotherhood. Material civilization, in all its parts and in all times, grows out of a spiritual root; and only faith leads to sight, only the things unseen and eternal create those which are seen and temporal.

The two Theologies at the present time which stand opposed to each other here are not Calvinism and Armenianism, not Trinitarianism and Unitarianism, not Naturalism and Supernaturalism. But they are the Theology of discouragement and fear on one side, that of courage and hope on the other. The one thinks men must be driven to God by terror: the other seeks to attract them by love. The one has no faith in man, believes him wholly evil, believes sin to be the essential part of him. The other

believes reason a divine light in the soul, and encourages
it to act freely; trusts in his conscience enlightened by
truth, and appeals to it confidently; relies on his heart,
and seeks to inspire it with generous affections and disinterested love. That this Theology of faith is to triumph
over that of fear who can doubt? All the best thought,
the deepest religion, the noblest aspiration of the age,
flows in this direction. Whether our handful of Unitarian Churches is ever to become a great multitude or
not, I do not know; but I am sure that the spirit which
inspired the soul of Channing is to lead the future age,
and make the churches which are to be. It is not now a
question of Unity or Trinity, but something far deeper
and much more important. While endeavoring to settle
the logical terms of Christ's divinity and humanity, we
have been led up higher to the sight of the Divine Father
and the Human Brotherhood. Like Saul, the son of Kish,
we went out to seek our father's asses, and have found a
kingdom.

We have recently been told about a Boston Theology.
If there is any thing which deserves to be called a Boston
Theology it is this doctrine of courage and hope. For it
is shared by all the leading minds of all Protestant denominations in this city. Whatever eminent man comes
here, no matter what he was when he came, finds himself, ere long, moving in this direction. The shackles of
tradition and formality fall from his limbs, his eyes open
to a new light; and he also becomes the happy herald of
a new and better day.

But a better word still, if one is wanted by which to
localize these ideas, would be "The New England Theology." For in every part of New England, from the

beginning; in every one of the multiform sects, whose little spires and baby-house churches have spotted our barren and rocky hills, there have never failed men of this true Apostolic succession; men believing in truth, and brave to utter it; believing that God loves truth better than falsehood; that he desires no one to tell a lie for his glory, or to speak words of wind in his behalf. With all our narrowness, our bigotry, our controversial bitterness, our persecuting zeal, — of which, God knows, we have had enough in New England, — the heart of New England has been always free, manly, and rational. Yes: all the way from Moses Stuart to William Ellery Channing, all along the road from the lecture-rooms on the hills of Andover to the tribune of Theodore Parker standing silent in the Music Hall, we have had this same brave element of a manly Theology. This has been the handful of salt which has saved New England. Hence it is that from the days of the early Puritans, men and women, of Harry Vane, Mrs. Hutchinson, and Roger Williams, who stood up for the rights of the human soul against priestly tyranny, down through the ministers of the Revolution who went with their people to the camp of Washington at Cambridge; down to the days of the Beechers, — there has never failed a man in the New England pulpit to stand up for justice, freedom, and humanity. From our bare hill-tops New England men and women have looked up to the sky and seen it not always nor wholly black with superstitious clouds, but its infinite depths of blue interpenetrated evermore with the warm living light of a God of Love. And therefore has New England been the fountain of Progress, the fruitful parent of Reforms, "the lovely mother of yet more lovely children."

I have quoted several striking passages from the Apostle Paul. One expresses his longing for greater excellence, and declares that he forgets every thing already attained, and is reaching out for better things, for more truth and more love. Another passage calls on his disciples to think for themselves, and be rational Christians, not children in understanding. A third asserts that he is the minister of the spirit of the gospel, not its letter; a fourth that his religion is not one of fear, but of power and love and a sound mind; a fifth says, Stand fast in freedom, and be liberal Christians; and in other places he exhorts his brethren not to be narrow, nor bigoted; but to look at every thing beautiful, lovely, true, and good, no matter where they find it. But a little while before he said these things Paul himself was one of the most narrow, and intolerant of men, opposed to progress wholly. What made this great change in his soul? It was that he had found a true Theology. He learned from Christ to trust simply in the divine love for pardon and salvation. He learned that God was the God of Heathen and Pagans as well as of Jews. He learned that no ritual, ceremony, sacraments nor forms, but only the sight of God as a Father and Friend, can really save the soul from its diseases, and fill it with immortal life. A true Theology was the secret of Paul's immense progress, and of his wonderful power to awaken and convert others. There are many who suppose his Theology obscure and severe. But when we penetrate the veil of Jewish language, we find it one of Freedom, of Reason, of Love, manly and tender, generous and intelligent. And this same Theology passing in its essence from Paul to Augustine, to Luther, to Wesley, has always been the motive power of human civilization and human development. It has been the friend of free thought, liberty of conscience, and universal progress.

I mean then by a true Theology what Paul meant when he said that God "has not given to us a spirit of fear, but of power, and of love, and of a sound mind." I mean what he said when he declared that God had made him a minister of the New Testament, not of the letter but of the spirit; for the letter killeth, but the spirit giveth life.

I mean the Theology which places the substance above the form; the thing before the name; which looks at the fact, not at the label.

Let us then, brethren, who call ourselves Unitarians, be glad and grateful for the gospel of faith and hope which we enjoy. And let us give to others what we have ourselves received. If it be true, as we have tried to show, that human progress depends largely on a true Theology we cannot help mankind more than by diffusing widely that which God has given us of his truth. Freely you have received, freely give. You who have always lived in this community, surrounded by this mellow warm light of peace and freedom, do not know, cannot tell, what those suffer who have been taught from early childhood to fear God, and to distrust his light in their soul. Do your part in spreading abroad the beams of a better day. Give to the world that religion which is not a spirit of fear, but of power, and of love, and of a sound mind.

THE RISE AND DECLINE

OF THE

ROMISH CHURCH.

———

By ATHANASE COQUEREL, Fils.

THE RISE AND DECLINE

OF THE

ROMISH CHURCH.

WE live in a time of great and manifold changes. There is one church that for centuries has had her principal glory in asserting that she never has changed, — that she has at all times been exactly the same; but now she can hardly deny that either in accordance with her own will, or by the force of circumstances, very great changes have been wrought in her during the last few years. This, if it is true, must change also the nature, the system, the course of our controversy with her. The controversy between the two churches has not always, perhaps, been quite fair; and I should not like to be unfair to any adversary, whoever he may be. I should not be at ease in my conscience if I thought I had been unfair to any thing, especially to any thing religious, of whatever kind that religion may be; because in any religion, even the most imperfect, there is some aspiration from this earth to the sky; at least, from human souls to what they hope or believe to be God. And especially I could not pardon myself for being in any way unjust to that great church which has for centuries comforted and sustained a multitude of souls, and made them better and happier by her teachings. It is a Christian church; and though I think that Romish Christianity has been in a very great degree alloyed, and mixed with grave errors, — and that is exactly what I wish to show, — yet, even under that veil of human errors, I recognize, I acknowledge, religion, Christianity; and therefore I bow before it.

I think, however, the changes that have taken place have not altered the essential character of the Roman Church. I think the changes that have happened are in conformity with the nature of that church; really were to be expected, and have nothing absolutely new in them. We might, perhaps, for a long time have seen them coming; and, if we had had foresight enough, we might have seen them from the very first times of that church. Let us try to understand exactly what she is, what she means; let us try to see what there is under that name, "Roman Catholic Church." She calls herself *catholic*, which means *universal*, and at the same time she has a local name. She is for the whole world; but at the same time she belongs to one city, and she bears the name of that city. Why? This is the question; and though it seems only a question of name, I think we shall find by other ways that it is a question of facts. A second advance requires a change in our polemics with Roman authority. A new science has been created in our time, which gives us better means of judging and studying other churches than our own; that science is called the comparative history of religions. In England Max Müller, in France Burnouf, and in this country James Freeman Clarke, have compared the history of several religions. According to that comparative history, there are rules to be understood, to be acknowledged, in the development of religion. One of the rules which I think we can deduce from any comparative history of religion may be a startling one; and I will use a very homely comparison, to make myself perfectly understood. Have you ever seen over a shop door a sign-board, where the name of the old shop-keeper was painted; and, when his successor came in, he had the same board covered with a new color, and his own name painted over the old one? But in time the new paint wore off, so that the old name reappeared under the new, in such a way that it became perhaps difficult to distinguish clearly which letters or lines belonged to the old, and which to the new. If this image appears somewhat too familiar, let me ask you if you remember what scholars call a palimpsest. Sometimes in the Middle Ages it was difficult to find well-prepared parchment on which to write, and there were a great many monks who had nothing else to do — and it was the best use they could make of their time — but write or copy the Bible or other religious books. When they found parchments where were copied the comedies and tragedies or other works of the heathen, they thought those were of very little use, and they could very easily have the writing on those parchments washed out, or covered over with white paint, in such a way that what had been written there was no more visible. Then on those parchments they would write the Bible, or sermons, or any document they thought useful. But the same thing happened then that happened with the sign-board, — the old writing reappeared after a time; the white covering spread over the page disappeared. And thus it happens that scholars are sometimes pondering for a long time over a page from a sermon of Saint Augustine, or John Chrysostom, in which they find a verse from some comedy of Terence or Aristophanes; then they have perhaps some trouble in making out which is comedy and which is sermon, in distinguishing exactly what of the writing is old and what is new; and they have not always perfectly succeeded in that effort.

Now what we see in the sign-board we see also in the religion of the different churches, when a whole multitude, at one time, pass from one worship to another. Then, against their will, and perhaps without their knowing it, they never come into the pale of their new church empty-handed: they carry with them a number of ideas, and habits, and turns of thought, which they had found in their old worship. And thus, after a time, when the fervor of the early days is over, you find in the new religion, or new worship, a real palimpsest: the old one is reappearing under the new. That makes itself manifest in a good many ways; sometimes in ways the most strange and unexpected.

If you ask me, now, remembering this rule, what means the name, "Roman Catholic Church," I answer: Christianity absorbed into itself the Roman empire; the Roman empire became Christian in a very few years, with a most rapid, with a most admirable sway; souls became conquered in large numbers; they became Christian. But afterwards it appeared that they were not so perfectly unheathenized as they were thought to be, or as they thought themselves: many of their heathenish habits of life, thoughts, and customs remained even in their very worship. Thus, after Christianity had absorbed the Roman world, it appeared that the Roman world had penetrated and impregnated the whole of Christianity; and this is the Roman Catholic Church. She is Christian, but she is full of the errors and superstitions that belonged to the old Roman heathenish world.

To understand what this means we must now try to comprehend what the old Roman genius was. Here I ask you not to confound it with the Greek genius, which was in many respects highly superior, but which had, at that time, passed away in a large measure, and been replaced everywhere by the Roman genius. What were the especial traits of character of the Romans? The first, and a very striking one to those who have travelled and studied in those countries, is a most vivacious love for tradition. In Rome, at the present day, you find things that are done, that are said, that are believed, that are liked, because they were two thousand years ago, without the people themselves having a very clear notion of it. Their custom — and it is born in their flesh, and in their blood — is to look backwards, and to see in the past the motives and the precedents for their acts and for their belief. Of this I could quote to you a number of instances. I will choose but one. The first time I was in Rome I stopped, as every traveller does, on the *Piazza del Popolo*. In the midst of that square is an obelisk, and on one side of the pedestal of that obelisk is written: "This monument was brought to Rome by the High Pontiff, Cæsar Augustus." I went round the monument, and on the other face of the same pedestal I read : "This monument, brought to Rome by the High Pontiff, Cæsar Augustus, was placed in this square by the High Pontiff, Sextus V." And then I remembered that one of those High Pontiffs was a Roman heathen, an Emperor; and that the other was a Christian, was a priest, was a pope; and I was astonished, at first sight, to find on two faces of the same stone the same title given to those two representatives of very different religions. Afterwards, I observed that this was no extraordinary case, but that in many other places in Rome instances of the same kind were to be found. I inquired a little more deeply, perhaps, than some other travellers, into the meaning of those words. I asked myself why this pope, Sextus V., and this Emperor Augustus, should each be called "pontiff." What is the meaning of "pontiff"? "Pontiff" means bridge-maker, bridge-builder. Why are they called in that way? Here is the explanation of that fact. In the very first years of the existence of Rome, at a time of which we have a very fabulous history, and but few existing monuments, — the little town of Rome, not built on seven hills as is generally supposed; there are eleven of them now; then there were within the town less than seven even, — that little town had a great deal to fear from any enemy which should take one of the hills that were out of town, the Janiculum, because the Janiculum is higher than the others, and from that hill an enemy could very easily throw stones, fire, or any means of destruction, into the town. The Janiculum was separated from the town by the Tiber. Then the first necessity for the defence of that little town of Rome was to have a bridge. They had built a wooden bridge over the Tiber, and a great point of interest to the town was that this bridge should be kept always in good order, so that at any moment troops could pass over it. Then, with the special genius of the Romans, of which we have other instances, they ordained, curiously enough, that the men who were a corporation to take care of that bridge should be sacred; that their function, necessary to the defence of the town, should be considered holy; that they should be priests, and the highest of them was called "the high bridge-maker." So it happened that there was in Rome a corporation of bridge-makers, *pontifices*, of whom the head was the most sacred of all Romans, because in those days his life, and the life of his companions, was deemed necessary to the safety of the town. Things changed; very soon Rome was large enough not to care about the Janiculum; very soon Rome conquered a part of Italy, then the whole of Italy, and finally almost the whole of the world. But when once something is done in Rome, it remains done; when once a thing is said, it remains said, and is repeated; and thus it happened that the privilege of the bridge-makers' corporation, as beings sacred and holy, remained; and that privilege made everybody respect them; gave them a sort of moral power. Then kings wanted to be made High Bridge-makers; after kings, consuls; later, dictators; and, later, emperors themselves made themselves High Bridge-makers, which meant the most sacred persons in the town.

When Constantine, who is generally called the first Christian emperor, — but who was very far from being a real Christian, — when Constantine became nominally a Christian, he did not leave off being the high bridge-maker of the heathen. He remained high priest of the heathen at the same time he was a Christian emperor; and he found means, as well as his son after him, to keep the two functions. He acted on some occasions as high pontiff of the heathen; on other occasions, he called councils, presided over them, and sent them away when he had had enough of their presence; declared to the bishops that he was in some sense one of them, and acted to all intents and purposes as popes have acted after him. Thus that title remained the type of whatever was most sacred in Rome; and the bishop of Rome, when an opportunity came, — when the title had been lost in Rome by emperors, — took it up again. And thus we see on the same stone, at the present time in Rome, the name of a high bridge-maker who is a heathen emperor, and the name of a high bridge-maker who is a pope, who is the head of the Christian Catholic Church. Thus you see an old superstition, an old local superstition, established with a political meaning, has survived itself, has survived centuries, has survived the downfall of heathenism, and is at the present time flourishing. You all know that the present pope is called *Pontifex Maximus;* it is his title; and everywhere you see, even on the pieces of money, that Pio Nono is *Pontifex Maximus,* — the great bridge-maker, which means the highest of all priests, of all sacred beings. Thus has tradition, on that special spot, and in connection with the history and with the antiquities of that spot, established an authority unequalled anywhere else.

Though the Roman Catholic Church is special to that place, and inherits the local habits and traditions, it pretends also to universality. This is, again, perfectly Roman. The heathen Romans had thought for centuries that the world was made to be conquered by them; that unity was represented by Rome; that Rome was all in all; and at the present time the Pope, on Thursday of every Easter week, gives his solemn blessing, as you know, to the town first, and the world afterwards, — *urbi et orbi.* All countries, both hemispheres, all nations, all languages, are lost in that great unity. One town and one world, of which that town is the capital, — that was the wish, the hope of the heathenish Romans for centuries; and that has been the aim, the assumption of papal Rome for centuries also. When the present Pope said, on a celebrated day, after enumerating the great acts of his pontificate, that he had created more bishoprics than any other pope, he was right. He has created, on his own authority, bishoprics in Holland, in England, and in other countries; cut out bishoprics on the map of those countries. And he did that because, as pope, he is the spiritual sovereign of the world; because England and Holland belong to him; because Rome is the capital of the world; and he cuts off a part of any country, in America as well as in Europe, in order to make of it the see or dominion of a bishop. The old Roman idea was that nobody knew how to govern except Romans. They assumed — and often, if an unscrupulous government was the best of all, if a tyrannical government was the best of all, they were right — to govern better, more wisely, and with more acute politics, than any other nation. They said, "Other sciences, other arts, may be the share of other nations; but our share in the great things of this world is *government*." I hardly dare to speak Latin in an English country, because I cannot pronounce Latin as you do; but though I pronounce it as a Frenchman, which is, perhaps, a shade less bad than to pronounce it as you do in England and America, you may guess what I mean when I recall to the memory of some of you the famous lines of Virgil, where he says what must be, in this world, the function of the Romans: —

> "Tu regere imperio populos, Romane, memento;
> Hæ tibi erunt artes."

That is to say, "You Romans! remember that you are made to govern the nations; that must be your office; all the arts come after this; this is the special Roman art." I declare to you that at this present moment the clergy, the cardinals, the bishops, the prelates, the court of Rome, think, and have never ceased to think, that they are the people to govern better than any other political body; and that the government of the world has been providentially reserved to that town; first, in a temporal way, for the heathen; and, secondly, in a spiritual way, for the Christians, for the Catholic countries of the world. And as they believe spiritual things are a great deal more important than temporal things, they think their government is a great deal more important, and greatly superior to any government of any kind.

Let us now turn back a little again, and try more fully to understand what the old Roman genius was in its way of government. They governed by laws. You all have heard about Roman law, about Roman jurisprudence. It has been said for centuries that they were men who, better than any other, understood the art of making laws,—very precise, full of foresight, forgetting nothing, or few things, and giving in the most exact terms the decisions to be enforced in all possible cases, at least in all the cases with which they had occasion to deal. It is said also, it has always been said, that their laws were hard; but they accepted them, though hard: "*dura lex, sed lex.*" And certainly there was something noble and good in this respect for law, whatever the law was: there was something just, really in the interest of nations, in this love of law. But at that time this love of law was accompanied by the fact that the law was exceedingly hard in a great number of cases. Yet that hardness was in conformity with the general temperament of the nation at that time: the Romans were hard.

I have no time to stop to show you how different they were from the Greeks; but you remember that when the Greeks assembled in one of their great annual festivals, they heard music, they listened to poetry, they listened to the works of the historian; or they saw men run races, or engage in one of those contests that were not cruel, that were only displays of strength, agility, or training. That was the pleasure of the Greeks in their annual festival. What did the Romans do? You all know. They had immense amphitheatres where they assembled to see men kill one another. Their pleasure was to see people die, to see people suffer, to see people maimed, and weltering in their blood: that was their favorite amusement. And ambitious men in that day secured votes by bringing lions, hyenas, and tigers, in large numbers, to Rome, and by giving the people the diversion of seeing those animals killing men, devouring living men, women, and children, living Christians, often. That was the punishment in fashion at that time: Christian men, women, and children were killed, were devoured, were mangled before the eyes of the people, and for their pleasure. In their hardness they had a taste for the formal, precise execution of their law, whatever it might be. Christianity came and swept away their abominable pleasures, — this cruelty, which was contrary to every human feeling; but the habit of a sort of hardness, in the infliction of the penalties of law, remained in Rome more than it did in any other place. And this was allied to another feeling of a different nature, but which very well connected itself with it. I mean the Roman love for the literal in every thing. They did not like to understand any thing as metaphorical, as poetry: they liked to take every thing literally; and it was in consequence of this characteristic of the Roman mind that they were able to enforce their law. Even if the result of what the law demanded was absurd, they maintained, for the honor of the law, that it must be literally understood, and literally executed; and they permitted none of those different ways of alleviating the hardships of the law that have been in other places not only allowed, but ordered, by those in command. This is of extreme importance. Perhaps at first sight it does not strike you so, but it is. Remember from what country Christianity came. Christianity came from the East, came from Asia, came from the Jews. The Apostles, the first propagators of Christianity, were Oriental men, were Jews. I have seen part of the Levant, I have seen those very countries, and I can speak of it as a fact known for centuries, that the people of the Orient never speak otherwise than by images. They do not like the shortest way from one point to another; they make the way long. They use flowers, and rays of light, and moonshine, or any thing else that gives an image and color to their speech. They bring these things in continually, whatever may be the subject they speak of.

Perhaps I may give here an illustration that will make you understand me. I was in a house made of branches of trees, where lived a sheik. He told me that every thing in that house, his own person, his own family, were mine; and he said this with the greatest protestations. This is exactly the same as if you should say to a foreigner, coming into your house, "You are welcome." Nothing more. If, on going away, I had taken any thing from that house, the man would immediately have shot me; though he had given me every thing, even to his own person and his own family; because he would have had this idea: "This man is a thief; I have a thief in my house." If I had said, "But you gave me every thing in the house," he would have answered me, "You come from a country where people have no politeness. I gave you these things· that means *welcome*, and nothing more." Thus a man of the Orient never says any thing in the simple short way that Western nations do: they always want some poetry, some rhetoric, some image about it. And you must remember that many of the most admirable teachings of the Bible are in images, are in poetry, and are extremely beautiful and eloquent by their poetry. We are accustomed to this, so that we know that it is poetry; and we understand it. But the Romans, accustomed to their principle, that the law may be hard, but that law is law, and must be understood literally, and executed literally, understood every thing literally, and in that way they spoiled many of the great Christian truths. I will not here quote many instances, though it would be exceedingly easy to bring them in large numbers before you. I will take the most striking and best known of all. When our Lord, a few hours before being separated from his disciples, to die on the cross, gave them of the bread that was on the table, and said, "Eat, this is my body," it was absolutely impossible for Eastern people to misunderstand him; it was impossible for them not to understand that he meant, "This represents my body." The idea that what he held in the hands of his own body was his own body again; that he gave them his own body to eat, and that he ate some of it himself with them, — that idea could not for a moment have entered the head of one of those who were there. And if a multitude had been there, instead of the twelve Apostles, it would have been exactly the same. Nobody would have understood, when the Lord said, "I am the way," or when he said, "I am the door," that he was really, in fact, a path or a gate; everybody knew that he meant, "I am the leader; you must come with me; I show you the way." Everybody in the Orient understood that. But here comes the Roman genius, taking every thing literally; and they repeat, "He said, 'This is my body,' and this *is* his body." They repeat: "You Protestants do not accept the truth coming from the lips of your Master. He says, 'This is my body,' but you Protestants say, 'No, it is not his body, it represents his body.'" Thus it seems we are convicted of crime; it seems we will not accept the teachings of our Lord; yet we are perfectly true to his own meaning, to his real meaning, that could not be misunderstood in the East, but that was misunderstood when it was carried to Rome, a country where people gloried in taking every thing in a literal sense. So they did with many other most beautiful and delicate things in the Bible. The Roman genius — I cannot help saying it — had something clumsy in it. They were like giants, having very strong arms, and enormous hands, to take every thing, and to dominate over every thing. But any thing very delicate, very poetic, like flowers from the East, they could not touch without the flowers being broken and faded, losing their charm and their color. That was their way of treating many of the most beautiful things of the Bible, which they did not understand; which they made absurd or repulsive, by taking in a literal sense what was said, and ought to be taken, in a spiritual sense. They acted exactly as we should, if we received an Oriental letter and understood as literal every thing contained in it.

I will give another instance to make this clear. I remember having seen two letters, written one by a French General, and another by Abd-el-Kader, the chief of the enemies of the French in Algeria. These lette·s were intended to convey identically the same thing; that is to say, that some prisoners on one side were to be exchanged for the same number of prisoners on the other side. It had been decided that the French General and the Arab chief should say the same thing. I have seen both. The French General writes two lines; very clear, distinct, and polite, with nothing but the exact meaning he wanted to convey. But Abd-el-Kader, meaning to write the same thing, writes a whole page, about flowers, and jewels, and roses, and moonshine, and every thing of the kind. His intention was to say exactly the same thing, to convey identically the same meaning; but these things, translated from one language to another, pass, as a celebrated German scholar says, "from the Shemitic to the Japhetic; from the poetic language of the sons of Shem, to the precise language of the sons of Japhet." This has been the fault of the Roman Catholic Church in many dogmas, in many points of very high importance: the sons of Japhet could not understand what the sons of Shem meant. They thought they understood it, when they were entirely in error, and gave to it a meaning altogether different from what was intended.

I must add, that what helped them along in this belief of things, taken in a literal sense, was Roman superstition. In that town, and in Italy, have always prevailed the strangest superstitions. The most celebrated Romans, men whose wisdom and whose glory have filled the world, if they met, when they went out of their house in the morning, a hare in the way, re-entered their house on the instant, and renounced any thing they had to do, because meeting a hare was ominous of misfortune, and any thing they should undertake that day would result in their confusion or misfortune. When they put their foot in the wrong way, the left before the right, or the right before the left, on the stone at the entrance of a house, they stopped there and returned to their house, because every thing they should do in that house would prove unfortunate, since they had made a mistake in putting the wrong foot foremost when they entered the house.

So there were a multitude of superstitions. You know when they were to decide the greatest questions of peace or war, they consulted their sacred chickens. They gave them grains of wheat, and if the chickens ate it, or if they refused to eat it, or if they ate it too fast, or if the chickens let fall a grain of wheat from their mouths,— these signs meant that war would be successful, or that it would not be, and they decided according to these whether there should be a war or not. And those great magistrates, who were sometimes men of the greatest eminence, like Cicero, were augurs. You know what Cicero says, "Two of us cannot meet without laughing;" because they knew that their auguries were utterly worthless, but the multitude thought they were true. So the Romans were superstitious to the highest degree, and they have never ceased to be so. There is superstition in the marrow of their bones. Many Romans are ready to believe any thing to-day, at the present moment. I shall allude to a single fact. They all believe devoutly in the evil eye; that there

OF THE ROMISH CHURCH. 77

are people who, if they look at you, will bring upon you some horrible misfortune, disease, or death. They believe this so fully, that they have a gesture, representing with their fingers a pair of horns; and, when they meet any one who is supposed to have the evil eye, they endeavor, in a secret way, to make that sign, to prevent misfortune from coming upon them. It is believed, in Rome, that the present pope, who is to them God on earth, who is to them the successor and vicar of Jesus Christ, that he, as a man, has the evil eye. And when he passes through the streets of Rome, a great many women, devoutly kneeling before him, with their heads almost in the dust, craving to receive his blessing, as he passes in his carriage, will, under their aprons, make this sign, to preserve themselves from the effects of the evil eye. This is no disparagement to his person; they think that the poor man cannot help it; that there is no ill will in it; that it is fate; he has the evil eye.

I could cite many other instances of this superstition; perhaps it will be enough to refer to one more, and one that disgusted me completely. It is the worship with which they surround the *Santo Bambino.* There is on the Capitoline Hill a church that was formerly a heathen temple, and which has kept an old name, "*Ara Cæli*," or "altar of Heaven." In that church, the Franciscan monks keep a very ugly doll. This doll is said to have been sculptured out of one of the olive-trees on the Mount of Olives, and then Saint Luke is supposed to have painted it over. Saint Luke must have been the painter of the poorest daubs that ever were in the world, and the angels who took it to him must have been very far from being connoisseurs of painting. This doll is covered with diamonds, emeralds, sapphires, and other precious stones, of greatest price. It is kept in a box on the altar, and, when you ask to see it, the monks pray before the door, they light tapers, they produce the box, and then the box is opened, and you see the hideous little wooden image. Now, this *Santo Bambino* is supposed to have healing properties. He heals people, when they are rich enough to pay a good salary to him; he is not a physician who heals for nothing. He has a magnificent carriage of his own, and servants with his own livery; and, when any rich man wants to be cured by him, the *Santo Bambino* goes in his own carriage to the man's house, carried on the knees of Franciscan monks, and cures the patient, — if he can. Such is the belief of the country. But I could not see any very great difference between that doll and the idols that the old Romans had, and used in the same way. The idea is this: they suppose that the *Santo Bambino* represents Christ as a little child.

Not only were the old Romans superstitious, but we know, by historical testimony coming from the heathen themselves, that at the time when Christianity appeared there was an increase of superstition; there was a general feeling of a want of something definite, something like a sort of atonement; and at that time all sorts of ceremonies, all sorts of bloody sacrifices, were introduced from Syria, from Libya, from the most remote countries, and the Romans tried to find for their consciences some satisfaction in those rites. For instance, you all know they had a custom of having their sins expiated by means of what they called *taurobolium*. A man had a grave dug in the ground, and then over that grave was put a marble slab, with a great many holes in it, like a sieve. In that grave the man stretched himself at full length, and over the marble slab a bull was killed, in such a way that the blood fell through the holes into the grave. When the bull was taken away, and the marble slab was lifted, the man rose out of that grave perfectly covered with the blood of the bull, entirely bathed in that blood. Then he was supposed to be a new man, supposed to be washed of all his sins. He believed that from that moment the anger of the gods had passed to the bull, and that the blood of the bull had been shed instead of his own. We find in Ovid, one of the poets of the time, the prayer of a man for whom was about to be offered up the sacrifice of the black hen. He asks the gods to take the heart of the hen instead of his own, the fibres of the hen's body instead of the fibres of his own body. The poor black hen was sacrificed in the most cruel way they could find; she must suffer as long as possible, because then the anger of some god who was supposed to pursue the man found full satisfaction. The ferocity of the god had ample satisfaction in the torture of the poor black hen, and the sins of the man were expiated. Then there was superstition upon superstition, because, when the mangled remains of the unfortunate hen were thrown into the street, if any person unconsciously put his foot on that body, then he became the inheritor of the crimes of the first man, and of the anger of the gods. They had a special name for those bloody remains of the sacrificed fowl: they called them *purgamentum*, because they thought that such a sacrifice purged a man of his sins. As nobody dared lift or touch the body of the victim, they put a fence around it; and, as long as there remained on the ground in the streets of Rome a vestige of the poor bird, nobody would tread on that place; and the fence was put there to prevent this. These were the superstitions of that time; and Plutarch wrote a treatise to which he gives the title Δεισιδαιμονία, which is translated very often by the word "superstition;" but it means more than that, it means "terror of the gods." It means that feeling which was more and more prevailing in the Roman world, that the gods were to be feared; that there was anger in heaven; that the earth could not defend itself against the bad will of a supernatural power. We can very well understand that when Christianity was preached to those people they were happy to take that religion of hope, that religion of regeneration and sanctification. It was to them a marvellous deliverance to be out of that old doctrine and in the new one. But they carried with them many habits of thought, many things which were inherent in the ancient religion. Among those things was the habit of multiplying the divine being. They had been for a long series of centuries polytheists, believing in many gods. With their superstitious fears, they were always afraid there were not gods enough. That was saying a good deal, for they had more than 30,000 of them at the time of Christ. It was recognized that nobody could even know them all by name.

Again you will excuse me if I use here a very familiar illustration to make the leading thought of polytheism understood.

You know that in fairy tales the fairies are always called in to the festival at the baptism of the infant child. The intention is to invite them all, but there is always one forgotten; and that one curses the child in some way or other; and then all the gifts of all the good fairies cannot prevent the child from suffering, at least for a time, from

OF THE ROMISH CHURCH. 81

the bad will of the one that has been forgotten. This involves the essential idea of polytheists. They had always the thought that all the good gods whom they worshipped could not prevent any malevolent one who had been neglected from hurting them; and they were always in search of that one. They were always making altars "to the unknown god or gods," to be certain in that way to include them all. They were constantly asking what gods were worshipped in such a country, in such a place; and if it was a god that was not known among them, straightway they prepared a place for his worship. They said, "He has no existence, very likely; but if he has, if he lives, then we must sacrifice to him, to prevent his spoiling the happiness that the other good gods wish to give us." So there was an incessant adding to the immense number of gods. At the time of Christ, they had so many of them that, from the time a grain of corn was put into the ground to the time the harvest commenced, they had nine different deities who in succession took charge of the corn that had been put into the ground, and thus it passed from one god to another. Nine of them were necessary while the grain was in the ground. Thus, when the heathen became Christians, they had been in the constant habit of adding gods to their heaven, of adding good men to their gods, and also men not good, but whom they feared, — for all the emperors were made gods the moment they died, so that one of them, who was rather a wit, when he was dying said, "I feel that I am becoming a god." The heathen had become so habituated to this that, when they became Christians, they continued very naturally to multiply the number of the objects of worship. They soon

4*

ceased to make the slightest difference between Christ and the Father. In good time they unconsciously put Mary, the mother of Christ, above Christ; now, without ever having this intention, they put, in fact, Mary above the Father. And so on, adding always a new god to a new worship, and always making the new worship as binding and as efficacious as possible, to satisfy that polytheistic craving. They did not understand their error in keeping between the infinite God and themselves an immense number of minor deities. This craving was unwholesome, but very sincere. That unconscious wish to multiply gods and make saints has continued to this day; and no pope has canonized so many saints as the present one, who is always trying to show that he does more in this way than any of his predecessors.

This will suffice to give you an idea of what the old spirit of Rome was, the whole tendency of the Roman mind, and what was brought by them into the church. I must now ask you to go in imagination with me to the tomb of one of those old Romans, who were not burned, according to the custom of that period, say the Scipios. Suppose one of the Scipios taken out of his tomb; and bring him into a Roman Catholic Church: do you think he will be very much astonished? He will be astonished at one thing, — by the crucifix, the image of the crucified Son of God. That was completely contrary to the Roman ideal and their habit of thought. But all the other things he will see will not astonish him at all. He had seen them all his life in his own time. You believe, perhaps, that the shape of a Roman Catholic Church at Rome will astonish a pagan? Not at all. Cato had given the Romans the pleasure of enjoying,

OF THE ROMISH CHURCH. 83

for the first time, a portico with three ranges of columns, the middle aisle being broader than the others; and at the end was what we call an apse, but the ancients a conch. The end was rounded off, and thrown into the form of a semi-circle, and the tribunal for the prætor or judge was placed in that half-circle at the end. This portico was called a *stoa basilica*, and the first Roman Christian churches were built on that plan. Afterwards, the idea came of making the church in the shape of a cross; and then a smaller basilica was placed across the other, forming the transept of the church. But those long ranges of columns remained, with the same wide space in the middle, and narrower aisles on either side. The basilica was the form of public buildings most in fashion in Rome at that time. There the gothic style was never popular. Even now, of four or five hundred churches in Rome, only one, the Minerva, is gothic. When Christian architecture was born, Christian architecture accepted the heathen plan.

In the new church, in that *basilica*, what do we find? We find holy water at the door. That was exactly what you found in the pagan temple, only it was called lustral water. In the temple, my Scipio, who goes with me, recognizes all his old habits of thought, all the old emblems of his religious devotion. He sees a number of statues, or images; but he has seen those all his life. There is not only a central shrine, but there are small chapels. The saints have a golden circle round their heads: Christians call it the *aura*, the ancients called it the *nimbus;* but it was exactly the same thing. They had it around the heads of their deities in painting and sculpture, and so on. There are censers and there are tapers burning there; and there are all the ornaments a pagan was accustomed to see in his temple. All those things had been kept, had been re-established, and the pagans had brought them with them into the Catholic churches. When I went for the first time to Naples, the man who showed me the museum there showed me feet, legs, and arms, hands, eyes, and ears, in stone. He said, "These are *ex voto.*" People who were ill gave to some of the gods, the ones they chose, these things as marks of gratitude for having been cured. The cicerone told me, "You see, sir, it is exactly the same thing we have in our churches." And so it is. In all the churches in Naples and Rome, and in the Roman Catholic churches all over Spain and France, you see, in wax, in gold, in silver, and in stone, such legs and arms, eyes and ears. It is exactly the same thing. The heathen man said to his god, "I will pay you by this mark of honor and gratitude, by this mark of your power and your glory, if you cure me." The Roman Catholic says exactly the same thing to a saint, to the Virgin, sometimes to Jesus, and very rarely to God.

I cannot mention here all the other details, like funeral services at the end of the year, like funeral chapels, like many other institutions that exist in the Roman Catholic Church, that are practised every day in it, and that are exactly the same, so far as religious ideas go, as were practised in the pagan churches. But I must add something of more consequence than that, about the worship of human beings, and especially of the worship of the Virgin Mary. It was nothing new to the Pagans to worship a woman, and especially to worship a virgin. That was one of the ideas the most familiar to their devotion. In Rome they had the temple of Hestia or Vesta, who was supposed to be a virgin; and she had around her nuns who were pledged to live in celibacy, and punished by death if they did not remain true to their vow. In Greece it was the same thing with Pallas. Perhaps you all know that in Athens, the largest, most perfect, and most beautiful of the Greek temples — immensely superior to any edifice I ever saw in any country — is called the Parthenon, which means the Virgin Temple. That temple is the temple of Pallas, — Athene, or Minerva, — who was the principal deity of Athens. Thus that idea was perfectly familiar to them, and they only kept it, and brought it with them into Christianity.

I have spoken of monks. You must not believe that the monks are by any means a Roman Catholic invention. In the East there have been monks in all times and in all religions. It seems to have been a special habit or taste of the people of the East to give some men no other business, no other work to do, but to live in solitude, and pray for them; and some men have always, in those very hot countries, where it is exceedingly tiresome to work, liked to live in perpetual prayer better than any other more fatiguing labor. We find the monk in all times and countries in the East, then in the West; and he has been imported from paganism into Christianity, like all the rest. I do not believe there is a religion more completely contrary to the monastic feeling than the religion of Christ. I do not think there was ever a type more radically contrary to the type of the monk, than the figure of Christ as we find it in the Bible. However, that old monkish spirit of the Orient was always known to the Romans from the beginning; for they had priests and monks from the time their city began. That spirit has, like other things, been smuggled into the Church, though it was contrary to the spirit of Christianity.

I must recall one last rite of great importance. Both the old Romans and the old Jews had, as a principal part of their worship, the rite of sacrifice. The origin of it was simply this: that men in the first place possessed nothing but flocks, and they gave to God one head of their flock, one sheep, or one bull, as being the only riches they had to give. Before they had houses, before they had garments, before they had any other thing, — money they were very far from having, — men had to eat, and they had flocks because they wanted to have meat to eat; and thus they gave to God the only necessity of life to them, the only thing they understood the importance of. And they gave him the whole animal, not reserving to themselves any part of it, in some cases; in other cases, a part of it only, making a meal of the rest for themselves. To give a part to God was one essential element of their worship, the rite of sacrifice; and we find that the rite grew out of that, and nothing else. It was a habit deeply rooted in the Roman mind, and at the same time already familiar to the Jews; and when those Christians who had been Jews spoke of Christ to the Romans, they could not prevent that Roman or Jewish habit from taking double force, and double space in religion. What happened? It happened that the old Romans and old Jews wanted a sacrifice; wanted to give something to God; wanted a victim; and then came this strange fact, very easy to understand however, of which we find traces in the first days of Christianity, — that there was no better victim to offer to God than Christ. When they had identified completely Christ with the Father, then there was no greater victim to offer to God than God himself. Therefore, they had a sacrifice that is called "the mass." You know the official name is "sacrifice of the mass." It consists in this. The priest takes the host, which is merely bread, — it is nothing but a little flour and water, made into bread, — he pronounces the consecrating words; then, after he pronounces them, there is no bread, there is no flour; instead of the bread, instead of the flour, there is Jesus Christ. According to the Council of Trent, that *is* Jesus Christ, his body, his blood, his soul, and his divinity; it is Jesus Christ; is perfect God. And this has been, by an old Roman Catholic writer, very clearly expressed in these three words: "The priest, what is he? what does he do? *Creatus Creatorem creat.*" He is a creature who creates the Creator. After that comes the second great part of the sacrifice of the mass. There is God, and the priest sacrifices God to God. And how? *Sacrificat manducando.* That is to say, according to the formal explanation, he sacrifices God by eating God. This is the sacrifice of the mass. If the Roman mind had not been accustomed, as I have shown you, to superstition, to all literalism, to the love of the law and the letter, even when the law or the letter was absurd, they would not easily have accepted all this; but with their turn of mind, with their way of taking things, that was exactly what they wished for, and that was what they adopted. Not at once: it was very long in elaborating itself. It was so completely, I cannot say otherwise, so completely absurd, that it required a great deal of time to make it so precise; but they attained to that at last, and they could not but do so. See, then, what a man the priest is. He has before him bread, and he makes God; he afterwards sacrifices God;

he is almost a God himself. At the moment when he makes God, he seems to be superior to God; at the moment when he sacrifices God, by eating him, he seems superior to God. Thence comes the immense power of the priesthood, of priestcraft. And as if this were not enough, in the mass, as you know, the priest has not only the host, but he has the wine, the cup. The other members of the church have not the cup, because they must not be equa. to the priest even in the communion; even in the act of uniting themselves with God. Laymen cannot arrive at the height of glory to which the priest arrives; they must eat the host when it is given to them, but they cannot touch the cup; that is reserved to the priest, a sort of heavenly, or divine, or godlike character. Even as the Romans had respected their old bridge-makers, their old *pontifices*, their old priests, whom they considered the bulwarks of their town, they respected afterwards the priests of the Roman Catholic Church. So the mass was established, with all its consequences.

This is not all. I must explain exactly how a part of the heathenish religion answered, in the time of Jesus, the wants of the heathen better than the more natural religion of the Christians. At the time of Christ, many Romans did not believe in thirty thousand gods and in all the absurd and indecent history of those thirty thousand deities, but they had a form of worship that had become purer and purer. They had what they called "Mysteries." In Greece, and in Rome also, there were "Mysteries." These were ceremonies in which great philosophic and religious lessons were given. There exists a very touching letter from Plutarch to his wife, written at the time he lost his only daughter, and when they were in the deepest affliction

and desolation. He writes to his wife, who was separated
from him at that time, a very kind and loving letter, trying
to give her comfort and hope. He says to her, "Remember
the beautiful things we have seen together in the Mysteries
of Bacchus." You must not believe, as many would at
first believe, that the Mysteries of Bacchus were nothing
but drunkenness and disorder: they were something else.
They were like the Mysteries of Ceres, the Goddess of Corn,
and like the representations, in other cases, of the immortality of the soul. They were a sort of tragedy in which,
less by word than by singing, and by acting especially,
was shown to men that, when the body is interred in
the ground, the soul lives, and the soul shall rise to fulness of life. A grain of wheat hidden in the ground remained hidden there for weeks before coming to life.
That was the emblem of the new life of immortality. Now,
this teaching, good in itself, true in itself, but given in
dramatic images, was at that time the very best, soundest,
most human, and most natural part of heathenism. And
then it happened that Mysteries were acted, not only in
the heathen churches, but in Christian churches; that the
history of Christ, that the death of Christ, that the resurrection of Christ, took the place of the resurrection of
Proserpine, the daughter of Ceres, who represented wheat
and corn; and then Christianity became a sort of subject
of sacred myths, sacred plays, that were very devoutly
acted, and that kept their title of "Mysteries." As soon
as we see something of the dark ages, and what the practice of worship was, we see this same thing. It is going
on in all countries in some measure. You may see it in
the Roman Catholic churches during Easter week. You
may see then that, when Christ dies, all the lights are put

out, save one very small light, because that represents the moment when the sky was covered with darkness at his death. And you hear in a choir some persons sing the words of the people who screamed " Crucify him!" and others repeating the words of Caiaphas and the words of Christ. This "Mystery," this serious, devout play, is acted in all Roman Catholic churches. When Christ is dead, the host is taken away from the altar, and it is carried into the tomb, carried into some lower chapel, from which it comes back to the great altar on Easter morning, on the day of the resurrection. That solemn play is going on in all Roman Catholic countries at the present time, and that is a "Mystery." Such is also the "Mystery" that was played in Germany, at Oberammergau (Bavaria), during the last year, and is played there every ten years. It is a devout, religious, serious, dramatic representation of our Lord's suffering, death, and resurrection. The mass in itself was in the beginning a Mystery; it is often called so; it is often called in old Roman Catholic books and often in modern ones the "Mystery of the Mass." It was a representation of the death and sacrifice of Jesus; but the Roman Catholic spirit coming in declared that this Mystery was not, like others, a mere representation, a sacred play, but a reality; and according to the doctrine proclaimed by the Council of Trent, three hundred years ago, the sacrifice of the mass is much more than a representation of Christ's death, of Christ's sacrifice, for he is sacrificed anew, he suffers death really anew. And it has been declared, because some Protestant opponents were astonished at it, that every time any priest says mass,— and every priest must say mass at least once every day,— every time a priest says mass, Christ suffers again, and dies again, sacrificed by the priest for the redemption of human kind. This is the doctrine of the mass, and this gives it a very tragic, grand, and solemn effect in the eyes of those who believe in it. Yet this again is nothing but Roman literalism, the Roman way of taking every thing literally.

Is all this real Christianity? At all events I have said enough, I hope, to give you an idea of the way in which the religion of Jesus of Nazareth, as he was called, preached by him on the hills of Galilee, — a religion that was quite spirit, and quite truth; a religion that had at that time no bleeding, no consecrated man, but that was alive by the Spirit of God in the conscience and in the hearts of men, — how that religion, purely spiritual as it was, became all the pomp, all the exterior complications, all the dramatic intricacies of the Church of Rome.

And here I stop to ask again, Can all this suit the urgent necessities of our times? Is that the truth after which our souls hunger and thirst?

Now I must, before I end, say a few words to you about the late changes. Do those changes make matters better or worse? Let us pass over ages and centuries, and come to the present day, because I say we must make some change in our way of resisting the Church of Rome. I must state, and very rapidly, what these changes are. There are three of them. The first is, that a new dogma has been established. The new dogma amounts to this, without going into details, that Mary, the mother of Christ, was created, at the moment she began to exist, exempt from original sin. All human beings are guilty of Adam's sin, with one exception, and that exception is Mary. That exception dates from the very first instant of her existence.

She never was, even in thought or in feeling, a sinner; she is consequently out of the pale of humanity; she is not a human being; she is more than a woman, she is something godlike from before her birth. That is the dogma. It is not new; it was invented in Spain; it is a Spanish, an Andalusian dogma. It was invented at a time when the Catholics in Spain were laboring very hard to expel from their country the Moors, the African Moslems, who were masters of a great part of Spain, and who had more science, more art, and more literary culture than the Christians of Spain, but who had absurd doctrines about the family and about religion, as well you know. Nothing could displease them more, could astonish them more, or could confound all their ideas more, than to tell them that a woman was godlike. They thought, as all Moslems have thought, that a woman had no soul; and here was a woman who was a goddess before her birth, who was always a goddess. This was something absolutely incredible to them, and it showed the great difference between Christians and Moslems, between Spaniards and Arabs. This became the general rule among the Spaniards of the southern part of the country, in Andalusia especially; and when they met one another they did not salute with words of good greeting, but for centuries it was the habit in Andalusia, when one Spaniard met another, to say to him, *Ave Maria purissima*, and the other answered, *Sin pecado concepida*, which means that that dogma was proclaimed every time two persons met. This dogma has been taken into special favor by the very powerful order of Jesuits. They thought it was important to the church; it was putting Mary in the highest honor, to have that dogma become the law of the church. But up to the present century, up to last year in the Roman Catholic Church, people could believe it or not; now the Pope has declared that henceforth every man who does not believe that dogma is eternally lost and damned. This he has decreed, after consulting with some bishops, with whom he conferred about it, but declaring that he did so of his own accord, because, as pope, he had a right to decide on that. He said, it is no new doctrine; it has always been in the church. As the great writer Father Perrone wrote, "That dogma has been developing itself in the church a long time." When I saw the Church of Rome speaking of a dogma "developing itself," I thought, This is the beginning of the end. If they understand that dogmas develop themselves, that they have not fallen like aerolites from the heavens, it seems to me that that is the end of infallibility. Some people think it was the beginning of infallibility, that it was the Pope for the first time declaring a dogma for all men without consulting officially or legally any one, and that when he had done this he had augmented his power. I must remark here, that when a pope is very weak, the general rule is, he does something extremely strong. When he is extremely weak, politically, materially, he generally makes some great demonstration of spiritual power. When Pope Gregorius VII. kept Henry in his shirt a whole night at the door of the castle of Canossa without opening the door to him, saying, "You are a sinner, do penance,"— when he did that, the Pope had been expelled from Rome, he had lost Rome, therefore he must prove his immense spiritual power, because his temporal power was lost. And when the present Pope has done acts of authority greater than any other pope, it has not been because he was strong, but because he was weak; to remain on his throne he wanted to have the bayonets of Louis Bonaparte to keep him in power. His own subjects would very soon have shown him a second time the way to the frontier, if they had not been prevented by the bayonets of that man. Thus the Pope did more towards asserting and confirming his own power than any of his two hundred and fifty odd predecessors. When afterwards he took a new step, it was in continuance of this. He called a council when three hundred years had elapsed since an œcumenical council had been called. I know old Roman Catholic families who had been waiting for centuries for the moment when an œcumenical council should assemble, to denounce before that council the encroachments of the Pope, and to ask that the popedom be kept within bounds for the future. Pio IX. had an œcumenical council called, and held it in his own house, in the Vatican. And there, in one end of one of the transepts of the immense church of Saint Peter, the Pope had himself declared infallible by the council. Thus all the other councils which had been the hope of such persons in the church as could not accept every word of the Pope, all those councils have been sacrificed, have abdicated, in the last of them, at the foot of the Pope. Now, the Roman Catholic Church has become very logically, what it ought to become, the same thing in the spiritual world that the Roman Empire became in the temporal world. The Roman Emperor was every thing; there had been priests and magistrates who had great powers; then the emperor made himself dictator, consul, tribune of the people; made himself high bridge-maker; took upon himself all dignities. He was every thing; and then the whole Roman Empire was one man; and some-

times it happened that that man was a mad man like
Caligula, who said, " I am sorry that all men have not one
head that I might cut it off." Such was the unity of the
Roman Empire, and we see the same fact in the Roman
Catholic Church to this extent, that there is one human
brain that thinks for all Roman Catholics in the world,
and if that human brain decides that such a thing is or is
not, all other human brains must believe it, or be damned
eternally; there is no choice. This is perfectly logical;
this is not an unexpected change; this must have come
to pass. As the Pope became physically weak, the more
absolute became the necessity that this should be done.
Now, he is weak, he has lost Rome. Although it was
not in my way, I passed through Rome a few months ago
for the purpose of seeing Rome free, and it was an immense joy to see that. I had seen Rome groaning under
that proud, domineering government of the priests, who
declared that their government was the best in the world,
while the whole world called it emphatically *il mal governo*. Now I have seen it free; and I think no Bonaparte
of France, nor any French Government, nor any other
government, had any right to give up Rome to the priests,
to prevent the Romans from being masters in their own
house, from being free in their own city. I must declare
to you, that if in one sense the Roman Catholic Church
has lost a great deal because she has lost that great
tradition, lost that long habit of ruling in Rome, and the
high prestige that comes from it, yet the Roman Catholic
Church has gained more perhaps than she has lost in this.
You must not believe that the Roman Catholic Church is
to disappear to-morrow, or the next day: that shall not
happen. There are hundreds of thousands of souls who

like better to have one man on a throne thinking for them, taking on his conscience and his honor the question of their salvation, — they like that better than to think for themselves; and there will be Roman Catholic churches for a long time to come. They will even be stronger in one sense, because that temporal power was so exercised that it caused great weakness; and now the Pope will be strengthened; will find more interest and sympathy, because he is a king without a crown, a king without a throne: in his weakness he will find new strength.

What must we do, we Protestants, in the presence of this fact? Must we exaggerate, must we be unfair in our attacks? No. Must we go to sleep, thinking there is nothing to do? No, not that either. We must work; we must work steadily to give light and instruction to all. We have here, — and I have tried in a very rapid way to give you an idea of it, — we have here history. That is the greatest of weapons in such a case as this. Usurpers never like history, because they know very well that history condemns them. We must make history known, make the facts known, and proclaim liberty and the rights of the human conscience. We must do that over the whole world. I do not believe that Protestantism, as it has often been said, is nothing else but Roman Catholicism stripped of some of its abuses, and without some of its errors. It is something else. If there were time, and I could begin now instead of ending, I would try to show you that in the history of Protestantism, and even before Protestantism appeared, there has always been, next to that stream of power of Roman Catholicism, always becoming stronger and more encroaching up to these last days, another current of protest; there have always been men struggling for faith with liberty, who said, "That cannot be;" who understood better the Gospel, who liked the spirit of the Gospel, the spirit of God in Christ, better than the spirit of Rome. For centuries their mouths may have been closed; their speaking and teaching punished by death; but always they became more and more numerous, and active, and vigorous; and then came the great day of Luther. Protestantism has not been a negation, a remnant of Roman Catholicism, the negative side of Christianity. I cannot adopt that idea in the least. True. Protestantism is full of the spirit of the Gospel; it is the living soul of Christ in the Church, it embodies the perfect conviction that there is truth, that there is salvation, that there is liberty, in the Gospel, and nowhere else so completely.

Now, we must consider the Roman Catholic Church as being an organization of power, the most dreadful, the most tyrannical, the most crushing organization of power that ever was. It is the master-piece of Roman genius. It has been preparing during centuries, and it has been complete only since yesterday. It is a great organization against liberty, against man's rights, against man's conscience, for the honor of a church and of a man. And this we must resist, too. In my country, I declare that the cause of all our ills, the fact that is at the basis of all our suffering and all our misfortunes, is nothing else than Roman Catholicism. This is against the conscience of many souls; this throws many people into sheer Atheism, because they see no choice between kissing the shoe of the Pope, as is done in ceremonies, and denying the existence of God. So they deny God rather than submit to the Pope. We must give them sound teaching, religious teaching; we must give them the Gospel. And I came to this country to say these things to you; to ask you to help us with all your might, and with all your heart, to do what is necessary should be done in France to-day; what will be necessary to be done in this country sooner or later, and what will be necessary to be done in all countries, to show more and more that "where is the Spirit of the Lord, there is liberty."

SELFHOOD AND SACRIFICE.

By ORVILLE DEWEY.

SELFHOOD AND SACRIFICE.

THE title which I have chosen for this discourse, is Selfhood and Sacrifice. My purpose is, to consider what place these principles have in human culture. I use the word, selfhood, rather than self-regard or self-interest, because I wish to go back to the original principle — selfhood, according to the analogy of our language, describing the simple and absolute condition in which self exists; as manhood does that of man, or childhood, that of a child. And I say sacrifice, rather than self-sacrifice, because the true principle does not require the sacrifice of our highest self, but only of that which unlawfully hinders outflow from self.

The subject of culture has been brought before the public of late, by Professor Huxley, and Matthew Arnold, and Mr. Shairp. I do not propose to enter into the questions which have engaged their able pens, but to go back to those primary and foundation principles, which I have proposed to consider — the one of which is the centre, and the other, the circumference of human culture, — Selfhood and Sacrifice.

It is the object of this course of lectures, in part at least as I understand it, to discuss this subject — to discuss, *i.e.* the principles and grounds, on which right reason and rational Christianity propose to build up a good and exalted character. Now with regard to what Christianity teaches, has it never occurred to you, or has it never seemed to you, in reading the Gospels, that they appeal to self-interest, to the desire to be saved, in a way that is at variance with the loftiest motives? But it is appealed to, and therefore is, in some sense, sanctioned. And yet, as if this self-interest were something wrong, the prevalence of it in the world, the world's selfishness in other words, is represented by many preachers, as if it were the sum of all wickedness, the proof indeed, of total depravity. Here then, it seems to me, whether we look at Christianity or at the teachings of the pulpit, there is urgent need of discrimination. And there is another aspect of the same subject, which seems to require attention; and that is what is called, individualism — the mentally living, if not for, yet in and out of ourselves; claiming to find all the springs and forces of faith and culture within ourselves, to the exclusion of the proper influence of society, of Christianity, of the whole great realm of the past, by which we have been trained and formed; individualism, which says, "I belong to myself, and to nobody else, and do not choose to be brought or organized into any system of faith or action with anybody else." This, indeed, is an extreme to which, perhaps, but few minds go; but there is a tendency of this kind, which needs to be looked into.

Now there is a way of thinking, in matters of practical expediency, to which I confess that I am committed by my life-long reflections; and which has always prevented me from going to the extreme with any party, whether in reforms, in politics, in religious systems, or in any thing else; and that is, to look to the mean in things; to look upon human nature and human culture, as held in the balance between opposing principles. With this view, I shall first undertake to show that the principle of self-regard, or of individualism, is right and lawful — is indeed, an essential principle of culture.

There is a remarkable passage in the old "Theologia Germánica," which hits, I think, the very point in this matter of self-regard. Speaking of its highest man, it says, "All thought of self, all self-seeking, self-will, and what cometh thereof, must be utterly lost, surrendered and given over to God, *except in so far as they are necessary to make up a person.*" This personality, this stand-point, we must hold to, go where we will.

But let me state more precisely what it is, that is here conceded, and must be maintained; and why it is important to defend and justify it. I call it selfhood; and the word, I conceive, is philosophically necessary to meet the case. Because it is a principle, that goes behind selfishness; and of which selfishness is the excess and abuse. Selfishness calculates, overreaches, circumvents. But selfhood is simpler. It is the instinctive, instantaneous, uncalculating rush of our faculties, to preserve, protect and help ourselves. Selfishness proposes to take advantage of others; selfhood only to take care of itself. It is not, as a principle of our nature, a depraved instinct; animals possess it. It is not moral, or immoral, but simply *un*moral. It is a simple force, necessary to our self-preservation, to our individuality, to our personality. The highest moral natures feel it as well as the lowest. The martyr, who gives up every thing else, holds his integrity fast and dear. It is written of the great Martyr, that, "for the joy that was set before him, he endured the cross, despising the shame." No being that is not an idiot, can be divested of all care and regard for himself. And not only does necessity enforce, but justice defends the principle. If happiness is a good, and there are two equal amounts of it, the one of which is mine, and the other my neighbor's, I may in strict justice, value and desire my own as much as his. If I love his more than my own, I go beyond the commandment. It is not worth while to put any Utopian strain upon the bond of virtue; nay, it does positive harm.

Yet this is constantly done; to the injury of virtue, of conscience, and of a proper self-respect. In our theories of culture, we demand of ourselves, what is impossible, what is unjust to ourselves, what repudiates a part of the very nature we would cultivate. We demand of ourselves, and we suppose that Christianity demands of us, a certain unattainable perfection, — or what we call perfection, — a sinking of ourselves out of sight, and an absorption into the love of God and men, quite beyond our reach: and failing of that — thinking it entirely out of our sphere, we give up the proper rational endeavor to be Christians. We make the highest virtue something exceptional, instead of regarding it as a prize for us all. We imagine that some few have attained it; that Jesus did, and that a few persons, denominated *saints*, have approached him; but that for the common run of men, this is all out of the question. The fact is, that Christianity is regarded by many, as an enigma, a secret of the initiated, as an idle vision or hard exaction — not as a rational culture. Listen to the conversation of the mart or the drawing-room, you will find that the high Christian law is but a mocking dream in their eyes. " Giving to him that asketh, and from him that would borrow, turning not away, and to him that takes from us our coat, giving our cloak also; and turning the other cheek to the smiter;"—what is this, they say, but extravagance and fanaticism? As if they did not know that there is such a figure of speech as hyperbole; and that it was perfectly natural, in a society where the poor and the weak were trodden under foot, for the greatest heart that ever was, thus to pour out itself in pleadings for sympathy, commiseration and kindness. But the same Master said, "It is profitable for thee—it is better for thee," to have some of thy pleasures cut off—thine offending hand or eye; rather *that*, than to have thy whole being whelmed in misery.

It is really necessary in this matter, not only to vindicate Christianity as a reasonable religion, but to vindicate human nature to itself; to save it from the abjectness of feeling that the necessity of self-help is an ignoble necessity. Men say, "Yes, we are all selfish, we are all bad;" and they sink into discouragement or apathy, under that view.

The conditions of true culture are attracting increased attention at the present time; and it is natural that they should, when men's minds are getting rid of theologic definitions and assumptions, and are coming to take broad and manly views of the subject. I am endeavoring to make my humble contribution to it; and with this view, to show, in the first place, what part our very selfhood, both of right and of necessity, has in it.

This principle lies in the very roots of our being; and it is developed earliest in our nature. Before the love of right, of virtue, of truth, appears this self-regard. Disinterestedness is of later growth. Infancy comes into the world like a royal heir, and takes possession, as if the world were made for itself alone. Itself is all it knows; it will by and by, take a wider range. There is a natural process of improvement in the very progress of life. "You will get better," says a dramatic satirist,[1] "as you get older; all men do. They are worst in childhood, improve in manhood, and get ready, in old age, for another world. Youth with its beauty and grace, would seem bestowed on us, for some such reason, as to make us partly endurable, till we have time to become so of ourselves, without their aid, when they leave us. The sweetest child we all smile on, for his pleasant want of the whole world to break up, or suck in his mouth, seeing no other good in it — would be roughly handled by that world's inhabitants, if he retained those angelic, infantile desires, when he has grown six feet high, black and bearded; but little by little, he sees fit to forego claim after claim on the world, puts up with a less and less share of its good as his proper portion, and when the octogenarian asks barely for a sup of gruel or a fire of dry sticks, and thanks you as for his full allowance and right in the common good of life, — hoping nobody will murder him — he who began by asking and expecting the whole world to bow down in worship to him — why, I say, he is advanced far onward, very far, nearly out of sight."

This advancement, thus springing out of the very experience of life, I am yet to consider, and have it most at heart to consider. It is of such priceless worth, it so embraces all that is noble in humanity, that the importance of the opposite principle, is liable to be quite overlooked. Selfishness, which is the excess of a just self-regard, is the

[1] Browning: A Soul's Tragedy, p. 250.

one form of all evil in the world. The world cries out upon it, and heaps upon it every epithet, expressive of meanness, baseness and guilt. And let it bear the branding scorn; but let us not fail to see, though selfishness be the satirist's mark, and the philosopher's reproach, and the theologian's argument, the real nature and value of the principle, from which it proceeds.

Selfhood I have preferred to call it; self-love, be it, if you please. It is that, which satire and false criticism have misconstrued, when they have said that love of kindred, of friends, of country, of God himself, is but self-love. The mistake arises from that primal and vital part and participation which ourself has in every thing that we enjoy or love or adore. This magnificent *I*— and I emphasize it, because all meanness is thought to be concentred in that word — this mysterious and magnificent *I*— this that one means, when he says I — we may utter, but can never explain, nor fully express it. There are great men in the world, whose lives are of far more importance than mine — statesmen, commanders, kings — but *I* — no being can feel an intenser interest in his individuality than I do in mine; no being can be of more importance to himself than I am to myself; the very poles of thought and being turn upon that slender line; that simple unity, like the unit in figures, swells to infinite multiplication; that one letter, that single stroke of pen or type, may be varied and complicated, till it writes the history of the world. " I think, therefore I am," said the philosopher; but the bare utterance of the word I, yields a vaster inference. No animal ever knew what that word means. It is some time before the little child learns to say, I. It says, "Willy or Ellen wants this or that — will go here or there." What is insanity, but the wreck of this personality? The victim loses himself. And the morally insane, the prodigal, when he returns to reason and virtue, comes to himself.

"A man's self," says Thackeray, "must always be serious to him, under whatever mask or disguise or uniform he presents it to the public." Yes, though it were as mime, harlequin, jester fool almost; nor could there be a more deplorable or desperate condition for a human being, than to account himself nothing, or nothing worth, or worthy only to be the butt of universal scorn and contempt. From this utter ruin, every man is protected by that mysterious and momentous personality that dwells within him. We may be little in comparison with the general mass of interests, little in comparison with kingdoms, little in comparison with the swelling grandeur of thrones and empires, little in comparison with the great orb that rolls round the sun, and bears millions of such; but we are forever great in the sense of individual destiny. *This* swells beyond kingships, grandeurs, empires, worlds, to infinitude and eternity.

There is another element in this selfhood, to be considered, besides its conscious importance, and that is free will—itself also unmoral, but indispensable. For imagine a rational being to be placed in this world, *without* free will. He can choose neither wrong nor right. He has a conscience, but no freedom; no power to choose any thing. It is, I think, an incongruous and impossible kind of existence; but imagine it. Evils, troubles, temptations press against this being, and he can do nothing; he cannot even will to resist. Could there be a condition more horrible? No; man is a nobler and happier being than this amounts to. Free will is put in him, on purpose to fight the great battle against evil. He could not fight, if he could not will. He could not choose the right, without being free to choose the wrong; for choosing one path without being at liberty to take the other, would be no choosing. Free will is to fight the battle. It is a glorious prerogative. And man, I believe, is out of all proportion, happier, with this power, all its aberrations included, than he would be without it. I am glad for my part, that I am not passing through this world, like a car on a railroad, or turning round like a wheel in a mill; that I can go, this way or that, take one path or another; that I can read, or write, or study, or labor, or do business; and that when the great trial-hour, between right and wrong, comes, though I may choose the wrong, yet that I *can* choose the right. What better would there be for me than this—what better constitution of a rational nature? I know of no better possible.

Selfhood, then—this interest in ourselves, being seen to be right, and the play of free will which is a part of it desirable; let us turn finally to the useful working of the principle. You may have said in listening to me thus far, " What need of insisting so much upon self-regard, which we all perfectly well understand?" I doubt whether it is so well understood; and this must be my apology. We have seen that the principle is native and necessary to us; let us look a moment, at its utility.

I am put in charge of myself—of my life, first of all. So strong is the impulse to keep and defend it, that self-preservation has been called the first law of our being. But that argues an antecedent fact—self-appreciation. Why preserve that which we value not? We defend ourself, because we prize ourself. We defend our life, with the instant rush of all our faculties to the rescue. "Very selfish," one may say; "And why does a man care so much for himself; he isn't worth it." He can't help it. He obeys the primal bond; he is a law to himself. Is it not well? Man's life would perish in a thousand ways, if he did not thus care for it. The great, universal and most effective guardianship over human life everywhere, is — not government nor law, not guns nor battlements, not sympathy, not society — but this self-care.

I am put in charge of my own comfort, of my sustenance. I must provide for it. And to provide for it, I must have property — house, land, stores, means — something that must be my own, and not another's. If I were an animal, I might find food and shelter in the common storehouse of nature's bounty. But I have other wants; if I have no provision for them that is my own; if some godless International League, or Agrarian Law, could break down all the rights of property, there would be an end to industry, to order, to comfort, and eventually to life itself. Whatever evils, whatever monstrous crimes come of the love of gain, its extinction would be infinitely worse.

I am put in charge of my good name, my place among men. I must regard it. I am sinking to recklessness about virtue if I cease to value approbation. Even the martyr, looking to God alone, seeks approval. And good men's approbation is the reflection of that. To seek honor from men at the expense of principle, is what the Master condemns — not the desire of honor. It has been made a question whether the love of approbation should be appealed to, in schools. It cannot be kept out, from there, nor from anywhere else. If it could, if the vast network of social regards, in which men are now held, were torn asunder, society would fall to pieces.

Finally, I am put in charge of my virtue — of that above all. And that I must get and keep for myself; no other can do it for me. Another may stretch out the hand to defend me from a fatal blow; another may endow me with wealth; another may give me the praise I do not deserve; but no friendly intervention, no deed of gift, no flattery, no falsity, can give me inward truth and integrity. That solemn point in human experience, that question upon which every thing hangs — shall I do right? — or shall I do wrong? — is shrouded in the secrecy and silence of my own mind. All the power in the world, cannot do for me the thing that I must do for myself. To me, to me, the decision is committed.

Now what I have been saying, is this; it is well that that self-regard, upon which so much is devolved, should be strong; that there should be no apathy, no indifference, upon this point; that if ever a man wanders away into recklessness, into idleness, into disgrace, into utter moral delinquency and lawlessness, he should be brought to a stand, and brought back again, if possible, by this intense and uncontrollable regard for himself — for his own well-being. I do not resolve every thing in human nature, into the desire of well being. I do not say that the love of life, of property, of reputation, still less of virtue, is the same as the love of happiness; but I say that to the pursuit of all these a man is urged, driven, almost forced, by this love of his own well-being; nay more to the pursuit of the highest eventually, and that, by the very laws of his nature.

Let us now turn to the other principle which I propose

to discuss — that which opens the whole field of our culture — the principle that carries us out of, and beyond ourselves.

It has been no part of my design, in discussing the principle of selfhood, to show the hinderance to culture, and the evil every way, that come from the abuse of it. That will be sufficiently manifest, if it be made to appear, that all culture and happiness are found in the opposite direction. But if I wanted to put this in the strongest light, I should point to the pain and obstruction which are experienced in a diseased self-consciousness. It would be a powerful argument for that going out of self, which I am about to speak of. Self, if it is a necessary stand-point, is yet liable to be always in our way. A morbid anxiety about our position, our credit with men, the good or ill opinion others have of our talents, tastes or merits, causes more misery, I am inclined to think, than any other form of human selfishness. See a company of persons, inthralled with music, charmed by eloquence, transported by some heroic action set before them; and they forget themselves; they do not think, how they look, how they are dressed, what others think of them, in their common delight.

The sense of this, I believe it was, that lay at the bottom of the old Buddhist doctrine of Nirwana — *i.e.*, self-oblivion. To lose this wearisome, diseased self, seemed to Gautama, the great apostle of Buddhism, to be the chief good. Nirwana has been taken to mean absolute annihilation. I do not believe the Buddhists meant that; for to me, it is incredible, that any great sect, numbering millions, should have so totally given up the natural love of existence, and desire of immortality; and Max Müller

SELFHOOD AND SACRIFICE. 113

and others have brought that construction of the Buddhist creed, into doubt. Individuals may go that length. Unhappy Blanco White, tortured in body and mind, could say that he desired no more of life, here or hereafter. A German naturalist could say, "Blessed be the death hour — the time when I shall cease to be." But this revolt against self and very self-existence, whether ancient or modern, I advert to, only to show the necessity of going out from it, in order to build up the kingdom of God within us. It is notable; it is suggestive; but it is neither healthy, nor true to human nature. Far truer is that admirable little poem of David Wasson's, originally entitled " Bugle Notes," which in unfolding the blessing and joy of existence, touches, I think, the deepest and divinest sense of things.

But let us proceed to consider the law of sacrifice — not sacrifice of happiness nor improvement, but the finding of both, in going out from self, to that which is beyond and above it.

A man's thought starts from himself; but if it stopped there, he would be nothing. All philosophy, science, knowledge presuppose certain original faculties and intuitions; but not to cultivate or carry them out, would leave their possessor to be the mere root or germ of a man. A line in geometry presupposes a point; but unless the point is extended, there can be no geometry; it is a point barren of all science, of all culture.

Every intellectual step is a step out of one's self. The philosopher who studies *himself*, that he may understand his own mind and nature, is but studying himself objectively; his very self *then* lies out of himself, and is an abstraction to him. And the mathematician, the astronomer, the naturalist, the poet, the artist, each one goes out of himself. His subject, his theorem, his picture it is, that draws him — not reward, not reputation. Doubtless Newton or Herschel, when he left his diagram or his telescope, and seated himself in the bosom of his family, might say, "We must live; I must have income; and if public or private men offer to remunerate and sustain me, it is right that they should do so." But the moment he plunges into deep philosophic meditation, he forgets all that. Nature has more than a bridal charm, science more than golden treasures, truth more than pontifical authority, to its votaries. Not wooing, but worship, is found at its shrines and altars. In the grand hierarchies of science, of literature, of art, there is a veritable priesthood, as pure, as unworldly, as can be found in any church. It is delightful to look upon its work, upon its calm and loving enthusiasm. The naturalist brings under his microscope, the smallest and most unattractive specimen of organized matter, and goes into ecstasies over it, that might seem ridiculous; but no, this is a piece of *holy nature* — a link in the chain of its majestic harmonies.

And so every intellectual laborer, when his work is noblest, forgets himself — the lawyer in his case, the preacher in his sermon, the physician in his patient. Is it not true then, and is it not noteworthy, that all the intellectual treasures that are gathered to form the noblest humanity, all the intellectual forces that are bearing it onward, come of self-forgetting?

Equally true is it — more true if possible, in the moral field. The man who is revolving around himself, must move in a very small circle. Vanity, self-conceit, thinking much of one's self, may be the foible of some able and learned men, but never of the greatest men: because the wider is the circle of a man's thought or knowledge, at the more points does he see and feel his limitations. Vanity is always professional, never philosophic. It belongs to a narrow, technical, never to the largest, moral culture. And all the moral *forces* in the world, are strongest, divinest, when clearest of self. When the public man seeks his own advancement, more than the public weal, he is no more a statesman, but a mere politician; and when the reformer cares more for his own opinion than for the end to be gained, the people will not regard nor respect him. The world may be very selfish, but it will have honesty in those whom it permits to serve it.

The truth is that the whole culture of the world, is built on sacrifice; and all the nobleness in the world lies in that. To show that, it is only necessary to point to those classes of men and spheres of action, which exert the widest influence upon the improvement and welfare of mankind. They will all be found to bear that mark.

Look, first, at the professional teachers of the world — the authors, artists, professors, schoolmasters, clergymen. In returns of worldly goods, their services have been paid less, than any other equal ability and accomplishment in the world. Doubtless there have been exceptions; some English bishops and Roman prelates have been rich; and some authors and artists have gained a modest competence. More are doing it now, and yet more will. But the great body of intellectual laborers, has been poor. The instruction of the world, has been carried on by perpetual sacrifice. A grand army of teachers — authors, artists, schoolmasters, professors, heads of colleges — have been through ages, carrying on the war against ignorance; but no triumphal procession has been decreed to it; no spoils of conquered provinces have come to its coffers; no crown imperial has invested with pomp and power. In lonely watch-towers the fires of genius have burned, but to waste and consume the lamp of life, while they gave light to the world.

It is no answer to say that the victims of intellectual toil, broken down in health or fortune, have counted their work, a privilege and joy. As well deny the martyr's sacrifice, because he has joyed in his integrity. And many of the world's intellectual benefactors, have been martyrs. Socrates died in prison, as a public malefactor; for the healing wisdom he offered his people, deadly poison was the reward. Homer had a lot so obscure, at least, that nobody knew his birthplace; and indeed some modern critics are denying that there ever was any Homer. Plato travelled back and forth from his home in Athens to the court of the Syracusan tyrant, regarded indeed and feared, but persecuted and in peril of life; nay, and once sold for a slave. Cicero shared a worse fate. Dante, all his life knew, as he expressed it, —

> "How salt was a stranger's bread,
> How hard the path still up and down to tread,
> A stranger's stairs."

Copernicus and Galileo found science no more profitable than Dante found poetry. Shakspeare had a home; but too poorly endowed to stand long in his name, after he left it; the income upon which he retired was barely two or three hundred pounds a year; and so little did his contemporaries know or think of him, that the critics hunt in vain for the details of his private life. "The mighty space of his large honors," shrinks to an obscure myth of a life in theatres of London or on the banks of the Avon.

I might go on to speak, but it needs not, of the noble philanthropists and missionaries, often spoken of lightly in these days, because what is noblest must endure the severest criticism; of inventors, seldom rewarded for their sagacity and the immense benefits they have conferred upon the world; of soldiers, our own especially, buried by thousands, in unknown graves — green, would we fain say, green forever be the mounds that cover them! Let processions of men and women and children, every year, bring flowers, bring garlands of honor, to their lowly tombs!

But there is another form of self-consecration which is yet more essential, and which is universal. And yet *because* it is essential and universal, the very life-spring of the world's growth; because it is no signal benefit, but the common blessing of our existence; because it moulds our unconscious infancy, and mingles with our thoughtless childhood, and is an incorporate part of our being, it is apt to be overlooked and forgotten. The sap that flows up through the roots of the world — it is out of sight. The stately growths we *see;* the trees that drop balsam and healing upon the nations, we *see;* the schools, the universities, the hospitals, which beneficence has builded, we *see;* but the stream that, through all ages, is flowing from sire to son, is a hidden current.

It is one of the miracles of the world — this life that is forever losing, merging itself in a new life. We talk of martyrdoms; but there are ten thousands of martyrdoms, of which the world never hears. Beautiful it is to die for our country; beautiful it is to surrender life for the cause

of religious freedom; beautiful to *go forth*, to bear help
and healing to the sick, the wounded, the outcast and forlorn; but there are those who *stay at home*, alone, unknown,
uncelebrated, to do and to bear more than is ever done, in
one brief act of heroism or hour of martyrdom. In ten
thousand homes are those, whose life-long care and anxiety
wear and waste them to the grave. They count it no
praise; they consider it no sacrifice. I speak not, but for
the simple truth, of that which to me, is too holy for eulogy.
But meet it is, that a generation coming into life, which
owes its training and culture and preservation to a generation that is passing away, should be sensible of this truth—
of this solemn mystery of Providence—of this law of
sacrifice, of this outflow from self into domestic, into social
life, which lies at the very roots of the world.

There is one further application of the principle of disinterestedness, which goes beyond classes and instances
such as I have mentioned, and embraces men simply as
fellow-men. Much has been said among us of late years,
and none too much, of the dangers of an extreme individualism. We began as a religious body, in a strong
assertion of the rights of individual opinion; and we went
on in that spirit for a considerable time; till it seemed, at
length, as if we were liable to lose all coherence and to
fall to pieces in utter disintegration. But a few years ago,
moving in that zig-zag line which marks all human progress, we awoke to the dangers of the situation; and happily found that if we could not agree upon any technical
definition of Christian faith, we *could* combine for Christian
work. The National Conference was formed; a new impulse was given; new funds were poured into our treasury;
we are circulating books and tracts more widely than we

have ever done before; we are helping feeble churches and founding new ones, besides doing something for missions abroad: in short, we are trying to do the work which, in common with other Christian communions, properly belongs to us.

But there is another movement, which I regard with equal interest, and which promises in fact, to go deeper than any thing else we can do. I allude to those Unions, in which, I think the city of Providence leads the way: and in which New Bedford, Worcester, and Brooklyn have followed the example. These associations provide a public room or rooms, well lighted and warmed, for those who will, to resort to them; but especially for the young, who most need good culture, entertainment and encouragement; and in these rooms are found books, pictures, games, and music perhaps; and classes for regular instruction may be formed, and lectures occasionally given, or discussions held; in fact, whatever will contribute to the general improvement and to the pleasant and profitable passing of social evenings, may be introduced. This kind of institution is especially adapted to our smaller cities; and may be extended to our country villages. Our people in the country, live too much apart and alone; and besides the direct advantages of these gatherings together, a mutual acquaintance and a kindly feeling would be promoted, which are of scarcely less importance.

Let me add that there is a new ideal of life, which, I think, is slowly arising among us; and which, when it is fully carried out, I believe, will make an impression upon society, never before seen in the world. This is the idea of mutual helpfulness; of every man's living not to himself, but to God, in loving and helping his kind. Helpfulness, I say — that which Mr. Ruskin describes as the most glorious attribute of God himself; and which has so seized upon his imagination, that he ventures to substitute for "Holy, holy, holy is the Lord," Helpful, helpful, helpful, is the Lord God Almighty! This will not do; but it indicates a glorious tendency of modern thought. The old ideal of life has been, to get together the means of comfort and enjoyment; to get wealth, to get a fine house, to get luxuries for wassail and feasting, or to get books and pictures; and then to sit down and enjoy all this good estate, and transmit it to fortunate heirs, with little thought of others — with some charities perhaps, but without taking into heart or life, the common weal, happiness and improvement of all around.

What a millennium would it begin, if, instead of this, every man should be thinking, just so far as he can go beyond taking care of his own body and soul, what he can do for others — not in any merely eleemosynary way; not merely to instruct and improve men, with the pharisaic assumption of being better or better off than they; but by acting a brotherly part towards them, speaking neighborly words, doing neighborly deeds, smoothing the path, softening the lot, seeing all erring and sorrow, and joy and worth, as if they were their own; and wherever there is any difficulty or trial or need, to "lend a hand." Whenever such a spirit enters into and pervades society, it will make a world, compared with which, *our* time will sink back among the dark ages.

In short, when is it, that a man does and is, the highest that he is capable of? The answer is, when forgetting himself, forgetting advantage, gain, praise, fame, he pours himself out, in intellectual or moral, and, any way, beneficent activity. When does culture or art in him attain to the highest? It is when going beyond all thoughts of culture and art, he flings himself, in perfect sympathy and free communion, into the great mass of human interests. It is so that the greatest things have been achieved in all the higher fields of human effort — in writing, in eloquence, in painting and sculpture and music; and it is so, especially, that the doers of great things, have become the noblest men. "Art for art's sake," has been the motto for culture, with some. And to a certain extent, that is true. It is fine to work for the perfection of the work, and without any intrusion of self. But a man may work so, upon a theme of little or no significance to the world's improvement or welfare. He may work so, with small thoughts, small ideals, for which nobody cares, or has any reason to care. But so can he not work grandly, however finished be the result. Art is for the sake of something beyond itself. Only when it goes out into great ideals that mingle themselves with the widest culture and improvement of men, only when it strikes for the right, for liberty, for country, for the common weal, does it achieve its end.

We have had literature enough, and have it now, in which the writer seems hardly to go beyond himself — writing out of himself and into himself — occupied with making fine sentences, without any earnest intent; and which readers, used to feed upon the honest bread of plain English speech, hardly know what to make of. Very fine, these sparkling sentences may be, very beautiful, very apt to strike with admiration; but they divert attention with surprises, or cover up thought with coruscations. They are like gems that lie scattered upon the table; they are not wrought into any well-woven fabric; they do not move *on* the subject to any conclusion.

Men may win great admiration and great fame, but not great love; though they gain, perhaps, as much as they give. Only by writing out of the bosom of a great humanity *to* the great humanity, can one fill the measure of good art or good culture. Even Goethe, of whom Professor Seeley says, that "he found every thing interesting except the fact that Napoleon was trampling upon Germany"—a fatal exception: even Goethe, with all his art, his marvellous versatility and fine accomplishment, failed to reach the highest place, either in the best self-culture, or in men's best love. *Savant*, poet, novelist, of high mark, as he was, he has no such place as Newton, Wordsworth, and Walter Scott, in men's love. Schiller and Richter, I believe, are more beloved in Germany, than Goethe.

In mere art, in perfection of style, no writers have equalled Homer and Shakspeare. But *they* did not say, "Art for art's sake." They had no thought but to communicate their thought. If singular felicities appear in their style, little eddyings of exquisitely turned conceits, as especially in Shakspeare, they made a part of, and swept on the strong current of their ideas. They were not introduced for their own sake, or merely to please the writer.

It has been said that great authors are born of great occasions. Some remarkable era, some turn or tide in human thought, or in human affairs, have borne them on to their supreme greatness. Will not the time come, when men shall so look into the depths of the human heart, into the tragic or blissful experiences of all human life, that no great era shall be necessary to make great writers?

I believe it. I believe in a perpetual human progress — progress in every kind, material, mental, moral, religious, divine; and I greatly desire to say a few words in close, if you will indulge me upon this point. For I found this faith in progress, on the two principles which I have been considering in this lecture. Selfhood obliges a man to take care of himself. To go out of himself is the only way, in which he can take care of himself — can take care, that is to say, of his own improvement and happiness. In selfhood, necessary as it is, there is no virtue, and little joy. Outflow from it — love, generosity, disinterestedness — embraces the whole sphere of our culture and welfare.

Can there be any doubt upon either of these points — either the culture or welfare?

Upon the culture, I say; upon what makes for human improvement. There is evil enough in the world; but what nation or age ever approved of it? What people ever praised selfishness, injustice, falsifying of speech or trust? No literature ever celebrated them. No religion ever enjoined them. No laws ever enacted them. Imagine a law that proposed to reward villains and to punish honest men. The world would spit upon it. Imagine a book or essay or poem or oration, that plainly set about to tell what a beautiful and noble thing it is, to lie, to defraud, to wrong, corrupt, and ruin our fellows. No man ever had the face to do such a thing. No; books may have taught such things, but they never taught them as noble things. The man never lived, that would stand up and say, "It is a glorious thing to betray trust, or to ruin one's country, or to blaspheme God." Men do such things, but they don't reverence nor respect themselves for doing them.

This then being settled — and it is a stupendous fact — the right principle about culture, being thus set up, high and irrepealable in the human conscience and in the sentiments of all mankind — what says the common judgment of men about the happiness or misery of following the right? Does it say — "It is a blessed thing to be a bad man; it is good and wise to be a base or cruel man." Does it say — "Happy is the miser, the knave, the drunkard.' No, it does not. There is temptation to do wrong; *that* all know; there is a notion that it may promote some temporary interest or pleasure; there is a disposition in many, to prefer some sensual gratification to the purer satisfactions of the higher nature; but there is, at the same time, a deep-founded conviction, that misery in the long run must follow sin; that the everlasting law of God has so ordained it to *be;* and that only the pure, the noble, the heroic, the good and godlike affections can ever make such a nature as ours, content and happy.

Here then is another stupendous principle settled. And now, I say, this being is a lover of happiness. He is not wise; he is not clear-seeing; he is not good either — *i.e.*, he is not fixedly and determinately good; he is weak too; he is easily misled; he is often rebellious to the higher laws of his nature; but — I hold to that — he is a lover of happiness; and happiness, he knows, can never be found, but in obedience to those higher laws. He is a lover of happiness, I say; he cannot be worse off, without wishing to be better off; if he is sick, he wants to be well; if his roof lets in the rain, he will have it repaired; if the meanest implement he uses, is broken, he will have it mended. Is it not natural — is it not inevitable, that this tendency should yet develop itself in the higher concerns of his being? Is it not in the natural order of things, that the higher should at length gain the ascendency over the lower, the stronger over the weaker, the nobler over the meaner? How can it be thought — how can it *be*, in the realm of Infinite Beneficence and Wisdom, that meanness and vileness, sin and ruin should be strong and prevail, and gain victory upon victory, and spread curse beyond curse, and draw their dark trail over the bright eternity of ages!

No, in the order of things, this cannot be. Grant that there are evils, difficulties, obstacles in the way. But in the order of things, principles do not give way before temporary disturbances. Law does not yield to confusion. Gravitation binds the earth, notwithstanding all the turmoil upon its bosom. Light prevails over darkness, though cloud and storm and night interrupt its course. The *moral* turmoil upon earth's bosom, war and outbreak and widespread disaster, the cloud and storm and darkness of human passions and vices, the bitter struggles and sorrows of humanity, the dark shadows of earthly strife and pain and sin, are yet to give place to immutable law, to all-conquering might and right, to everlasting day.

I am as sure of it, as I am of the being of God — as I am of my own being. The principles of progress are laid in human nature. If man did not care for himself, I should have no hope of him. If he could not go out from himself, and find therein his improvement, virtue and happiness, I should have no hope of him. But these two principles yoked together, in the Heaven-ordained frame of our being, will draw on to victory.

THE RELATION OF JESUS

TO THE

PRESENT AGE.

By CHARLES CARROLL EVERETT.

THE RELATION OF JESUS

TO THE

PRESENT AGE.

THE writer to the Hebrews affirms that Jesus Christ is "the same yesterday, to-day, and for ever." Paul exclaims to the Corinthians, "Though we have known Christ after the flesh, yet now henceforth know we him no more." Christ was the same; yet before the generation that he left upon the earth had passed away his relation to the earth had changed. Thus does the work of Christ shape itself afresh to meet the needs of every generation. Compare together the Christ of the first century, the Christ of the thirteenth, the Christ of the sixteenth, and the Christ of the nineteenth centuries, and you would hardly think they all represent the same personality. Christ is always the same. His work is always substantially the same; but because the ages change, the method of this work changes. The same needs always exist in the heart of humanity, but in different ages these needs manifest themselves in different ways, and are to be met by different instrumentalities. And, further, it is not merely because the needs of humanity continually change their aspect that the work of Christ is ever changing. No age is a recipient alone. There is no action without reaction

Each age contributes something to the work of Christ. It adds new forces, new methods, new machinery. Its spirit, and by this I mean its real, vital, energizing spirit, becomes united with the spirit of Christ, as it is present and active in the world.

In considering the relation of Christ to the present age, we have then to consider it under two aspects. We have to consider each as a giver, and each as a receiver. We may help to make this double relation clear by saying that Christ is present to this nineteenth century at once as a problem and as a power. No questions have stirred more deeply the heart of the age than those which have to do with the person and the office of Christ. The answers to these questions shape the aspect in which he stands to the age, and become therefore parts and elements of the power by which he acts upon the world. But this statement does not exhaust the twofold relation of which I speak. That which the age gives to Christ is not merely its thought about him. The secular thought and life of the age bring their contribution, they are themselves a contribution to him. They furnish one part of that complete organism of which Christ furnishes the other. If the age, in any fundamental forms of its thought and life, seems to stand in opposition to Christ, this apparent opposition is only the antithesis of elements which belong together. If what we call the spirit of the age seems, in any respect, to stand in opposition to the spirit of Christ, this only shows the need that each has of the other. The spirit of this nineteenth century needs the spirit of Christ, and the spirit of Christ needs the spirit of this nineteenth century. It is not then merely that the thought of the age clears away something of the obscurity and the misconception that have gathered about the person and the work of Christ. If all he said and did were as truly comprehended now as they could have been at the first, no less real, no less important, would be the offering which this age would bring to him. Neither does the fact, that the work of Christ needs the work, and that his spirit needs the spirit, of the century in which we live, necessarily imply any imperfection in his original work, or any thing originally lacking in his spirit. The question as to what he had in reserve, as to the limit, or the lack of limit, of his insight and comprehension, is one that I do not need, and do not intend here to raise. There is a kind of work that cannot be done all at once. There is a fulness of spirit that cannot manifest itself all at once. It is sufficient to know that Christ recognized this fact as well as we can. He affirmed it as clearly and as confidently as it is possible for us to do. "I have," he said to his disciples, "yet many things to say unto you, but ye cannot bear them now. Howbeit, when he, the Spirit of truth, is come, he shall lead you into all truth." All, so far as we can see, that it was possible for any spirit to do at one moment, Christ did. He infused into the world a spirit of love and faith and consecration, a principle of enthusiasm for humanity. He added to these the vitalizing power that came from his personality. This he did, and with this he was forced to be content. He told us the nature of his work, and foretold to us its history. It was to be as a little leaven which a woman hideth in a measure of meal till the whole is leavened. He hid in the world the leaven of his truth. That was all that he could do. It is for us to witness, and to contribute to, the completion of his work.

In considering the theme before us, I shall speak, first,

of the external history of Christ, next of his teaching, and finally of his personality, in their relation to the present age.

In considering the relation of Christ to the present age, we are met, then, first by the most external form of this relation. The external history of Christ, the very framework of many of his highest and purest teachings, contains elements that are utterly opposed to the habits of thought which are most peculiar to the present century. I refer to whatever in the history of Christ implies the exercise of any miraculous power by him.

The idea of a miracle is opposed to the fundamental axioms of the popular thought of the present. The writers who best represent this thought do not hold it necessary to disprove the fact of miracles. They simply affirm, with Strauss, that the time is past when a miracle can be believed. On the other hand, the miraculous is inextricably intertwined with the history of Christ. We find miracles recognized, not merely in records the genuineness of which has, with or without reason, been suspected. In Epistles of Paul, the genuineness of which no critic of repute has ever dreamed of assailing, the miraculous element is recognized as distinctly as in the Gospels. We have at least the testimony of Paul — one of the grandest souls that ever lived, a man whom we know and honor as we know and honor few — that he believed himself to have wrought miracles, and that he believed the other apostles had done and were in the habit of doing the same. And we further have his testimony, with that of others indorsed by him, in regard to the most important of the miracles of Jesus; namely, the manifestation by Jesus of himself to his disciples after his death.

Here is a collision between the form of the external manifestation of Christ and the spirit of the age. The age itself has given such prominence to this that we cannot overlook it. The idea of miracle is so foreign to the spirit of the age that it has a fascination for it. It has less importance than any thing else in the history of Jesus, and yet nothing has more occupied the thoughts of the thinkers of the present generation.

For the reasons already stated, we must concede a certain degree of right to both sides of the great controversy. If we cannot eliminate the miraculous from the history of Jesus, neither can we, nor would we if we could, eliminate from the spirit of the age that element which finds it hard to accept a miracle. The very antagonism between the two, the right which each maintains being granted, shows the need that each has of the other. Each has a contribution for the other which could be received from no other source.

In the first place, the absolute incredulity with which the most thorough representatives of the thought of the time receive any story of the miraculous shows that now, for the first time, a miracle is seen to be in the truest sense of the word a miracle. To the child or the savage a miracle is hardly possible. Either every thing is a miracle or nothing is. It is only as the absoluteness of law is recognized that a miracle, which is in appearance a violation of this law, begins to produce its full impression. The present age has placed behind miracle a mighty background of law. From out this does miracle first stand forth in its true nature, as something demanding yet defying credence. Those who blame the spirit of the age for lack of faith in this direction should at least give it credit for this immense contribution to the idea of miracle, by which, for the first time, a miracle stands forth absolutely in its true nature.

Not only does the spirit of the age thus furnish to miracles the background that they need: it furnishes to them also a content. The thought of law does not stop with the background of laws of which I spoke. Laws may be finite: law is infinite. The miracle sets at defiance the great background of recognized laws; but itself can be only the manifestation of some higher, grander, more comprehensive law. Thus does a miracle more truly than ever before come as a real revelation. For the first time it has its full and logical meaning. It was before expected to prove something which from the nature of the case it could not prove. No miracle, however stupendous, can prove the truth of a principle in morals. It can show, indeed, some superiority, in some respect, in him who works the miracle; but this superiority may not be of a nature to demand implicit confidence towards the person in all respects. It may be like the superiority of the European over the ignorant savage. The missionary may win the trust of the simple barbarian by sending a message written upon a chip; but the sailor, bringing the seeds of all the vices of civilization, can "make the chip speak" as well as the missionary. But when the miracle testifies of the comprehensive law which it manifests, then first does it have a meaning which cannot be wrested out of it. Nay, then first does it become really sublime. Before, it was a single meteor flashing in short-lived brightness across the sky. Now, it is the first manifestation of a vast system of worlds of which we had not dreamed. Such is the contribution which the spirit of the age, through the very antagonism of which I spoke, makes to the miracles which constitute so much of the external form in which Christ meets it.

On the other hand, miracle brings a no less important contribution to the spirit of the age. This spirit tends, not only to look upon law as absolute, but to look upon the system of laws which it has discovered as final. These laws tend continually to become narrow and hard. They tend to become merely a system of physical forces. There is danger that the spirit may become shut up within these physical laws as in a prison-house. The miracle demonstrates to the senses that these physical laws are not absolute, even in their own realm; that these physical forces are encompassed and interpenetrated by spiritual forces; that matter is at the last subordinate to spirit. It may not reveal the nature of these spiritual forces; but it does reveal their presence. All do not need this demonstration. The same truth may be reached in other ways. The laws of thought reveal it. The spiritual consciousness may be sufficient unto itself. Christ himself regarded his miracles as of comparatively small account. He wrought them because he was moved to use whatever power he had to bless mankind. If he healed the sick, it was because he loved to heal them. He sympathized with sorrow and suffering, and, so far as he could, would remove their cause. But the miracles carry, as we have seen, their own revelation with them; and they have their place, however lowly, in regard even to the spiritual consciousness. The albatross, we are told, with all its magnificent sweep of wing, cannot lift itself from the flat surface of the deck on which it may be lying. Just because its wings are so strong and large, it needs to be lifted a little, that they may have space to move, that they may have freedom to smite the air. When this freedom has been given it, then it mounts upward, sustained by its own inherent strength. So is it, sometimes, with the spirit. It has strength of its own. It has a self-sustaining power. But it sometimes needs to be lifted a little way above the dead level of its daily life, above the plane of physical relations, before its wings find strength and freedom to beat the air. Then, leaving its temporary support behind it, it mounts in glad flight heavenward. Such help many have found, and may yet find, in the miracles of Jesus. The miracle may lift the level surface of life as if into a wave, from the crest of which the spirit may start upon its flight.

From the external manifestation of the history of Christ, and the external relations in which through this he stands to the present age, we pass to the inner power of this life. Within these external manifestations we find his teachings. We have, then, next to consider the relation in which Christ stands to the present age as a teacher. We shall find here the same twofold relation which we have found before; and the external may thus stand as a type and illustration of the internal. We will first consider, under this aspect, the basis and form of the teaching of Christ, and next its substance.

The spirit of the age is truth-seeking. We speak often of the eagerness for wealth that marks the age. I think that when, from the distant future, men shall look back upon this period of the world's history, the search for wealth will not be seen to fill the place that to us it seems to occupy. The age will be seen to be animated by a nobler quest than this. The search for truth will be seen to be the quest by which it is marked most really. We speak of the corruption of the age, of the trickeries of trade, of the unscrupulousness of speculation, of the pretence and display of fashion, of the venality of politics. All this is true. These things deserve the denunciation of the moralist and the preacher. But behind all this is the life which truly marks the age. It is the life of patient, earnest, honest search for truth. I believe that never and nowhere has there been manifested, to so great extent, such conscientious and self-forgetful love of truth for its own sake as may be found in the scientific investigations of the present day. Such accuracy of research, such microscopic delicacy of measurement, such patient and unprejudiced examination, I believe to be unequalled in the history of man. This proves that, in spite of the frauds and falseness of which I spoke, the age is really sound at heart. Theologians sometimes speak of the flippancy and conceit of the science of the day. The terms would be more true applied in the opposite direction. Theology is more open to such charges than science. A love of truth that would fling away even the highest glory of the earth and the hope of heaven, if so be truth may stand pure and perfect, has something sublime about it. Well might the theologian take a lesson from the man of science in regard to this consecration to truth. For theology, with its presumption, its prejudice, its pretence, its glossing over of difficulties, its leaning upon authority which it feels at heart is not authority, its saying what it does not exactly believe, that it may not contradict those who perhaps do not believe exactly what they say, may well stand ashamed in the presence of the science of the day that has left all to follow truth. Theology should give to science not tolerance, not patronage, but reverence. While it utters fearlessly the truth that is given it to speak, it should in its turn seat itself as a learner at the feet of science, and seek not only to gather the facts which it has to teach, but to catch something of its spirit, the spirit that loves truth, and that will suffer nothing to take the place of this.

But Christ was not a truth-seeker. It does not appear that he ever doubted or questioned. Pilate asked the question, What is truth? It does not appear that Jesus ever did. Jesus came not to seek the truth, but to announce it. "To this end," he cried, "was I born, and for this cause came I into the world, that I should bear witness unto the truth." He came to bear witness unto the truth, but it was truth that came to him without his seeking. Neither does it appear that Christ loved truth above all things. To the Jesuit there is something better than truth, and to this he will sacrifice truth itself. I assert nothing like this in regard to Christ. Truth was to him fundamental and essential. He would not accept or tolerate what was false. But still to know was not the great object of his life. There was something better to him than truth; namely, life. He would rather be than know. At his touch truth sprang into life. If he came to bear witness to the truth, this was only a step in his grander work, the work which he proclaimed at the very beginning of his mission, when he cried, "I am come that they might have life, and that they might have it more abundantly." And, further, Christ did not merely teach life through truth: he taught truth through life. "If any man," he said, "will do his will, he shall know of the doctrine." And John was full of the spirit of his Master when he cried, "The life is the light of men."

We see more clearly the antithesis between Christ as a teacher on the one side, and the present age on the other, in this fact: viz., that Christ speaks with authority to an age which rejects authority. The cry of the age, in the world of the intellect as well as in that of politics, is for liberty. But to this age, as to every age, Christ comes as a master. "My yoke," he says, "is easy;" but it is a yoke none the less.

If the relation of Christ to his truth is so different from that of the spirit of the age to its truth, it must follow that the two forms of truth rest on different bases. The faculties by which the age seeks truth must be different from those through which the truth came unsought to Jesus. This age seeks truth by the discriminating and investigating power of the understanding. Truth came to Jesus through the intuitions of the soul. In him the moral and spiritual faculties were full of strength. He lived as naturally in the world of spiritual realities as other men live in the world of physical realities. As we need only open our eyes and see, so his spirit had only to open its eyes and it saw. As the voices of the outward world come to us without our listening for them, so the voice of God came to him whether he would or no. And this was the ground of the authority with which he spoke. Whoever speaks from the moral and spiritual consciousness to the moral and spiritual consciousness may and must speak with authority. We may illustrate this by an extreme case. When a man is lurking for the commission of some crime, or after he has committed it, he feels the mastery of all innocent things. The rustle of a leaf may excite his dread. To a voice denouncing his crime, or crime like his, he listens as to the voice of God.

This recognition of the mastery of a higher degree of life after its own kind is felt at every stage of moral and spiritual development. If the soul be comparatively guilty, it recognizes this mastery with dread. If it be comparatively innocent, it recognizes it with joy. Such was the authority with which Jesus spoke. Though he spoke with authority, what he said did not rest on this authority. It was the authority with which the awakened calls to the sleeper, bidding him awake, for the world is bright with the morning. The voice penetrates to the obscured consciousness of the sleeper. He stirs himself, he opens his eyes, and rejoices for himself in the morning brightness. So Christ called to a sleeping world. Nay, he called to those who were dead in trespasses and sin, and they that were dead heard the voice of the Son of Man and lived.

If the truth taught by Jesus and the truth that is sought by the present age rest on such different bases, they must be, we should suppose, in some respects different each from the other. But, if each be truth, they must be the complements each of the other. And, if they are the complements each of the other, they must need one another. Each must be imperfect without the other. Each must find a certain confirmation and support from the other, and each must complete for the other the circle of truth. We are thus led to look at some points in the teaching of Christ, and to see how these complete and are completed by the truth which the present age seeks and finds.

In the first place, Christ teaches us of the loving providence of God. He awakens in our hearts all childlike instincts of trust and confidence. He tells us that God is our father, that his love watches over all his children, that it follows the prodigal in his wandering and greets him on his return, that even a sparrow does not fall to the earth without it. This teaching is sufficient for the spiritual necessities of our nature. The spirit that has adopted these principles into itself will live a strong and blessed life. They have been the inspiration of the centuries ever since Christ uttered them. They contain all that could be told of God in the age when Jesus lived. But they do not exhaust the truth of God. They leave space for misconception. Love may be universal, and yet be not without caprice. Providence may watch over all, and yet in every case be only a special providence. God may watch over every individual of the race, but over each merely as an individual. If there may be the caprices of love, then it is not a long step to the possibility of caprices which spring from the lack of love. Love may alternate with hate. If each individual be dealt with singly, as though he existed by himself, the step is not a long one to the thought of discrimination between individuals. The caprices of love may become favoritism, and the special favor shown to one implies the neglect of another. All these things are foreign from the spirit and the teaching of Christ. They contradict the fundamental principles of his teaching. And yet, men's habits of thought being such as they were, the teaching of Christ could not be absolutely fortified against them. He told men that the love of God was like the sunshine that visits all alike, but the words passed through their ears unheeded. Thus Christianity all along has been corrupted by misrepresentations of its truth in which the thought of love had suggested caprice, and the thought of special love and special providence had suggested the thought of favoritism, and favoritism had suggested discrimination and neglect. All men were seen to stand in the presence of God as individuals, which is true; and merely as individuals, which is false.

The truth that God is love needs to be supplemented by another truth; namely this, that God is Law. The great truth of the absoluteness of law cannot be taught in a single lesson. No man can tell it to another. It must be demonstrated to be believed. It must be shown in its myriad and unvarying applications to all forms of being before it can be felt as a reality. One must see for one's self the grand march of the order of the universe, the unfailing sequence of cause and effect, the mathematical exactness of the correlation of all the forces of the world, before one can have a sense of the truth which lies at the basis and forms the culmination of scientific thought today. This truth has not been reached suddenly. The ages have been groping after it. This age has reached, by slow and patient thought, a comprehension of this truth which is its inspiration. The ages to come will only add to it new illustrations as they follow its mighty sweep. This truth is what seems at times to put this age into antagonism with the spirit of Christ. It is really the offering which the thought of the age brings to Christ. The teaching of Christ needs, as we have seen, this truth as its complement. The antithesis between the two shows the intimate relationship between them. When we bring the two together in one thought, we have the most sublime conception that ever dawned upon the mind of man. The truth of Christ finds a body: the truth of the age finds a soul. On the one side, all possibility of caprice is driven from our thought of God. The lov-

of God, as strong and tender as the lips of Jesus could describe it, is seen to be as regular and as calm as the movements of the heavens. This truth only adds to the strength and the clearness of our thought of the love of God. We see demonstrated before us how his care pursues all things, how not a sparrow falls to the earth unfollowed by this watchful providence, how every grain of dust that floats in the summer sun has its place and work in the great whole, not a single mote forgotten. We learn in what direction to look for the action and succor of this providence. We do not look for it to come to us in weakness, but in strength. We see that this perfect order is the truest providence, that the care of each is most perfect that recognizes each in its relations to all the rest. So soon as we recognize the divinity of law and the love that is enshrined in it, we feel the omnipresent might of this divinity, the omnipotence of this love. The restlessness and passion of our hearts are stilled. Trust in God takes on the peace and the calmness of the heavens. Such is the offering which the age brings to Christ. It brings a body in which his spirit may incarnate itself afresh.

The result of the union of the thought of the age with the thought of Christ may be seen in all the relations in which the soul stands to God. Christ bade his followers preach his gospel to every creature. The age has taught us the necessity of educating and civilizing the barbarian, if we would christianize him. Christ taught us to love the sinner while hating sin. This has seemed to some paradoxical; but the age has removed some of the difficulty by showing how much of what we call character is the result of inherited tendencies and outward circumstances. Jesus taught the doctrine of immortality. Men have tended to look upon the future life as something standing over against the present. The age teaches us that such a break in life is impossible, that if there be an immortality it must lie hidden in the present. It teaches, too, that the judgments of God, if there be a God, are never arbitrary. He does not hold blessing in one hand and cursing in another, and give each, by an outward bestowal, as he may see that it is deserved. Men's acts drag their consequences after them. Thus the old Scripture phrases are just coming to their meaning. It is not an angry God that pursues the sinner: it is his own sin that has found him out. Men do reap the fruit of their own sowing. There is no scientific truth of the day that stands in any stronger antagonism to the truth of Christ than is implied in such antitheses as have been referred to. Even the theories of development, so rife at present, do not stand in the way of Christ. Christ looks not downward but upward, not backward but forward. Such theories, if established, would only show the progressive power of spirit, the omnipotence of life.

But if the thought of Jesus needs that of the present age, still more does the thought of the age need that of Jesus. If the spirit needs a body, still more does the body need a spirit. The laws, the forces on which the thought of the age dwells, until this divineness is added to them are hard and cold. The body, which could carry on all the functions of its life, yet without life, would be a machine, perfect indeed and wonderful, but a machine none the less. The thought of the age, taken by itself, uninspired by Christian truth, tends to drag down the soul, to imprison it in mere mechanism, to take from it its divine inspiration; and while we need the thought of the present age to illustrate to us the methods of God's dealings with the soul, none the less does the thought of the age need the knowledge that there is a soul. Among all the forces of the universe, the power of the soul, the culmination of them all, is apt to be lost sight of. The thought of the age tends to look upon things from without, and to lose that which is their essence. It needs the voice that shall awaken its own inner life, and thus bring it to a consciousness of the life that lies at the heart of all things.

Thus we see how the thought of Christ and the thought of the age need and complement each other. The thought of Christ is spiritual, the thought of the age tends to become material. In this world we are neither wholly spiritual nor wholly material. And we must bear in mind that the two elements should not exist over against one another in our thought. We must not hold the two conceptions, however opposite they may appear, as two. In life the spirit and the body do not exist as two but as one. As soon as they exist as two, there is death. So must the truth of Jesus and the truth of this present age be blended in one thought. We must not say love and law, but love in law. We must not see the divine power setting at work forces that by their natural operation shall reward or punish the spirit. We must see the divine power working in and through these forces. Then, as science makes us feel that we are encompassed by law, the words will not need translating to us; for we shall feel that we are encompassed by God.

The relation which we have found to exist between the intellectual teaching of Christ and the thought of the age is no less marked between the moral teaching of Christ and the life of the age. The moral teaching of Christ is absolutely true. It is as true as his thought of God; yet like that it needs its complemental truth. Further, the moral teaching of Christ needs instrumentalities. Love, however strong, cannot work without means. The heart needs the hands and the feet.

In both of these respects the age brings its offering to Christ. Christ teaches love and self-sacrifice. He bids us do for others as we would have them do for us. He bids us give to him that asks, and lend to him that would borrow. These principles are the very life of society. They are the very truth of God. But yet these principles carried out, without explanation and qualification, would produce harm as well as good. The church of every age, in striving to carry out these precepts, has done much good; but it has done much harm also. It has done good by bringing succor to the lives that needed it. It has done immeasurable good by keeping alive on the earth the spirit of Christian love. Men have been blest by the power of the spirit, even more than by its specific acts of mercy. But, while it has relieved the poor, it has too often tended to perpetuate poverty. Indiscriminate alms-giving, mere alms-giving, is the very mother of pauperism. We see in some Catholic countries how the alms-giving which the church has taught in the very words of Christ has degraded whole populations, has taken from manhood its real dignity and strength. We need, then, not only the principle of love, but also a knowledge of all social laws. The science of political economy must be understood; but this, like physical science, cannot be taught in a day. Ages must teach the lesson. The present age has only half learned it. But it has learned enough to bring a magnificent contribution to Christ. Christ bids us help men: the age, in its poor blundering way, is just beginning to tell us how to help them. It teaches that the best way to help the poor is to strike at the root of poverty. No less does the age furnish means for carrying out the principles of Jesus. It brings the ends of the earth together. Christ bids us love our neighbor. This age has made those from whom the sea parts us our neighbors. There is famine, or some more sudden calamity, on the other side of our continent, or in a foreign land. Christ bids us help those who need. How shall we carry sudden help unless we hear at once the story? How shall we send prompt help if there be no strong and swift messenger waiting at our door? But now the lightning tells the story the moment in which there is a story to be told, and the unwearied steam bears our gifts as soon as they can be gathered. The commands of Jesus are absolute. The power of the age to fulfil these commands is approaching absoluteness. Thus does the age add to the teaching of Christ the completeness that it needs.

But does not the age in turn need this teaching? Materialism and mechanism in thought are bad enough: they are worse in life. The life of the age has a tendency to materialism and mechanism. The science of political economy tends to become a hard system of rules, in which the spontaneous sympathy of the helper and the individuality of the helped are lost together. The eagerness of the world after material prosperity tends to a practical absorption in these ends. Thus we have the greed, the excitement, the madness, the display, the corruption that to so great an extent characterize the age. We have seen that there is a deeper life beneath this superficial one; but these evils, however superficial, need prompt and constant care lest they eat into the very heart. The body needs the spirit, or it will sink into decay.

I have spoken of the two elements which we are considering as if they stood simply over against one another. This is in some respects true. The thought and life of the age are, indeed, largely indebted to the stimulus of Christianity; but they are not, like the painting and architecture of the Middle Ages, the direct outgrowth of it. The science of the present day is self-developed and self-sustained. The machinery of the world has been invented for the world's uses. Its political economy has been thought out to facilitate its own ends.

But though the two elements, to some extent, stand over against one another, yet each, by its natural development, is approaching the other, and each is becoming penetrated by the other. On the one side, religion is catching the spirit of the age, and is approaching the clearness and accuracy of scientific thought. On the other side, science is becoming conscious of truth which is unattainable by its methods, and which is to it therefore the unknowable. Already does Herbert Spencer, who represents the foremost thought of the time, feel the awe of this mystery, and see gleaming through it something of the presence of the infinite love. The life of the age, also, by bringing men near to one another, tends to produce the sense of human brotherhood. Its vast business enterprise, in some of its aspects, does more for the cause of humanity than many a professed charity. Further, the age is, to some extent at least, directly inspired by Christianity. Its zeal for humanity, its sympathy with the oppressed and suffering everywhere, its gigantic and unparalleled charities, show it to be more truly Christian than any age that has preceded it.

If however, in spite of all this, we are sometimes tempted to doubt whether the power of the truth which Christ represents is to win the mastery, or whether it is destined to be lost in the great struggle, we must remember that its authority is that of elements that are fundamental in human nature. The spiritual instincts may be repressed: they cannot be exterminated. As in every little creek and inlet along the shore the water answers to the call of the ocean, and feels the might of the outgoing and the incoming tide, so in human life deep answers unto deep.

We must remember, too, that Christ is not a mere teacher. His power is not alone that of the truth he utters. It is no mere accident of history that the higher truth and life which we have been considering confront the age as Christian truth and life. They receive a power from their union with Christ which they could not have received, even had the thought of men attained to them, without this. We have looked at the external form of his life and at his teaching in their relation to the age. There is yet another step to take. There is still an inner reality to be unveiled. Behind the power of his teaching is the power of his personality. In this is found the climax of the antithesis in which he stands to the present. The tendency of the present age is, consciously or unconsciously, to disown personality. The laws which make the substance of its thought, the mechanism that makes the framework of its life, both tend to assert themselves against the power of a free personality. We may illustrate this by the modern method of warfare. In ancient times the victory depended on the strength of the individual arm and the courage of the individual heart. Now it depends more upon the drill of the army and the clear head of the general.

This tendency of the thought of the age is not based on error. It brings to our thought of personality the correction that it needs. The tendency of the past has been to look upon personality as existing by and for itself. It has recognized no limits to the power of freedom. Each individual stood by and for himself in the universe. Now we see a common element in all lives. All lives are entwined together. We see limits which freedom cannot pass. We understand something of the limits of each individual. We understand something of the laws of descent and of the power of education. Even the personality of Jesus does not stand by itself as it seemed to once. We see in him the power of the common nature. We see in him the effect of forces which had been in operation since the world was. He was no stranger upon the earth. He was the Son of God, but he was no less the Son of man. He was the flowering of a nation's history, the flowering of humanity. The flower is drawn forth by the sun, but it is drawn out from the plant. Even the sun can kindle the flame of no rose upon the bramble's stalk. While, however, the age teaches us what is the background out from which the power of personality stands forth, and what are the elements that are fused together in it, personality itself remains too much unrecognized. But, I repeat, the integrity of human nature can never be violated; and personality is the culmination of human nature. The power of a modern army, we have seen, depends largely on its drill; yet even here the impetuous courage of a leader may infuse a life into this vast machine that shall decide the victory. Mere signals, it is found, upon a ship will not answer the purpose of communication between the captain and the men. In times of peril, in the midst of the fury of the storm, the sailor needs the inspiration of the captain's voice, ringing with a force that is mightier than the tempest; namely, the force of human will and courage. No matter how mechanical the age may become, no matter how the idea of freedom may be eliminated from its thought, the great heart of humanity beats still in its bosom, and the voice of a strong, free personality will sooner or later arouse it to an answering consciousness. The very bands which it sets about personality will make its power more strongly felt when it is perceived. Its very knowledge of the elements that are united in it will make it feel more really the might of the force which can fuse these into one burning point.

Personality involves three elements. The first is freedom; the second, a purpose freely chosen; the third, devotion to this purpose. There is no slavery like sin. Absolute freedom, and thus absolute personality, can be found only in a nature wholly pure and unselfish. Christ was thus free. His purpose was the vastest that any human soul has grasped; and he gave himself to it with all the power of his nature. Thus Christ possessed the most intense personality ever felt upon the earth. His teaching came forth glowing with its fire. We feel to-day the effect which his personality produced upon those who came into direct contact with it. This influence has propagated itself from age to age. The Church grew out of it, and its influence is felt to-day far beyond the limits of the Church. Besides this indirect power of the personality of Jesus, we may feel its force directly, as we bring ourselves into personal relation with him. It has not lost its original might. It still tends to reproduce itself in the present.

The form in which truth first utters itself has a power which no subsequent repetition can equal. There is a kind of work that can be done only once. The first discoverer or announcer of any truth stands in a relation to it which no other can ever fill. Many navigators have crossed the sea, but there is only one Columbus. Many astronomers have searched the heavens, but there has been no second Newton. This fact is most noticeable in regard to truths that represent not merely the intellect, but the whole moral and spiritual nature of him who first uttered them in their fulness. There is a fact in science strange, apparently illogical, but yet unquestionable. It is this: The power of heat-bearing rays to pass through any resisting medium depends not upon the temperature of the rays, but upon that of the body from which they come. The heat-bearing rays of the sun that approach the earth hardly differ in temperature from the rays that are reflected from it; but the former pass almost unimpeded through the atmosphere by which the latter are to a great extent imprisoned. The rays reach the earth without difficulty, but are entrapped by the principle referred to, and remain to bless the world. The first have this power to pass through the atmosphere because they come direct from the burning body of the sun. The reflected rays have lost this power, because they proceed from the colder earth. This law is as true in the intellectual and spiritual as it is in the physical world. The power of moral and spiritual truths to penetrate to the hearts of men has this strange dependence upon the moral and spiritual power of him who utters them. The very spontaneity of this utterance is a revelation of this power. It is because the truth that Jesus uttered came forth from his glowing heart of love, it is because it sprang fresh and spontaneous from the intensity of his spiritual life, that it has such power to-day to touch the hearts of men. As the sun's rays preserve their penetrating force through all the interplanetary spaces, so the teachings of Christ have preserved it through all the reaches of history. No subsequent repetition of these truths can ever have quite the power that their first complete utterance still retains. And the power that they exercise is largely in this, that they excite in the hearts of men a spiritual life akin to that from which they originally sprang. Scientific truths are taught by demonstration. Spiritual truths are taught chiefly by stimulating the spiritual life. When we live merely in the contemplation of laws, in the study of external relations, our intellect is stimulated, but our moral and spiritual nature may be comparatively dormant. Our life is stimulated as we are brought into living relationship with the universe. As our inner nature is thus stimulated, as it rounds itself into completeness, the moral and spiritual consciousness is awakened. This is the reason why it so often happens that spiritual truths are so real in moments of sorrow. In its sorrow the soul lives wholly in love, and it receives the enlightenment of love. Our nation had almost forgotten God; but in those terrible years of war, when every soul was full of life and earnestness, the earth and the heavens were full of God. Our nation's history became transparent to us, as the history of the Hebrews was transparent to them, and we saw God's providence in it all. Theology has wrestled vainly with science. In such a struggle it will always be the loser. Christian theology can never conquer science. Christian life must absorb science into itself.

The truths that Jesus uttered, as they have been absorbed into the common thought of men, or as they are received directly from the record of his life, have a mighty power to purify the thought and elevate the hearts of men. But I think that the greatest power of Christ to-day is that of imparting his life to the men and women who are now living in the world. The power of the Church will depend upon its power to receive this life and to impart it. It is well to have a true theology; but the church that has the most of the life of Christ will accomplish the most for men. It brings to this truth-seeking and law-investigating age the pure personality which it needs. And it will at last possess the truest theology, for now and evermore it is the life that is the light of men.

THE MYTHICAL ELEMENT

IN THE

NEW TESTAMENT.

By FREDERIC HENRY HEDGE.

THE MYTHICAL ELEMENT

IN THE

NEW TESTAMENT.

"Φιλοσοφώτερον καὶ σπουδαιότερον ποίησις ἱστορίας ἐστιν."
ARISTOTLE.

WHEN Dr. Strauss, thirty-five years ago, in his "Life of Jesus," advanced and applied to the narrative of the New Testament a theory of interpretation, in principle the same with that which a Christian Father of the third century had employed in his treatment of the Old, the theological world was profoundly shocked by what seemed to be the last impiety of criticism. A hundred champions rushed with drawn pen to the rescue of the old interpretation of the text. The truth of Christianity was supposed to be assailed; the belief in Christianity as divine revelation was felt to be imperilled by a theory which substituted mythical figment for historic fact. That no such harm was intended, or was likely to ensue from his labors, the author himself assures us in the preface to that extraordinary work. "The inner kernel of Christian faith," he declares, "is entirely independent of all such criticism. Christ's supernatural birth, his miracles, his resurrection and ascension, remain eternal truths, however their reality as facts of history may be called in question."

In this declaration I find a fitting text for the following discourse.

How far does the cause of Christianity depend on the facts, or alleged facts, of the Gospel narrative? Or, to state the question in other words, Is the truth of Christianity identical and conterminous with the literal truth of its record?

It is obvious at the start that a certain amount of historic truth must be assumed as implied in the very existence of any religion which dates from a personal founder whose thought it professes to embody, and whose name it bears. Christianity purports to be founded on the ministry of a Jewish teacher, entitled by his followers "the Christ." We have the testimony of a nearly contemporary Latin historian to the fact that an individual so named was the leader of a numerous body of religionists, and was put to death by command of Pontius Pilate, in the reign of Tiberius. But, without this confirmation, the very existence of the Christian Church compels us to accept as historic facts, the ministry of Jesus, the strong impression of his word and character, his purity of manners and moral greatness, his life of beneficent action, his martyr death, and his manifestation to his disciples after death, however that manifestation be conceived, whether as subjective experience or as objective reality. So much, beyond all reasonable question, must stand as history, vouched by documentary evidence, and by the existence, in the first century, of a church universally diffused, which affirmed these facts as the ground of its being, and in the strength of them overcame the world.

But, observe, it is Christianity that assures the truth of these facts, and not the facts that prove Christianity. To base the truth of Christianity on the credibility, in every particular, of the Gospel record; to measure the claims of the religion by the strict historic verity of all the narrative of the New Testament, is to prejudice the Christian cause in the judgment of competent critics. It is to challenge the cavil and counter-demonstration of unbelief.

Christianity assures the truth of certain facts; but by no means of all the facts affirmed by the writers of the New Testament. Faith in Christianity as divine dispensation does not imply, and must not be held to the belief, as veritable history, of all that is recorded in the Gospel. Not the historic sense, but the spiritual import; not the facts, but the ideas of the Gospel, are the genuine topics of faith.

Christianity, like every other religion, has its mythology, — a mythology so intertwined with the veritable facts of its early history, so braided and welded with its first beginnings, that history and myth are not always distinguishable the one from the other. Every historic religion, that has won for itself a conspicuous place in the world's history, has evolved from a core of fact a nimbus of legendary matter which criticism cannot always separate, and which the popular faith does not seek to separate, from the solid parts of the system. And in one view the legends or myths which gather around the initial stage of any religion are as true as the vouched and substantial facts of its record: they are a product of the same spirit working, in the one case, in the acts and experiences; in the other, in the visions, the ideas, the literary activity of the faithful. It is one and the same motive that inspires both the writer and the doer.

When I speak of historic religions, I mean such as trace

their origin to some historic personage, and bear the impress of his idea, in contradistinction to those which have sprung from unknown sources, the wild growths of nature-worship as found in ancient Egypt, in the Indian and Scandinavian peninsulas, and in Greece.

No distinction in religion is so fundamental as that between the wild religions and those which have sprung from the word of a human sower going forth to sow; the religions of sense and those of reflection, the "natural" and the "revealed." The prime characteristic of the former is polytheism; that of the latter, monotheism. Mosaism, Mohammedism, Buddhism, — so far as it knows any God, — even Parsism, is monotheistic in as much as its dualism is resolvable into the final triumph and supremacy of the good. No founder of a religion ever taught a plurality of gods.

Another characteristic of the wild religions is their transitoriness. The Egyptian, the Greco-Roman, the Scandinavian, perished long ago. Bramanism, the last survivor of the ancient polytheisms, is fast melting beneath the advancing heats of Islam and the Brahmo Somaj. The "revealed" religions on the contrary are permanent. No religion of historic origin, so far as I know, has ever died out. Judaism, the eldest of them, still flourishes: never since the destruction of Jerusalem has it flourished with a greener leaf than now. Mohammedism is pushing its conquests faster than Christianity in the East, Parsism is still strong in Bengal, Buddhism in one or another form calls a third part of the population of the globe its own.

All religions have their mythologies, but with this distinction: polytheism is mythical in principle as well as form, in soul as well as body, and mythical throughout. Its whole being is myth. Whatever of scientific or historic truth may be hidden in any of its legends, such as the labors of Herakles, the fire-theft of Prometheus, or the rape of Europa, is matter of pure conjecture. In the "revealed" religions, on the contrary, the mythical is incidental, not principial, and always subordinate to doctrine or fact. Always the truth shines through the myth, explains it, justifies it.

Before proceeding any farther, I desire to explain what I mean by myth in this connection. I shall not attempt a philosophic definition, but content myself with this general determination. I call any story a myth which for good reasons is not to be taken historically, and yet is not a wilful fabrication with intent to deceive, but the natural growth of wonder and tradition, or a product of the Spirit uttering itself in a narrative form. The myth may be the result of exaggeration, the expansion of a veritable fact which gathers increments and a *posse comitatus* of additions as it travels from mouth to ear and ear to mouth in the carriage of verbal report; or it may be the reflection of a fact in the mind of a writer, who reproduces it in his writing with the color and proportions it has taken in his conception; or it may be the poetic embodiment of a mental experience; or it may be what Strauss calls "the deposit[1] of an idea," and another critic "an idea shaped into fact." I think we have examples of all these mythical formations in the New Testament; and I hold that the credit of the Gospel in things essential is nowise impaired, nor the claim of Christianity as divine revelation compromised, by a frank admission of

[1] Niederschlag.

this admixture of fancy with fact in its record. On the contrary, I deem it important, in view of the vulgar radicalism which confounds the Christian dispensation and its record, soul and body, in one judgment, to separate the literary question from the spiritual, and to free the cause of faith from the burden of the letter.

It has been assumed that the proof of divine revelation rests on precisely those portions of the record which are most offensive to unbelief. On this assumption the Christian apologists of a former generation grounded their plea. Prove that we have the testimony of eye-witnesses to the miracles recorded in the Gospels, and Christianity is shown to be a divine revelation. In the absence of such proof (the inference is) Christianity can no longer claim to be, in the words of Paul, "the power of God unto salvation." This is substantially Paley's argument. Planting himself on the premise that revelation is impossible without miracles, in which it is implied that miracles prove revelation, he labors to establish two propositions: 1. "That there is satisfactory evidence that many professing to be original witnesses of the Christian miracles passed their lives in dangers, labors, and sufferings, voluntarily undergone in attestation of the accounts which they delivered, and solely in consequence of their belief in those accounts; and that they also submitted from the same motives to new rules of conduct." 2. "That there is *not* satisfactory evidence that persons pretending to be original witnesses of any other similar miracles have acted in the same manner in attestation of the accounts which they delivered, and solely in consequence of their belief in the truth of those accounts." The argument is stated with the characteristic clearness of the author, and as well supported perhaps as Anglican church-erudition in those days would allow; but the case is not made out, and, if it were, the argument fails to satisfy the sceptical mind of to-day. To say nothing of its gross misconception of the nature of revelation, which it makes external instead of internal, a stunning of the senses instead of mental illumination, an appeal to prodigy and not its own sufficient witness, — waiving this objection, the argument fails when confronted with the fact that, in spite of the evidence which scholars and critics the most learned and acute of all time have arrayed in support of the genuineness of the Gospels, the number is nowise diminished, but rather increases, of intelligent minds that find themselves unable, on the faith of any book, however ancient, to receive as authentic a tale of wonders which contradict their experience of the limits of human ability and their faith in the continuity of nature. For myself, I beg to say, in passing, I am not of this number. I do not feel the force of the objection against miracles drawn from this alleged constancy of nature, which it seems to me reduces the course of human events to a dead mechanical sequence, makes no allowance for any reserved power in nature or any incalculable forces of the Spirit, and virtually rules God, the present inworking God, out of the universe. I can believe in any miracle which does not actually and demonstrably contravene and nullify ascertained laws, however phenomenally foreign to nature's ordinary course. But the possibility of miracles is one thing, the possibility of proving them another. With such views as these objectors entertain of the constancy of nature, I confess that no testimony, not even the written affidavit of a dozen witnesses taken on the spot, supposing that we had it, would suffice to convince me of the truth of marvels occurring two thousand years ago, of the kind recounted in the Gospels. My Christian prepossessions might incline me to believe in them: the weight of evidence would not. No wise defender of the Christian cause, at the present day, will rest his plea on the issue to which Paley committed its claims. After all that Biblical critics and antiquarian research have raked from the dust of antiquity in proof of the genuineness and authenticity of the books of the New Testament, credibility still labors with the fact that the age in which these books were received and put in circulation was one in which the science of criticism as developed by the moderns — the science which scrutinizes statements, balances evidence for and against, and sifts the true from the false — did not exist; an age when a boundless credulity disposed men to believe in wonders as readily as in ordinary events, requiring no stronger proof in the case of the former than sufficed to establish the latter, — viz., hearsay and vulgar report; an age when literary honesty was a virtue almost unknown, and when, consequently, literary forgeries were as common as genuine productions, and transcribers of sacred books did not scruple to alter the text in the interest of personal views and doctrinal prepossessions. The newly discovered Sinaitic Code, the earliest known manuscript of the New Testament, dates from the fourth century. Tischendorf the discoverer, a very orthodox critic, speaks without reserve of the license in the treatment of the text apparent in this manuscript, — a license, he says, especially characteristic of the first three centuries.

These considerations, though they do not discredit the essential facts of the Gospel history, — facts assured to us, as I have said, by the very existence of the Christian Church, — might seem to excuse the hesitation of the sceptic in accepting, on the faith of the record, incidental marvels of a kind very difficult of proof at best. I recall in this connection the remarkable saying of an English divine of the seventeenth century. "So great, in the early ages," says Bishop Fell, "was the license of fiction, and so prone the facility of believing, that the credibility of history has been gravely embarrassed thereby; and not only the secular world, but the Church of God, has reason to complain of its mythical periods." [1]

It is not in the interest of criticism, much less of a wilful iconoclasm, from which my whole nature revolts, but of Christian faith, that I advocate the supposition of a mythical element in the New Testament. I am well aware that in this advocacy I shall lack the consent of many good people who identify the cause of religion with its accidents, and fancy that the sanctuary is in danger when a blind is raised to let in new light. I respect the piety that clings to idols which Truth has outgrown, as Paul at Athens respected the religion which worshipped ignorantly the unknown God. But Truth once seen will draw piety after it, and new sanctities will replace the old. No Protestant in these days feels himself bound to accept as history the ecclesiastical legends of the post-apostolic age. Some of them are quite as significant as some of those embodied in the canon; but no Protestant scruples to reject as spurious the story of the caldron of boiling oil into which St. John was thrown by order of the

---

[1] Tanta fuit primis seculis fingendi licentia, tam prona in credendo facilitas, ut rerum gestarum fides graviter exinde laboraverit, nec orbis tantum terrarum sed et Dei ecclesia de temporibus suis mythicis merito queratur.

Emperor Domitian, and from which he escaped unharmed, or that of the lioness which licked the feet of Thecla in the circus at Antioch, or Peter's encounter with Christ in the suburbs of Rome. If we talk of evidence, I do not see but the miracles said to be performed by the relics of martyrs at Milan, attested by St. Augustine, and those of St. Cuthbert of Durham, attested by the venerable Bede, are as well substantiated as the opening of the prison doors and the liberation of the Apostles by an angel, attested by Luke. The Church of Rome makes no such distinction between the first and the following centuries: she indorses the miracles of all alike. But modern Protestantism draws a line of sharp separation between the apostolic and the post-apostolic ages. On the farther side the portents are all genuine historic facts: on the hither side they are all figments. While John the Evangelist, the last of the twelve, yet breathed, a miracle was still possible: his breath departed, it became an impossibility for evermore. And yet when Conyers Middleton first ran this line between the ages, and published his refutation of the claim of continued miraculous power in the Church, religious sensibility experienced a shock as great as that inflicted in our day by Strauss, and resented with equal indignation the affront to Christian faith. The author of the "Free Inquiry" published in 1748 was assailed by opponents, who "insinuate" he tells us "fears and jealousies of I know not what consequences dangerous to Christianity, ruinous to the faith of history, and introductive of universal scepticism." The larger work had been preceded by an "Introductory Discourse" put forth as a feeler of the public pulse; for "I began," he says, "to think it a duty which candor and prudence prescribed, not to alarm the public at once with an argument so strange and so little understood, nor to hazard an experiment so big with consequences till I had at first given out some sketch or general plan of what I was projecting." The experiment which required such careful preparation was to ascertain how far the English public in the middle of the eighteenth century would bear to have it said that the miracles affirmed by Augustine and Chrysostom and Jerome, as occurring in their day, were not as worthy of credit as any of the wonders recorded in the New Testament. Up to that time, English Protestants as well as Romanists had given equal credence to both, and esteemed the former as essential to Christian faith as the latter. Men like Waterland and Dodwell and Archbishop Tillotson held that miracles continued in the Church until the close of the third century, and were even occasionally witnessed in the fourth. Whiston, the consistent Arian, maintained their continuance up to the establishment of the Athanasian doctrine in 381, and "that as soon as the Church became Athanasian, antichristian, and popish, they ceased immediately; and the Devil lent it his own cheating and fatal powers instead."

To me, I confess, the position of the Church of Rome in this matter seems less indefensible than that of Middleton and modern Protestantism. Either deny the possibility of miracles altogether to finite powers, or admit their possibility in the second century, and the third century, as well as the first, and in all centuries whenever a worthy occasion demands such agency. I can see no reason for separating, as Middleton does, the age of the Apostles from all succeeding. Had he drawn the line between the miracles of Christ and those ascribed to his followers, the principle of division would have been more intelligible, and more admissible on the ground of ecclesiastical orthodoxy.

But the question here is not of the possibility or probability of miracles, as such, in one age rather than another. It is a question simply of Biblical interpretation,— whether the literal sense of the record is in every case the true sense, whether history or fiction is the key to certain Scriptures. Those who insist on the verbal inspiration of the New Testament will be apt to likewise insist on the literal historic sense of every part of every narrative. And yet that mode of interpretation is by no means a necessary consequence or logical outcome of that theory. Origen believed in the verbal inspiration of the Old Testament, but Origen did not accept in their literal sense the Hebrew theophanies: he allegorized whatever seemed to him to degrade the idea of God. The Spirit can utter itself in fiction as well as fact, and in communicating with Oriental minds was quite as likely to do so. And surely, for those who reject the notion of verbal inspiration, the way is open, in perfect consistency with Christian faith, for such interpretation as reason may approve or the credit of the record be thought to require. The credit of the record will sometimes require an allegorical interpretation instead of a literal one.

It is a childish limitation which in reading stories can feel no interest in any thing but fact; and a childish misconception which supposes that where the form is narrative, historic fact must needs be the substance. Recount to a little child a fable of Pilpay or Æsop, and his questions betray his inability to apprehend it otherwise than as literal fact. He has no doubt of the truth of the story; "what did the lion say then?" he asks; and "what did the fox do next?" The maturer mind has also no doubt of the truth of the story, but sees that its truth is the moral it embodies. Of many of the Gospel stories the moral contained in them is the real truth. In the height of our late civil war there appeared in a popular journal a story entitled "A Man without a Country," related with such artistic verisimilitude, such minuteness of detail, such grave official references, that many who read it not once suspected the clever invention, and felt themselves somewhat aggrieved when apprised that fiction, not fact, had conveyed the moral intended by the genial author. But those who saw from the first through the veil of fiction the needful truth and the patriotic intent were not less edified than if they had believed the characters real, and every incident vouched by contemporary record. The story of William Tell was once universally received as authentic history: it was written in the hearts of the people of Uri, and so religiously were all its incidents cherished, that when a book appeared discrediting the sacred tradition it was publicly burned by the hangman at Altorf. For five centuries the chapel on the shore of the Lake of the Four Cantons has commemorated a hero whose very existence is now questioned, of whom contemporary annals know nothing, of whose tyrant Gessler the well-kept records of the Canton exhibit no trace, whose apple placed as a mark for the father's arrow on the head of his child is proved to have done a foregone service in an elder Danish tale. The story resolves itself into an idea. That idea is all that concerns us; and that idea survives, inexpugnable to criticism, a truth for evermore. In the world of ideas there is still a William Tell who defied the tyrant at Altorf, and slew him at Küsnacht, and whose image will live while the mountains stand that gave it birth.

And so all that is memorable out of the past, all that tradition has preserved, the veritable facts of history as well as the myths of legendary lore, pass finally into ideas. Only as ideas they survive, only as ideas have they any abiding value. The anecdote recorded of Aristides — his writing his own name at the request of an ignorant citizen on the shell that should condemn him — embodies a noble idea which has floated down to us from the head-waters of Grecian history. Do we care to know the evidence on which it rests? If by critical investigation the fact were made doubtful, would that doubt at all impair the truth of the idea? The story of Damon and Pythias, reported by Valerius Maximus, for aught that we know, may be a myth: suppose it could be proved to be so, the truth that is in it would be none the less precious. We do not receive it on the faith of the historian, but on the faith of its own intrinsic beauty. There is scarcely a fact in the annals of mankind so vouched and ascertained as to be beyond the reach of historic doubt, if any delver in ancient documents, or curious sceptic, shall see fit to call it in question. But, however the fact may be questioned, the idea remains. We have lived to see apologies for Judas Iscariot, and the literary rehabilitation of Henry VIII. But Judas is none the less, in popular tradition, the typical traitor, the impersonation of devilish malice; and Henry VIII. is no less the remorseless tyrant whose will was his God. When Napoleon I. pronounced all history a fable agreed on, he reasoned better perhaps than he knew. The agreement is the thing essential; but that agreement is never complete, is never final. Every original writer of history finds something to qualify, and often something to reverse, in the judgment of his predecessors. How can it be otherwise, when even eye-witnesses disagree in their observation and report of the same transaction; when even in a matter so recent as the siege of Paris, or the conflagration of Chicago, the verification of facts is embarrassed by contradictory accounts? The best that history yields to philosophic thought is not facts, but ideas. These are all that remain at last when the tale is told, — all, at least, that the mind can appropriate, all that profits in historical studies, the intellectual harvest of the past. A fact means nothing until thought has transmuted it into itself: its value is simply the idea it subtends. Homer's heroes are as true in this sense as those of Plutarch. Ajax and Hector are as real to me as Cimon or Lysander; Don Quixote's battle with the windmills which Cervantes imagined is as real as the battle of Lepanto in which Cervantes fought; and Shakespeare's Hamlet is incomparably more real than the Prince of Denmark whom Saxo Grammaticus chronicles.

I do not underrate the importance of facts on their own historic plane. The historian, as annalist, is bound by the rules of his craft with conscientious investigation to ascertain, substantiate, and establish, if he can, the precise facts of the period he explores. I only contend that historic truth is not the only truth; that a fact, — if I may use that term in this connection for want of a better, — that a fact which is not historically true may yet be true on a higher plane than that of history, true to reason, to moral and religious sentiment and human need. The story of Christ's temptation is none the less true, but a great deal more so, when the narrative which embodies the interior psychological fact is conceived as myth, than when it is interpreted as veritable history. The truth that concerns us is that the Son of Man "was tempted in all points as we are," not that he was taken by the Devil and set on a pinnacle of the Temple, and thence spirited away "into an exceeding high mountain."

We have now attained a point of view from which to estimate on the one hand the real import of what I have ventured to call the myths of the New Testament, and on the other hand to overrule the petulant radicalism which, not distinguishing truth of idea from truth of fact, contemns these legends, and perhaps contemns the Gospel, on their account. I have wished to show how unessential it is to the right enjoyment or profitable use of those portions of the record that we receive them as fact; to show that, if we seize and appropriate the idea, those narratives are quite as edifying from a mythical as from an historical point of view; in other words, that the Holy Spirit may and does instruct by fiction as well as fact. If I am asked to draw the line which separates fact from fiction, or to fix the criterion by which to discriminate the one from the other, I answer that I do not pretend to decide this point for myself, much less should I presume to attempt to settle it for others. I am not disposed to dogmatize on the subject. It is a matter in which each must judge for himself. I will only say that for myself I do not place the line of demarcation between miracle and the unmiraculous, for the reason that it seems to me, as I said before, unphilosophical to make our every-day experience of the limits of human power and the capabilities of nature an absolute standard by which to measure the possible scope of the one or the other.

I content myself with a single illustration of what I regard as a mythical formation. My example is the story known as "The Annunciation." Luke alone, of all the evangelists, records the tale. The angel Gabriel is sent to a virgin named Mary, and surprises her with the tidings, "Thou shalt conceive in thy womb, and shalt bring forth a son, and shalt call his name Jesus. He shall be great, and shall be called the Son of the Highest. And the Lord God shall give unto him the throne of his father David. And he shall reign over the house of Jacob for ever, and of his kingdom there shall be no end." This beautiful legend, the most beautiful, I think, of all the legends connected with the birth of Christ, the favorite theme of Christian art, so lovingly handled by Fra Angelico, by Correggio, Raphael, Titian, Andrea del Sarto, and a host of others, is best understood as a Jewish-Christian conception, taking an historic form and "shaped into a fact." The legend represents the humility and faith of a pious maiden communing with the heavenly Presence, drawing to herself divine revelations of grace and promise, and thus sanctioning the hope so dear to every Jewish maiden, — that of becoming the mother of the Messiah. The sudden inspiration of that hope is the angel of the Annunciation.

A word more. How far is our idea of Christ affected by a mode of interpretation which supposes a mingling of mythical with historic elements in the Gospel record? That idea is based on the representations of the evangelists. Will not our confidence in those representations be impaired by this view of their contents? I see no cause to apprehend a result so distressing to Christian faith. The mythical interpretation of certain portions of the Gospel has no appreciable bearing on the character of Christ. The impartial reader of the record must see that the evangelists did not invent that character; they did not make the Jesus of their story; on the contrary, it was he that made them. It is a true saying that only a Christ could invent a Christ. The Christ of history is a true reflection of the image which Jesus of Nazareth imprinted on the mind of his contemporaries. In that image the spiritual greatness, the moral perfection, are not more conspicuous than the well-defined individuality which permeates the story, and which no genius could invent.

If the Christ of the Church, of Christian faith, is, as some will have it, an ideal being, it was Jesus of Nazareth who made the ideal. The ideal in him is simply the result of that disengagement from the earthly vestiture which death and distance work in all who live in history. By the very necessity of its function, history idealizes. The historic figure and the individual represented by it, though inseparably one in substance, are not so identical in outline that the one exactly covers the other, no more and no less. The individual is the bodily presence as it dwells in space; the historic figure is the image of himself which the individual stamps on his time, and, so far as his record reaches, on all succeeding time, — his import to human kind. That image is a veritable portrait, but not in the sense of a *fac-simile*. A material portrait, a portrait painted with hands, if the painter understands his art, is not a *fac-simile:* it presents the chronic idea or characteristic mode, not the temporary accidents, "the fallings off, the vanishings," of the person portrayed. In the hero-galleries of Tradition, as in the visions of the Apocalypse, they are seen with white robes, and palms in their hands, and unwrinkled brows of grace, who in life were begrimed with the dust and furrowed with the cares of their time. St. Paul is there without his thorn in the flesh, Luther without his impatience, Washington without his fiery choler, Lincoln without his coarseness, Dante and Milton without their scorn. History strips off the indignities of earth when she dresses her heroes for immortality. And the transfigurations she gives us are nearer the truth than the limitations of ordinary life. The man is more truly himself in the epic strain of public action, with spirit braced and harness on, than in the subsidence and undress of the closet. It is not the gossiping anecdotes, the spoils of the ungirt private life, so dear to antiquaries and literary scavengers, but the things which history hastens to record, that show the man. We must take the life at full-tide; we must view it in its freest determination, in its supreme moment, to know the deepest that is in him. And the deepest that is in him is the true man. That is his idea, his mission to the world, his historic significance. It is this that concerns us in all the great actors of history, — the historic person, not the individual. And the more the historic person absorbs the individual, the higher we rise in the scale of being until we reach the idea of God, from which all individuality is excluded, and only the Person remains, filling space and time with the ceaseless procession of his being.

We misread the Gospel and reverse the true and divine order, if we suppose the ideal Christ to be an essence distilled from the historical. On the contrary, the ideal Christ is the root and ground of the historical; and without the antecedent idea inspiring, commanding, the history would never have been.

It has not been my intention in any thing I have said to make light of the record. The record to me is a literary relic of inestimable value, aboriginal memorial of the dearest and divinest appearance in human form that ever beamed on earthly scenes. I sympathize with every attempt to clear up and verify its minutest details, with the labors of all critics and archæologists devoted to this end. I rejoice in all topographical adjustments and illustrations; in all that local researches, following in the steps of "those blessed feet," have gleaned from the soil of Palestine. But all this is important only as it draws its inspiration from and leads my aspiration to the ideal Christ, "the same yesterday, to-day, and for ever." Dissociated from this idea, the acres of Palestine are as barren as any which the ebbing of a nation's life has left desolate.

THE PLACE OF MIND IN NATURE:

AND

INTUITION IN MAN.

By JAMES MARTINEAU.

THE PLACE OF MIND IN NATURE

AND

INTUITION IN MAN.

"Behold, there went forth a Sower to sow."—MARK iv. 3.

THAT the universe we see around us was not always there, is so little disputed, that every philosophy and every faith undertakes to tell how it came to be. They all assume, as the theatre of their problem, the field of space where all objects lie, and the track of time where events have reached the Now. But into these they carry, to aid them in representing the origin of things, such interpreting conceptions as may be most familiar to the knowledge or fancy of their age: first, the *fiat of Almighty Will*, which bade the void be filled, so that the light kindled, and the waters swayed, and the earth stood fast beneath the vault of sky; next, when the sway of poetry and force had yielded to the inventive arts, the idea of a *contriving and adapting power*, building and balancing the worlds to go smoothly and keep time together, and stocking them with self-moving and sensitive machines; and now, since physiology has got to the front, the analogy of *the seed or germ*, in itself the least of things, yet so prolific that, with history long enough, it will be as spawn upon the waters, and fill every waste with the creatures as they are. The prevalence of this newest metaphor betrays itself in the current language of science: we now "*unfold*" what we used to "*take to pieces;*" we "*develop*" the theory which we used to "*construct;*" we treat the system of the world as an "*organism*" rather than a "*mechanism;*" we search each of its members to see, not what it is *for*, but what it is *from;* and the doctrine of *Evolution* only applies the image of indefinite growth of the greater out of the less, till from some datum invisible to the microscope arises a teeming universe.

In dealing with these three conceptions, — of *Creation, Construction, Evolution,* — there is one thing on which Religion insists, viz., that *Mind is first, and rules for ever;* and, whatever the process be, is *its* process, moving towards congenial ends. Let this be granted, and it matters not by what path of method the Divine Thought advances, or how long it is upon the road. Whether it flashes into realization, like lightning out of Night; or fabricates, like a Demiurge, through a producing season, and then beholds the perfect work; or is for ever thinking into life the thoughts of beauty and the love of good; whether it calls its materials out of nothing, or finds them ready, and disposes of them from without; or throws them around as its own manifestation, and from within shapes its own purpose into blossom, — makes no difference that can be fatal to human piety. Time counts for nothing with the Eternal; and though it should appear that the system of the world and the ranks of being arose, not by a start of crystallization, but, like the grass or the forest, by silent and seasonal gradations, as true a worship may be paid to the Indwelling God who makes matter itself transparent with spiritual meanings, and breathes before us in the pulses of nature, and appeals to us in the sorrows of men, as to the pre-existing Deity who, from an infinite loneliness, suddenly became the Maker of all. Nay, if the poet always looks upon the world through a suppliant eye, craving to meet his own ideal and commune with it alive; if prayer is ever a "feeling after Him to find Him," the fervor and the joy of both must be best sustained, if they are conscious not only of the stillness of His presence, but of the movement of His thought, and never quit the date of His creative moments. In the idea, therefore, of a gradual unfolding of the creative plan, and the maturing of it by rules of growth, there is nothing necessarily prejudicial to piety; and so long as the Divine Mind is left in undisturbed supremacy, as the living All in all, the belief may even foster a larger, calmer, tenderer devotion, than the conceptions which it supersedes. But it is liable to a special illusion, which the others by their coarsely separating lines manage to escape. Taking all the causation of the world into the interior, instead of setting it to operate from without, it seems to dispense with God, and to lodge the power of indefinite development in the first seeds of things; and the apprehension seizes us, that as the oak will raise itself when the acorn and the elements are given, so from its germs might the universe emerge, though nothing Divine were there. The seeds no doubt were on the field; but who can say whether ever "a Sower went forth to sow"? So long as you plant the Supreme Cause at a distance from His own effects, and assign to Him a space or a time where nothing else can be, the conception of that separate and solitary existence, however barren, is secure. But in proportion as you think of Him as never in an empty field, waiting for a future beginning of activity, as you let Him mingle with the elements and blend with the natural life of things, there is a seeming danger lest His light should disappear behind the opaque material veil, and His Spirit be quenched amid the shadows of inexorable Law. This danger haunts our time. The doctrine of Evolution, setting itself to show how the greatest things may be brought out of the least, fills us with fear whether perhaps Mind may not be last instead of first, the hatched and full-fledged form of the protoplasmic egg; whether at the outset any thing was there but the raw rudiments of matter and force; whether the hierarchy of organized beings is not due to progressive differentiation of structure, and resolvable into splitting and agglutination of cells; whether the Intellect of man is more than blind instinct grown self-conscious, and shaping its beliefs by defining its own shadows; whether the Moral sense is not simply a trained acceptance of rules worked out by human interests, an inherited record of the utilities; so that Design in Nature, Security in the Intuitions of Reason, Divine Obligation in the law of Conscience, may all be an illusory semblance, a glory from the later and ideal days thrown back upon the beginning, as a golden sunset flings its light across the sky, and, as it sinks, dresses up the East again with borrowed splendor.

This doubt, which besets the whole intellectual religion of our time, assumes that we must *measure every nature in its beginnings;* admit nothing to belong to its essence except what is found in it then; and deny its reports of itself, so far as they depart from that original standard. It takes two forms, according as the doctrine of Evolution is applied to Man himself, or to the outward universe. In the former case, it infuses distrust into our self-knowledge, weakens our subjective religion or native faith in the intuitions of thought and conscience, and tempts us to imagine that the higher they are, the further are they from any assured solidity of base. In the latter case, it weakens our objective religion, suggests that there is no originating Mind, and that the divine look of the world is but the latest phase of its finished surface, instead of the incandescence of its inmost heart. Let us first glance at the theory of HUMAN evolution, and the moral illusions it is apt to foster.

I. Under the name of the "Experience Philosophy," this theory has long been applied to the *mind of the individual;* and has produced not a few admirable analyses of the formation of language and the tissue of thought; nor is there any legitimate objection to it, except so far as its simplifications are overstrained and cannot be made good. It undertakes, with a minimum of initial capacity, to account for the maximum of human genius and character: give it only the sensible pleasures and pains, the spontaneous muscular activity, and the law by which associated mental phenomena cling together; and out of these elements it will weave before your eyes the whole texture of the perfect inner life, be it the patterned story of imagination, the delicate web of the affections, or the seamless robe of moral purity. The outfit is that of the animal; the product but "a little lower than the angel." All the higher endowments — our apprehension of truth, our consciousness of duty, our self-sacrificing pity, our religious reverence — are in this view merely transformed sensations; the disinterested impulses are refinements spun out of the coarse fibre of self-love; the subtlest intellectual ideas are but elaborated perceptions of sight or touch; and the sense of Right, only interest or fear under a disguise. If this be so, how will the discovery affect our natural trust in the intimations of our supreme faculties? Does it not discharge as dreams their most assured revelations? By intuition of Reason we believe in the Law of Causality, in the infinitude of Space, in the relations of Number, in the reality of an outside world, in all the fundamental conceptions of Science; but here are they, one and all, recalled to the standard of Sense, which they seem to transcend, and emptied of any meaning beyond. By vision of Imagination we see an ideal beauty enfolding many a person and many a scene, and appealing to us as a pathetic light gleaming from within; but here we find it all resolved into curvature of lines and adjustments of color. By inspiration of Conscience we learn that our sin is the defiance of a Divine authority, and, though hid from every human eye, drives us into a wilderness of Exile, — for " the wicked fleeth, though no man pursueth;" but here we are told that the ultimate elements of good and evil are our own pleasures and pains, from which the moral sanction selects as its specialty the approbation and disapprobation of our fellow-men. Thus all the independent values which our higher faculties had claimed for their natural affections and beliefs are dissipated as fallacious; they are all based upon a *sentient measure* of worth which lies at the bottom; they are like paper money, refined contrivances representative of the ultimate gold of pleasure, but, where not interchangeable with this, intrinsically worthless. And so the feeling almost inevitably spreads, that we are dupes of our own characteristic capacities; that the loftier air into which they lift us is a

tinted and distorting medium, and shows us glories that
are not there; that the idea of an eternal Fount of
beauty, truth and goodness, behind the pleasingness and
concinnity of phenomena, is an illusion; and that the
tendency, irresistible as it is, to cling to this idea as something higher than its denial, is but a part of the romance.
Is this scepticism imaginary? Let any one, in studying
the modern writers of this school, compare the solid,
manly, sensible way in which they deal with every thing
on the physiological and sensational level, with their
manner towards all the convictions and sentiments usually
recognized as the supreme lights of our nature; the tone
now of forbearing indulgence, now of sickly appreciation,
often of hardly concealed contempt, that is heard beneath
the interminable conjectural analyses of Moral and Religious affections, — and he will feel the difference between
the honor that is paid to truth, and the constrained
patience towards what other men revere.

By a recent extension, the theory of Evolution has been
applied to the whole natural history of our race; and the
resources of *Habit*, already serviceable in explaining the
aptitudes of individuals, have been turned to account on
the larger scale of successive generations, transmitting by
inheritance the acquisitions hitherto made good. In the
training of a nature, the world thus becomes a permanent
school, the interruption of death is virtually abolished, and
life is laid open to continuous progress. By this immense
gain of power, it is supposed, all the differences which
separate Man from other animals may be accounted for as
gradual attainments; and many an intuition of the mind,
too immediate and self-evident to be a product of personal
experience, may yield to analysis as a more protracted

growth, and stand as the compend of ages of gathering feeling and condensing thought. Among creatures that herd together for common safety, each one learns to read the looks of anger or of good-will in its neighbors, and discovers what it is that brings upon him the one or other; and insensibly he forms to himself a rule for avoiding the displeasure and conciliating the favor in which he has so large an interest. This rudimentary experience imprints and records itself in the nervous organization, and descends to ulterior generations as an original and instinctive recoil from what offends and impulse towards what gratifies the feeling of the tribe: so that the lesson needs not be gone over again; but the offspring, taking up his education where the parent left off, accumulates his feeling, quickens his mental execution, and hands down fresh contributions to what at last emerges as a Moral Sense. In this way, it is contended, the Conscience is a hoarded fund of traditionary pressures of utility, gradually effacing the primitive vestiges of fear, and dispensing itself with an affluence of disinterested sympathy. And the religious consciousness that visits the soul in its remorse, of an invisible Witness and Judge who condemns the sin, comes, we are told, from the deification of public opinion, or the fancy that some dead hero's ghost still watches over the conduct of his clan.

This vast enlargement of the doctrine of Evolution, while increasing its power, and removing it from the reach of accurate tests, alters neither its principle nor its practical effect. It undertakes to exhibit the highest and the greatest in our nature as ulterior phenomena of the lowest and the least. And it usually treats as a superstition our natural reverence for the rational, moral, and religious intuitions as sources of independent insight and ultimate authority; and, in order to estimate them, translates them back into short-hand expressions of sensible experience and social utility. Nor can we wonder at this scepticism. If the only reality at bottom of the sense of duty is fear and submission to opinion, whatever it carries in it that transcends this ground, and persuades us of an Obligation in which fear and opinion have no voice, is an ideal addition got up within us by causes which produce in us all sorts of psychological figments. If the only facts that lie in our idea of Space are a set of feelings in the muscles and the skin and the eye, then whatever beliefs it involves which these cannot verify are naturally discredited, and treated as curiosities of artificial manufacture. If our human characteristics are throughout the developed instincts of the brute, differing only in degree, then the moment they present us with intuitions which are distinct *in kind*, they begin to play us false; and those who see through the cheat naturally warn us against them. And so we are constantly told that our highest attributes are only the lower that have lost their memory, and mistake themselves for something else.

It is not my present intention to call in question either of these varieties of evolution. Inadequate as the evidence of them both appears to be, I will suppose their case to be made out: and still, I submit, it does not justify the sceptical estimate which it habitually fosters of the intellectual, moral, and religious intuitions of the human mind. For,

(1) Though animal sensation, with its connected instinct, should be the raw material of our whole mental history, it is not on that account entitled *to measure*

all that comes after it, and stand as the boundary-line between fact and dream, between terra firma and "airy nothing." That which is first in Time has no necessary priority of rank in the scale of truth and reality; and the later-found may well be the greater existence and the more assured. If it is a development of Faculty, and not of incapacity, which the theory provides, the process must advance us into new light, and not withdraw us from clearer light behind: and we have reason to confide in the freshest gleams and inmost visions of to-day, and to discard whatever quenches and confuses them in the vague and turbid beginnings of the Past. With what plea will you exhort me, "If you would rid yourself of intellectual mysteries, come with us, and see the stuff your thought is made of: if you would stand free of ideal illusions, count with us the medullary waves that have run together into the flood-tide of what you call your conscience: if you would shake off superstition, look at the way in which the image of dead men will hang about the fancy of a savage, or the personification of an abstract quality imposes on the ignorance of simple times"? Is our wisdom to be gathered by going back to the age before our errors? And instead of consulting the maturity of thought, are we to peer into its cradle and seek oracles in its infant cries? If the last appeal be to the animal elements of experience, we can learn only by unlearning; and by shutting one after another of the hundred ideal eyes of the finished intellect, we shall have a chance of seeing and feeling things as they are. If nothing is to be deemed true but what the pre-human apes saw, then all the sciences must be illusory; with the suicidal result that, with them, this doctrine of Evolution must vanish too. Or if, stopping short of this extreme distrust of the acquired intuitions, you make a reservation in favor of the new visions of the intellect, what right can you show for discharging those of the conscience? The tacit assumption therefore that you upset a super-sensual belief, by tracing the history of its emergence among sensible conditions, is a groundless prejudice.

(2) Further, the question to be determined may be presented as a problem in physiology, to be resolved by corresponding rules: What is the *function* of certain parts of our human constitution, viz., the Reason and the Moral Faculty? Now it is a recognized principle that, in estimating function, you must study the organ, not in its rudimentary condition, before it has disengaged itself from adjacent admixtures and flung off the foreign elements, but in its perfect or differentiated state, so as to do its own work and nothing else. In order to give the idea of a timepiece to one who had it not, you would not send him to one of the curious mediæval clocks which could play a tune, and fire a gun, and announce the sunrise, and mark the tides, and report twenty miscellaneous things besides; but to the modern chronometer, simple and complete, that, telling only the moment, tells it perfectly. And in natural organizations, to learn the capabilities and project of any structure, you would not resort to the embryo where it is forming but not working: you would wait till it was born into the full presence of the elements with which it had to deal; not till then could you see how they played upon it, and what was its response to them. In conformity with this rule, whither would you betake yourself, if you want to measure the intrinsic competency of our intellectual faculty, and determine what its very nature

gives it to know? Would you take counsel of the nurse who held you "when you first opened your eyes to the light,"[1] or otherwise study "the first consciousness in any infant," "before the time when memory commences,"[2] and disregard every thing "subsequent to the first beginnings of intellectual life"?[3] On the contrary, you would avoid that soft inchoate promise of nature, only nominally born, where the very structures of its finer work have not yet set into their distinctive consistency and form; and will hold your peace till the faculty is awake and 'on its feet, and can clearly tell you what it sees for itself, and what it makes out at second-hand: just as, to gauge the lunar light, you must have patience while the thin crescent grows, and wait till the full orb is there. Still less can you take the report of the Moral Faculty from the confessions of the cradle, or from the quarrels and affections of the apes; the conditions being not yet present for the bare conception of a moral problem. The most that can be asked of an intuition is, that it shall keep pace with the cases as they arise, and be on the spot when it is wanted; and if you would know what provision our nature holds for dealing with its Duty and interpreting its guilt, you must go into the thick of its moral life, and bid it tell you what it sees from the swaying tides of temptation and of victory. The "purity" of intuitions is not "pristine," but ultimate; cleared at length from accidental and irrelevant dilutions, and with essence definitely crystallized, they realize and exhibit the idea that lay at the heart of all their tentatives, and constitutes their truth. Am I told that it is hopeless at so late an

---

[1] Mill's Examination of Hamilton, 3d ed. p. 172.
[2] Ibid.   [3] Ibid, p. 160.

hour to separate what is an indigenous gift from what is implanted by education? I reply, it no doubt requires, but it will not baffle, the hand of skilled analysis; it is a difficulty which, in other cases, we find it not impossible to overcome; for there are assuredly instincts and affections, strictly original and natural, that make no sign and play no part till our maturer years, yet which are readily distinguished from the products of artificial culture.

If, to find the functions of our higher faculties, we must look to their last stage, and not to their first, we at once recover and justify the ideal conceptions which the expositors of Evolution are accustomed to disparage as romance. For among these functions are present certain Intuitive beliefs — for the Reason, in Divine Causality; for the Conscience, in Divine Authority; together blending into the knowledge of a Supreme and Holy Mind. These august apprehensions we are entitled to declare are not the illusions, but the discoveries, of Man; who, by rising into them, is born into more of the Universe of things than any other being upon earth, and is made conscious of its transcendent and ultimate realities. If these trusts are indeed the growth of ages, from seeds invisibly dropped upon the field of time, be it so; it was not without hand: there was *a Sower* that went forth to sow.

II. We turn now to the Second Form of doubt raised by the doctrine of Evolution: under which it weakens our objective trust in an originating Mind.

A naturalist who to his own satisfaction has traced the pedigree of the human intellect, conscience, and religion, to Ascidian skin-bags sticking to the sea-side rocks, is not likely to arrest the genealogy there, at a stage so little fitted to serve as a starting-point of derivative being. Or, if his own retreat should go no further, others will take up the regressive race, and, soon passing the near and easy line into the vegetable kingdom, will work through its provinces to its lichen-spotted edge: and, after perhaps one shrinking look, will dare the leap into the dead realm beyond, and bring home the parentage of all to the primitive elements of "matter and force." To give effect to this extension over the universe at large of the theory of Evolution, the scientific imagination of our day has long been meditating its projected book of Genesis, and has already thrown out its special chapters here and there; and though the scenes of the drama as a whole are not yet arranged, the general plan is clear: that the Lucretian method is the true one; that nothing arises for a purpose, but only from a power; that no Divine Actor therefore is required, but only atoms extended, resisting, shaped, with spheres of mutual attraction and repulsion; that, with these *minima* to begin with, a growth will follow of itself by which the *maxima* will be reached; and that thus far the chief and latest thing it has done is the apparition of Mind in the human race and civilization in human society, conferring upon man the melancholy privilege of being, so far as he knows, at the summit of the universe.

The main support of this doctrine is found in two arguments, supplied respectively by physical science and by natural history; each of which we will pass under review.

i. The former relies on the new scientific conception of the *Unity of Force*. When Newton established the composition of Light in his treatise on Optics, and the law of Gravitation in his Principia, he conceived himself to be treating of two separate powers of nature, between which, quick as he was to seize unexpected relations, he dreamt of no interchange. Yet now it is understood that when collisions occur of bodies gravitating on opposite lines, the momenta that seem to be killed simply burst into light and heat. When Priestley's experiments detected the most important chemical element on the one hand, and the fundamental electrical laws on the other, he seemed to move on paths of research that had no contact. Yet, in the next generation, chemical compounds were resolved by electricity; which again turns up in exchange for magnetism, and can pass into motion, heat, and light. To see the transmigration of natural agency, trace only through a few of its links the effect of the sunshine on the tropic seas. So far as it warms the mass of waters, either directly or through the scorched shores that they wash, it stirs them into shifting layers and currents, and creates *mechanical* power. But it also removes the superficial film; and thus far spends itself, not in raising the temperature, but in changing the form from liquid to vapor, and so altering the specific gravity as to transfer what was on the deep to the level of the mountain-tops. It is the Pacific that climbs and crowns the Andes, resuming on the way the liquid state in the shape of clouds, and as it settles crystallizing into solid snow and ice. The original set of solar rays have now played their part, and made their escape elsewhere. But there is sunshine among the glaciers too, which soon begins to resolve the knot that has been tied, and restore what has been stolen. It sets free the waters that have been locked up, and lets their gravitation have its play upon their flow. As they dash through ravines, or linger in the plains, they steal into the roots of grass and tree, and by the tribute which they leave pass into the new shape of *vital* force. And if they pass the homesteads of industry, and raise the food of a civilized people, who can deny that they contribute not only to the organic, but to the *mental* life, and so have run the whole circuit from the lowest to the highest phase of power? That the return back may be traced from the highest to the lowest, is shown by every effort of thought and will; which through the medium of nervous energy in one direction sets in action the levers of the limbs, and in another works the laboratory of the organic life, and forms new chemical compounds, of which some are reserved for use, while others pass into the air as waste. Still further: all doubt of identity in the force which masks itself in these various shapes is said to be removed by the test of direct measurement before and after the change. The heating of a pound of water by one degree has its exact mechanical equivalent;[1] and a given store of elevated temperature will overcome the same weights, whether applied directly to lift them, or turned first into a thermo-electric current, so as to perform its task by deputy.[2] The inference drawn from the phenomena of which these are samples is no less than this: that each kind of force is convertible into any other, and undergoes neither gain nor loss upon the way; so that the sum-total remains for ever the same, and is only differently represented as the proportions change amongst the different forms of life, and between the organic and the inorganic realms. Hence arises the argument that, in having *any* force, you have virtually *all ;* and that, assuming only material atoms as depositories of mechanical resistance and momentum, you can supply a universe with an exhaustive

---

[1] Viz., the fall of 772 lbs. through a foot. See Mr. Joule's Experiments in Grove's Correlation of Physical Forces, p. 34, 5th ed.

[2] See Grove's Correlation, p. 255, 5th ed.

cosmogony, and dispense with the presence of Mind, except as one of its phenomena.

To test this argument, let us grant the data which are demanded, and imagine the primordial space charged with matter, in molecules or in masses, in motion or rest, as you may prefer. Put it under the law of gravitation, and invest it with what varieties you please of density and form. Thus constituted, it perfectly fulfils all the conditions you have asked; it presses, it moves, it propagates and distributes impulse, is liable to acceleration and retardation, and exhibits all the phenomena with which any treatise on Mechanics can properly deal. In order, however, to keep the problem clear within its limits, let us have it in the simplest form, and conceive the atoms to be all of *gold;* then, I would fain learn by what step the hypothesis proposes to effect its passage to the *chemical* forces and their innumerable results. *Heat* it may manage to reach by the friction and compression of the materials at its disposal; and its metal universe may thus have its solid, liquid, and gaseous provinces; but, beyond these varieties, its homogeneous particles cannot advance the history one hair's breadth through an eternity. It is not true, then, that the conditions which give the first type of force suffice to promote it to the second; and in order to start the world on its chemical career, you must enlarge its capital and present it with an outfit of *heterogeneous* constituents. Try, therefore, the effect of such a gift; fling into the pre-existing caldron the whole list of recognized elementary substances, and give leave to their affinities to work: we immediately gain an immense accession to our materials for the architecture and resources for the changes of the world, — the water and the air, the salts of the ocean, and

the earthy or rocky compounds that compose the crust of
the globe, and the variable states of magnetism and heat,
which throw the combinations into slow though constant
change. But with all your enlargement of data, turn
them as you will, at the end of every passage which they
explore, the *door of life* is closed against them still; and
though more than once it has been proclaimed that a way
has been found through, it has proved that the living thing
was on the wrong side to begin with. It is not true, therefore, that, from the two earlier stages of force, the ascent
can be made to the vital level; the ethereal fire yet remains in Heaven; and philosophy has not stretched forth
the Promethean arm that can bring it down. And if, once
more, we make you a present of this third phase of power,
and place at your disposal all that is contained beneath
and within the flora of the world, still your problem is no
easier than before; you cannot take a single step towards
the deduction of sensation and thought: neither at the
upper limit do the highest plants (the exogens) transcend
themselves and overbalance into animal existence; nor at
the lower, grope as you may among the sea-weeds and
sponges, can you persuade the sporules of the one to
develop into the other. It is again not true, therefore,
that, in virtue of the convertibility of force, the possession of any is the possession of the whole: we give you
all the forms but one; and that one looks calmly down on
your busy evolutions, and remains inaccessible. Is, then,
the transmigration of forces altogether an illusion? By
no means; but before one can exchange with another, *both
must be there ;* and to turn their equivalence into a universal formula, *all* must be there. With only one kind of
elementary matter, there can be no chemistry; with only

the chemical elements and their laws, no life; with only vital resources, as in the vegetable world, no beginning of mind. But let Thought and Will with their conditions once be there, and they will appropriate vital power; as life, once in possession, will ply the alembics and the test-tubes of its organic laboratory; and chemical affinity is no sooner on the field than it plays its game among the cohesions of simple gravitation. Hence it is impossible to work the theory of Evolution upwards from the bottom. If all force is to be conceived as One, its type must be looked for in the highest and all-comprehending term; and Mind must be conceived as there, and as divesting itself of some specialty at each step of its descent to a lower stratum of law, till represented at the base under the guise of simple Dynamics. Or, if you retain the forces in their plurality, then you must *assume* them *all* among your data, and confess, with one of the greatest living expositors of the phenomena of Development, that unless among your primordial elements you scatter already the germs of mind as well as the inferior elements, the Evolution can never be wrought out.[1] But surely a theory, which is content simply to assume in the germ whatever it has to turn out full-grown, throws no very brilliant light on the genesis of the Universe.

ii. The second and principal support of the doctrine under review is found in the realm of natural history, and in that province of it which is occupied by *living beings*. Here, it is said, in the field of observation nearest to us, we have evidence of a power in each nature to push itself and gain ground, as against all natures less favorably constituted. There is left open to it a certain range of possible

[1] Lotze's Mikrokosmus, B. iv. Kap. 2, Band ii. 33, seqq.

variations from the type of its present individuals, of which it may avail itself in any direction that may fortify its position; and even if its own instincts did not seize at once the line of greatest strength, still, out of its several tentatives, all the feeble results would fail to win a footing, and only the residuary successes would make good their ground. The ill-equipped troops of rival possibilities being always routed, however often they return, the well-armed alone are seen upon the field, and the world is in possession of "the fittest to live." We thus obtain a principle of self-adjusting adaptation of each being to its condition, without resorting to a designing care disposing of it from without; and its development is an experimental escape from past weakness, not a pre-conceived aim at a future perfection.

I have neither ability nor wish to criticise the particular indications of this law, drawn with an admirable patience and breadth of research, from every department of animated nature. Though the logical structure of the proof does not seem to me particularly solid, and the disproportion between the evidence and the conclusion is of necessity so enormous as to carry us no further than the discussion of an hypothesis, yet, for our present purpose, the thesis may pass as if established; and our scrutiny may be directed only to its bearings, should it be true.

(1) The genius of a country which has been the birth-place and chief home of Political Economy is naturally pleased by a theory of this kind; which invests its favorite lord and master, *Competition*, with an imperial crown and universal sway. But let us not deceive ourselves with mere abstract words and abbreviations, as if they could reform a world or even farm a sheep-walk. *Competition*

is not, like a primitive function of nature, an independent and original power, which can of itself do any thing: the term only describes a certain intensifying of power already there; making the difference, under particular conditions, between function latent and function exercised. It may therefore turn the less into the more; and it is reasonable to attribute to it an *increment* to known and secured effects; but not new and unknown effects, for which else there is no provision. It gives but a partial and superficial account of the phenomena with which it has' concern; of their degree; of their incidence here or there; of their occurrence now or then: of themselves in their characteristics it pre-supposes, and does not supply, the cause. To that cause, then, let us turn. Let us consider what must be upon the field, before competition can arise.

(2) It cannot act except in the presence of some *possibility of a better or worse*. A struggle out of relative disadvantage implies that a relative advantage is within grasp, — that there is a prize of promotion offered for the contest. The rivalry of beings eager for it is but an instrument for *making the best of things;* and only when flung into the midst of an indeterminate variety of alternative conditions can it find any scope. When it gets there and falls to work, what does it help us to account for? It accounts certainly for the triumph and *survivorship of the better*, but not for there *being a better to survive*. *Given*, the slow and the swift upon the same course, it makes it clear that the race will be to the swift; but it does not provide the fleeter feet by which the standard of speed is raised. Nay more; even for the prevalence of the better ("or fitter to live") it would not account, except on the assumption that whatever is *better* is *stronger* too; and a

universe in which this rule holds already indicates its divine constitution, and is pervaded by an ideal power unapproached by the forces of necessity. Thus the law of "natural selection," instead of dispensing with anterior causation and enabling the animal races to be their own Providence and do all their own work, distinctly testifies to a constitution of the world pre-arranged for progress, externally spread with large choice of conditions, and with internal provisions for seizing and realizing the best. On such a world, rich in open possibilities, of beauty, strength, affection, intellect, and character, they are planted and set free; charged with instincts eagerly urging them to secure the preferable line of each alternative; and disposing themselves, by the very conditions of equilibrium, into a natural hierarchy, in which the worthiest to live are in the ascendant, and the standard of life is for ever rising. What can look more like the field of a directing Will intent upon the good? Indeed, the doctrine of "natural selection" owes a large part of its verisimilitude to its skilful imitation of the conditions and method of Free-will; — the indeterminate varieties of possible movement; the presentation of these before a selective power; the determination of the problem by fitness for preference, — all these are features that would belong no less to the administration of a presiding Mind; and that, instead of resorting for the last solution to this high arbitrament, men of science should suppose it to be blindly fought out by the competing creatures, as if they were supreme, is one of the marvels which the professional intellect, whatever its department, more often exhibits than explains.

(3) But, before competition can arise, there must be,

besides the field of favorable possibility, *desire or instinct* to lay hold of its opportunities. Here it is that we touch the real dynamics of evolution, which rivalry can only bring to a somewhat higher pitch. Here, it must be admitted, there is at work a genuine principle of progression, the limits of which it is difficult to fix. Every being which is so far individuated as to be a separate centre of sensation, and of the balancing active spontaneity, is endowed with a self-asserting power, capable, on the field already supposed, of becoming a self-advancing power. Under its operation, there is no doubt, increasing differentiation of structure and refinement of function may be expected to emerge; nor is there any reason, except such as the facts of natural history may impose, why this process should be arrested at the boundaries of the species recognized in our present classifications. Possibly, if the slow increments of complexity in the organs of sentient beings on the globe were all mapped out before us, the whole teeming multitudes now peopling the land, the waters, and the air, might be seen radiating from a common centre in lines of various divergency, and, however remote their existing relations, might group themselves as one family. The speculative critic must here grant without stint all that the scheme of development can ask; and he must leave it to the naturalist and physiologist to break up the picture into sections, if they must. But then, *Why* must he grant it? Because here, having crossed the margin of animal life, we have, in its germ of feeling and idea, not merely a persistent, but a self-promoting force, able to turn to account whatever is below it; the mental power, even in its rudiments, dominating the vital, and constraining it to weave a finer organism;

and, for that end, to amend its application of the chemical forces, and make them better economize their command of mechanical force. Observe, however, that, if here we meet with a truly fruitful agency, capable of accomplishing difficult feats of new combination and delicate equilibrium, we meet with it *here first;* and the moment we fall back from the line of sentient life, and quit the scene of this eager, aggressive, and competing power, we part company with all principle of progress; and consequently lose the tendency to that increasing complexity of structure and subtlety of combination which distinguish the organic from the inorganic compounds. Below the level of life, there is no room for the operation of "natural selection." Its place is there occupied by another principle, for which no such wonders of constructive adaptation can be claimed; — I mean, the dynamic rule of *Action on the line of least resistance,* — a rule, the working of which is quite in the opposite direction. For evidently it goes against the establishment of unstable conditions of equilibrium, and must therefore be the enemy rather than the patron of the complex ingredients, the precarious tissues, and the multiplied relations, of sentient bodies; and on its own theatre must prevent the permanent formation of any but the simpler unions among the material elements. Accordingly, all the great enduring masses that form and fill the architecture of inorganic nature, — its limestone and clay, its oxides and salts, its water and air, — are compounds, or a mixture, of few and direct constituents. And the moment that life retreats and surrenders the organism it has built and held, the same antagonist principle enters on possession, and sets to work to destroy the intricate structure of "proximate principles" with their "compound radicals." With life and mind therefore there begins, whether by modified affinities or by removal of waste, a *tension* against these lower powers, carrying the being up to a greater or less height upon the wing; but with life it ends, leaving him then to the perpetual gravitation that completes the loftiest flight upon the ground. Within the limits of her Physics and Chemistry alone, Nature discloses no principle of progression, but only provisions for periodicity; and out of this realm, without further resources, she could never rise.

The downward tendency which sets in with any relaxation of the differentiating forces of life is evinced, not only in the extreme case of dissolution in death, but in the well-known relapse of organs which have been artificially developed into exceptional perfection back into their earlier state, when relieved of the strain and left to themselves. Under the tension of a directing mental interest, whether supplied by the animal's own instincts or by the controlling care of man, the organism yields itself to be moulded into more special and highly finished forms; and a series of ascending variations withdraws the nature from its original or first-known type. But wherever we can lift the tension off, the too skilful balance proves unstable, and the law of reversion reinstates the simpler conditions. Only on the higher levels of life do we find a self-working principle of progression: and, till we reach them, development wants its dynamics; and, though there may be evolution, it cannot be self-evolution.

These considerations appear to me to break the back of this formidable argument in the middle; and to show the impossibility of dispensing with the presence of Mind in any scene of ascending being, where the little is becoming great, and the dead alive, and the shapeless beautiful, and the sentient moral, and the moral spiritual. Is it not in truth a strange choice, to set up "*Evolution*," of all things, as the negation of *Purpose* pre-disposing what is to come? For what does the word mean, and whence is it borrowed? It means, to unfold from within; and it is taken from the history of the seed or embryo of living natures. And what is the seed but a casket of pre-arranged futurities, with its whole contents *prospective*, settled to be what they are by reference to ends still in the distance. If a grain of wheat be folded in a mummy-cloth and put into a catacomb, its germ for growing and its albumen for feeding sleep side by side, and never find each other out. But no sooner does it drop, thousands of years after, on the warm and moistened field, than their mutual play begins, and the plumule rises and lives upon its store till it is able to win its own maintenance from the ground. Not only are its two parts therefore relative to each other, but both are relative to conditions lying in another department of the world, — the clouds, the atmosphere, the soil; in the absence of which they remain barren and functionless : — and *this*, from a Cause that has no sense of relation! The human ear, moulded in the silent matrix of nature, is formed with a nerve susceptible to one influence alone, and that an absent one, the undulations of a medium into which it is not yet born; and, in anticipation of the whole musical scale with all its harmonies, furnishes itself with a microscopic grand-piano of three thousand stretched strings, each ready to respond to a different and definite number of aerial vibrations: — and *this*, from a Cause that never meant to bring together the inner organ and the outer medium, now hidden from each other! The eye, shaped in the dark, selects an exclusive sensibility to movements propagated from distant skies; and so weaves its tissues, and disposes its contents, and hangs its curtains, and adjusts its range of motion, as to meet every exigency of refraction and dispersion of the untried light, and be ready to paint in its interior the whole perspective of the undreamed world without: — and *this*, from a Cause incapable of having an end in view! Surely, nothing can be evolved that is not first involved; and if there be any thing which not only carries a definite future in it, but has the whole *rationale* of its present constitution grounded in that future, it is the embryo, whence, by a strange humor, this denial of final causes has chosen to borrow its name. Not more certainly is the statue that has yet to be, already potentially contained in the preconception and sketches of the artist, than the stately tree of the next century in the beech-mast that drops upon the ground; or the whole class of Birds, if you give them a common descent, in the eggs to which you choose to go back as first; or the entire system of nature in any germinal cell or other prolific *minimum* whence you suppose its organism to have been brought out. Evolution and Prospection are inseparable conceptions. Go back as you will, and try to propel the movement from behind instead of drawing it from before, development in a definite direction towards the realization of a dominant scheme of ascending relations is the sway of an overruling end. To take away the ideal basis of nature, yet construe it by the analogy of organic growth, will be for ever felt as a contradiction. It is to put out the eyes of the Past, in order to show us with what secure precision, amid distracting paths, and over chasms bridged by a hair, it selects its way into the Future.

If the Divine Idea will not retire at the bidding of our speculative science, but retains its place, it is natural to ask, what is its relation to the series of so-called Forces in the world? But the question is too large and deep to be answered here. Let it suffice to say, that there need not be any *overruling* of these forces by the will of God, so that the supernatural should disturb the natural; or any *supplementing* of them, so that He should fill up their deficiencies. Rather is His Thought related to them as, in Man, the mental force is related to all below it; turning them all to account for ideal ends, and sustaining the higher equilibrium which else would lapse into lower forms. More truly, yet equivalently, might we say, these supposed forces, which are only our intellectual interpretation of classes of perceived phenonema, are but varieties of His Will, the rules and methods of His determinate and legislated agency, in which, to keep faith with the universe of beings, He abnegates all change; but beyond which, in His transcendent relations with dependent and responsible minds, He has left a glorious margin for the free spiritual life, open to the sacredness of Personal Communion, and the hope of growing similitude.

THE RELATIONS

OF

ETHICS AND THEOLOGY.

By ANDREW P. PEABODY.

THE RELATIONS

OF

ETHICS AND THEOLOGY.

MY subject is the mutual relations of Ethics and Theology.

Ethics is the science of the Right; and we would first inquire whether this science is a mere department of theology, or whether it has its own independent existence, sphere, and office. Our opening question then is: What is the ground of right? Why are certain acts right, and certain other acts wrong? Are these characteristics incidental, arbitrary, created by circumstances; variable with time or place, or the intelligence of the agent; contingent on legislation, human or Divine? Or are they intrinsic, essential, independent of command, even of the Divine command?

We can best answer this question by considering what is implied in existence. Existence implies properties, and properties are fitnesses. Every object, by virtue of its existence, has its place, purpose, uses, relations. At every moment, each specific object is either in or out of its place, fulfilling or not fulfilling its purpose, subservient to or alienated from its uses, in accordance or out of harmony with its relations, and therefore in a state of fitness or of unfitness as regards other objects. Every object is at every moment under the control of the intelligent will either of the Supreme Being or of some finite being, and is by that will maintained either in or out of its place, purpose, uses, and relations, and thus in a state of fitness or unfitness as regards other objects. Every intelligent being, by virtue of his existence, bears certain definite relations to outward objects, his fellow-beings, and his Creator. At every moment each intelligent being is either faithful or unfaithful to these relations, and thus in a state of fitness or unfitness as regards outward objects and other beings. Thus fitness or unfitness may be predicated at every moment of every object in existence, of the volitions by which each object is controlled, and of every intelligent being with regard to his voluntary position in the universe. Fitness and unfitness are the ultimate ideas that underlie the terms *right* and *wrong*. These last are metaphorical terms: right, *rectus*, straight, upright, according to rule, and therefore *fit;* wrong, *wrung*, distorted, twisted out of place, abnormal, and therefore *unfit*. We are so constituted that we cannot help regarding fitness with esteem and complacency; unfitness, with disesteem and disapproval, even though we ourselves create it or impersonate it.

Fitness is the law by which alone we have the knowledge of sin, by which alone we justify or condemn ourselves. Duty has fitness for its only aim and end. To whatever object comes under our control its fit place or use is due; and our perception of that *due* constitutes our *duty*, and awakens in us a sense of obligation. To ourselves and to other beings and objects, our fidelity to our relations has in it an intrinsic fitness; that fitness is their and our due;

and the perception of that *due* constitutes our *duty*, and awakens in us a sense of obligation.

Conscience is the faculty by which we perceive fitness or unfitness. Its functions are not cognitive, but judicial. Its decisions are based upon our knowledge, real or imagined, from whatever source derived. It judges according to such law and evidence as it has; and its verdict is always, relatively, a genuine *verdict* (*verum dictum*), though potentially false and wrong by defect of our knowledge,—even as in a court of law an infallibly wise and incorruptibly just judge may pronounce an utterly erroneous and unjust decision, if he have before him a false statement of facts, or if the law which he is compelled to administer be unrighteous. What we call the education of conscience is merely the accumulation and verification of the materials on which conscience is to act; in fine, the discovery of fitnesses.

Permit me to illustrate the function of conscience by reference to a question now mooted in our community,—the question as to the moral fitness of the temperate use of fermented liquors. Among the aborigines of Congo and Dahomey, there being no settled industry, no mental activity, and no hygienic knowledge as to either body or mind, it seems fitting, and therefore right, to swallow all the strong drink that they can lay their hands upon; for it is fitted to produce immediate animal enjoyment,—the only good of which they have cognizance. Among civilized men, on the contrary, intoxication is universally known to be opposed to the fitnesses of body and mind, an abuse of alcoholic liquors, and an abuse of the drinker's own personality; and it is therefore condemned by all consciences, by none more heartily than by those of its victims. But there still remains open the question as to the moderate use of fermented liquors; and this is not, as it is commonly called, a question of conscience, but a mere question of fact, — of fitness or unfitness. Says one party, "Alcohol, in every form, and in the least quantity, is a virulent poison, and therefore unfit for body and mind." Says the other party, "Wine, moderately used, is healthful, salutary, restorative, and therefore fitted to body and mind." Change the opinion of the latter party, their consciences would at once take the other side; and, if they retained in precept and practice their present position, they would retain it self-condemned. Change the opinion of the former party, their consciences would assume the ground which they now assail. Demonstrate to the whole community — which physiology may one day do — the precise truth in this matter, there would remain no differences of conscientious judgment, whatever difference of practice might still continue.

From what has been said, it is necessarily inferred that right and wrong are not contingent on the knowledge of the moral agent. Unfitness, misuse, abuse, is none the less wrong because the result of ignorance. If the result of inevitable ignorance, it does not indeed imply an unfitness or derangement of the agent's own moral powers. Yet it is none the less out of harmony with the fitness of things. It deprives an object of its due use. It perverts to pernicious results what is salutary in its purpose. It lessens for the agent his aggregate of good and of happiness, and increases for him his aggregate of evil and of misery. In this sense — far more significant than that of arbitrary infliction — the maxim of jurisprudence, *Ignorantia legis neminem excusat* ("Ignorance of the law excuses no one"), is a fundamental principle of human nature.

We are now prepared to consider the relation of moral distinctions to theology. In the first place, if the ground which I have maintained be tenable, ethical science rests on a basis of its own, wholly independent of theology. Right and wrong, as moral distinctions, in no wise depend on the Divine will and law; nay, not even on the Divine existence. The atheist cannot escape or disown them. They are inseparable from existence. For whatever exists, no matter how it came into being, must needs have its due place, affinities, adaptations, uses; and an intelligent dweller among the things that are cannot but know something of their fitnesses and harmonies, and, so far as he acts upon them, cannot but feel the obligation to recognize their fitnesses, and thus to create or restore their harmonies. Even to the atheist, vice is a violation of fitnesses which he knows or may know. It is opposed to his conscientious judgment. He has with regard to it an inevitable sense of wrong. I can therefore conceive of an atheist's being — though I should have little hope that he would be — a rigidly virtuous man, and that on principle.

But while atheism does not obliterate moral distinctions, or cancel moral obligation, these distinctions are a refutation of atheism; and from the very fitness of things, which we have seen to be the ground of right, we draw demonstrative evidence of the being, unity, and moral perfectness of the Creator: so that the fundamental truths of theology rest on the same basis with the fundamental principles of ethics. Let me ask you to pursue this argument with me.

Every object, as I have said, must, by virtue of its existence, have its fit place and use; but, in a world that was the dice-work of chance, there would be myriads of probabilities to one against any specific object's attaining to its fit place and use. This must be the work of will alone. If chance can create, it cannot combine, co-ordinate, organize. If it can throw letters on the ground by the handful, it cannot arrange them into the Iliad or the Paradise Lost. If it can stain the sky or the earth with gorgeous tints, it cannot group them into a Madonna or a landscape. Its universe would be peopled by straylings, full of disjointed halves of pairs, — of objects thrown together in such chaotic heaps that seldom could any one object find its counterpart or subserve its end.

The opposite is the case in the actual world. The first discoveries which the first human being made were of the fitnesses of the objects around him to himself and to one another. With every added year his microcosm enlarged, so that, before he left the world, he had within his cognizance a range of fitnesses and uses sufficient to guide his own activity, and to enable him to predict its results, together with numerous other results not contingent on his own agency. Beyond this microcosm, indeed, lay a vast universe impenetrable to his search, in which he could trace no relations, no filaments of order; in which all seemed to him a medley of chaotic confusion, mutually intruding systems, clashing and jarring forces. On this realm of the unknown man has ever since been making perpetual aggressions; and every step of his progress has been the discovery of fitnesses, relations, reciprocal uses, among the most remote, diverse, and at first sight mutually hostile objects, classes, and systems. Natural history, physics, and chemistry, are the science of mutual fitnesses and uses among terrestrial objects. Astronomy is the science of harmonies among all the worlds, — of fitnesses in their relations and courses to the condition of things in our own planet, approximately to other bodies in the solar system, and, by ascertained analogies, to those distant orbs of which we know only that they stand and move ever in their order. Geology is the science of mutual fitnesses in former epochs and conditions of our own planet, and of prospective fitnesses in them to the needs and uses of the present epoch; so that by harmonies which run through unnumbered æons we are the heirs, and sustain our industries by the usufruct, of the ages, the great moments of whose history we are just beginning to read. Mathematical science reveals geometrical and numerical fitnesses, proportions, and harmonies, which are traced alike in the courses of the stars and in the collocation of the foliage on the tree, and which promise one day to give us the equation of the curve of the sea-shell, of the contour of the geranium-leaf, of the crest of the wave. There is still around us the realm of the unknown; yet not only are daily aggressions made upon it, but science has advanced so far as to render it certain that there is no department or object in the universe, which is not comprehended in this system of mutual fitnesses, harmonies, and uses.

Now consider the relation of organized being to this system. What is an organ? It is the capacity of perceiving, choosing, and utilizing a fitness. The rootlets of the tree by the river-side perceive the adjacent water, elongate themselves toward it, in a drought make convulsive and successful efforts to reach it; while the corolla of the heliotrope perceives the calorific rays, and turns toward their source in the heavens. The organs of the plant select from the elements around it such substances as are fitted to feed its growth, and appropriate them to its use, even though they be found in infinitesimal proportions, in masses of alien substance. In all this there is a semi-self-consciousness, corresponding, not indeed to the action of mind, but to that of the spontaneous life-processes in intelligent beings.

The animal carries us a step higher. His instincts are an unerring knowledge of fitnesses and uses within his sphere. He seeks what is fitted, shuns what is unfitted to his sustenance and growth, is never deceived when left to his own sagacity, and fails only when brought into anomalous relations with the superior knowledge of man. He lives, merely because he is conscious of the fitnesses of nature, and yields up his life to a stronger beast, in accordance with those same fitnesses — beneficent still — by which all realms of nature are kept fully stocked, yet never overstocked, with healthy and rejoicing life.

The fitness which thus pervades and unifies the entire creation, man as an animal perceives, as a living soul recognizes and comprehends; and to his consciousness it is an imperative law, obeyed always with self-approval, disobeyed only with self-condemnation. Of disobedience he alone is capable, yet he but partially. In order to live, he must obey in the vast majority of instances; still more must he obey, if he would have society, physical comfort, transient enjoyment of however low a type; and the most depraved wretch that walks the earth purchases his continued being by a thousand acts of unintended yet inevitable obedience to one of voluntary guilt. Man's law — the law which, in violating or scorning it, he cannot ignore or evade — is the very same fitness which runs through all inorganic nature, and which the semi-conscious tree, shrub, or flower, the imperfectly self-conscious bird, fish, or beast uniformly obeys.

Now can chance have evolved this universal fitness, and the sou's that own their allegiance to it? Is it not the clear self-revelation of a God, one, all-wise, omnipotent? Has it any other possible solution? Bears it not, in inscriptions that girdle the universe in letters of light, the declarations of the Hebrew seer, "In the beginning God created the heavens and the earth," and "The Lord our God is one Lord"? I am not disposed to cavil at the argument from design in the structure and adaptations of any one organized being; but immeasurably more cogent is this argument from a consenting universe, in which filaments of fitness, relation, and use cross and recross one another from bound to bound, from sun to star, from star to earth, from the greatest to the least, from the order of the heavens to the zoöphyte and the microscopic animalcule. In the human conscience I recognize at once the revelation and the perpetual witness of this all-pervading adaptation, this universal harmony. Conscience is the God within, not in figure, but in fact. It is the mode in which He who is enshrined in all being, who lives in all life, takes up his abode, holds his perpetual court, erects his eternal judgment-seat, within the human soul.

We pass to the consideration of the moral attributes of the Creator. I have spoken of moral distinctions as logically separable from and independent of the Divine nature. From this position alone can we establish the holiness, justice, and mercy of the Divine Being. In order to show this, let me ask your attention to the distinction between necessary and contingent truths; that is, between truths which have an intrinsic validity, which always were and cannot by any possibility be otherwise than true, and truths which were made true, which began to be, and the opposite of which might have been. Mathematical truth is necessary and absolute truth,—not made truth even by the ordinance of the Supreme Being, but truth from the very nature of things, truth co-eternal with God. Omnipotence cannot make two and two five, or render the sum of the angles of a triangle more or less than two right angles, or construct a square and a circle of both equal perimeter and equal surface. In our conception of mathematical truth we are conscious that it must have been true before all worlds, and would be equally true had no substance that could be measured or calculated ever been created. Every mathematical proposition is an inherent property or condition of the infinite space identical with the Divine omnipresence, or of the infinite duration identical with the Divine eternity.

Moral truth is of the same order, not contingent, but necessary, absolute. This is distinctly declared in one of the most sublime bursts of inspiration in the Hebrew Scriptures. If you will trace in the book of Proverbs the traits of Wisdom as personified throughout the first nine chapters, you will find that it is no other than a name for the inherent, immutable, eternal distinction between right and wrong. It is this Wisdom, who, so far from confessing herself as created, ordained, or subject, proclaims, "Jehovah possessed me in the beginning of his way, before his works of old. I was set up from everlasting, from the beginning, or ever the earth was. . .

When he prepared the heavens, I was there. . . . When he appointed the foundations of the earth, then I was by him, AS ONE BROUGHT UP WITH HIM; and I was daily his delight, rejoicing always before him."

It is only on the principle thus vividly set forth that we can affirm moral attributes of the Supreme Being. When we say that He is perfectly just, pure, holy, beneficent, we recognize a standard of judgment logically independent of his nature. We mean that the law of fitness, which He promulgates in the human conscience, and which is our only standard of right, is the self-elected law of his own being. Could we conceive of omnipotence and omniscience devoid of moral attributes, the decrees and acts of such a being would not be necessarily right. Omnipotence cannot make the wrong right, or the right wrong; nor can it indue either with the tendencies of the other, so that the wrong, that is, the unfitting, should produce ultimate good, or the right, that is, the fitting, should produce ultimate evil. God's decrees and acts are not right because they are his; but they are his because they are right. On no other ground, as I have said, can we affirm moral attributes of him. If his arbitrary sovereignty can indue with the characteristics of right that which has no intrinsic fitness, beauty, or utility, then the affirmation that He is holy, or just, or good, is simply equivalent to the absurd maxim of human despotism, "The king can do no wrong." It is only when we conceive of the abstract right as existing of necessity from a past eternity, and as a category of the Divine free-will and perfect prescience, in which the creation had its birth and its archetypes, that holiness, justice, and goodness, as applied to the Divine character, have any meaning.

We thus see that our ethical conceptions underlie our theology, and that, however explicit the words of revelation may be as to the Divine nature, he alone can understand them, who recognizes in his own heart the absoluteness and immutableness of moral distinctions. How many Christians have there been in every age since the primitive, who, in using the terms *just* and *holy* with reference to the Almighty, have employed them in an entirely different sense from that in which they are applied to human conduct, and with regard to supposed dispositions and acts, which in man they would call unjust and cruel! And this simply because they have attached no determinate meaning, but only a conventional and variable sense to ethical terms, and have imagined that arbitrary power could reverse moral distinctions, or that God could impose on man one law of right, and himself recognize another.

We have thus seen that theology is indebted to the fundamental principles of ethics for the most luculent demonstration of the being, omnipotence, and omniscience of God, and for the clear conception of his moral attributes.

We will now consider the reciprocal obligations of ethics to theology; and, in the first place, to Natural Religion. Pure theism attaches the Divine sanction to the verdicts of conscience, makes them the will, the voice of God, enforces them by his authority, and elevates the conception of virtue by establishing a close kindred between the virtuous man and the Ruler of the universe. And this is much, but not for many. It has raised some elect spirits to a degree of excellence which might put

Christians to shame. It has conjoined virtue with lofty devotion and earnest piety in a Socrates and a Marcus Antoninus, and refined it into a rare purity, chasteness, and tenderness of spirit in a Plutarch and an Epictetus. But on the masses of mankind, on the worldly and care-cumbered, on the unphilosophic and illiterate, it has exerted little or no influence. Moreover, while among the virtuous men of pre-Christian times and beyond the light of the Jewish revelation, we recognize some few of surpassing excellence, we find not a single ethical system, or body of moral precepts, which does not contain limitations, deficiencies, or enormities utterly revolting to the moral sense of Christendom. Thus Plato had lofty conceptions of virtue, but there are directions in which his precepts give free license to lust and cruelty; and even Socrates sanctioned by his unrebuking intimacy and fondness the leaders and ornaments of the most dissolute society in Athens.

The acme of extra-Christian piety, and consequently of moral excellence, is presented in the writings and lives of the later Stoics, whose incorruptible virtue affords the only relief to our weariness and disgust, as we trace the history of Rome through the profligacy of the declining commonwealth and the depravity of the empire. We find here the Simeons and Annas of the Pagan world, who, though with the fleshly arm they embraced not the Son of God, needed but to see him to adore and love him. Yet in nothing was Stoicism more faulty than in its exalted sense of virtue. For it had no charity for sin, no tolerance even for the inferior forms of goodness. It was the ethics of the unfallen. It proffered no hope of forgiveness; it let down no helping hand from the heavens; it uttered no voice from the eternal silence; it opened no Father's house and arms for the penitent. In Moore's "Lalla Rookh" the Peri, promised forgiveness and readmission to Paradise on condition of bringing to the eternal gate the gift most dear to heaven, returns in vain with the last drop of the patriot's blood. Again, when she brings the expiring sigh of the most faithful human love, the crystal bar moves not. Once more she seeks the earth, and bears back the tear of penitence that has fallen from a godless wretch melted into contrition by a child's prayer; and for this alone the golden hinges turn. Stoicism could boast in rich profusion the patriot's blood, could feed the torch of a love stronger than death; but it could not start the penitential tear, — it failed of the one gift of earth for which there is joy in heaven.

Let us rise, then, from the purest philosophy of the old world to Christianity in its ethical relations and offices.

Christianity, as a revelation, covers the entire field of human duty, and gives the knowledge of many fitnesses, recognized when once made known, but undiscoverable by man's unaided insight. The two truths which lie at the foundation of Christian ethics are human brotherhood and the immortality of the soul.

1. *Human brotherhood.* The visible differences of race, color, culture, religion, customs, are in themselves dissociating influences. Universal charity is hardly possible while these differences occupy the foreground. Slavery was a natural and congenial institution under Pagan auspices, and the idea of a missionary enterprise transcends the broadest philanthropy of heathenism. We find indeed in the ancient moralists, especially in the writings of Cicero and Seneca, many precepts of human-

ty toward slaves, but no clear recognition of the injustice inseparable from the state of slavery; nor have we in all ancient literature, unless it be in Seneca (in whom such sentiments might have had more or less directly a Christian origin), a single expression of a fellowship broad enough to embrace all diversities of condition, much less of race.[1] Even Socrates, while he expects himself to enter at death into the society of good men, and says that those who live philosophically will approach the nature of the gods, expresses the belief that worthy, industrious men who are not philosophers will, on dying, migrate into the bodies of ants, bees, or other hard-working members of the lower orders of animals.

The fraternity of our entire race — even without involving the mooted question of a common human parentage — is through Christianity established, not only by the Divine fatherhood so constantly proclaimed and so luculently manifested by Jesus, but equally by the unifying ministry of his death as a sacrifice for all, and by his parting commitment of " all the world " and " every creature " to the propagandism of his disciples. Though the spirit of this revelation has not yet been embodied in any community, it has inspired the life-work of many in every age; it has moulded reform and guided progress in social ethics throughout Christendom; it has twice swept the civilized world clean from domestic slavery; it has shaken every throne, is condemning every form of despotism,

---

[1] The verse so often quoted from Terence, "Homo sum; humani nihil a me alienum puto," will probably occur to many as inconsistent with my statement. The sentiment of this verse is, indeed, as it stands by itself, truly Christian; but in the Comedy from which it is quoted, so far from having a philanthropic significance, it is merely a busy-body's apology for impertinent interference with the concerns of his neighbor.

monopoly, and exclusiveness, and gives clear presage of a condition in which the old pre-Christian division of society into the preying and the preyed-upon will be totally obliterated.

2. *The immortality of the soul*, also, casts a light, at once broad and penetrating, upon and into every department of duty; for it is obvious, without detailed statement, that the fitnesses, needs, and obligations of a terrestrial being of brief duration, and those of a being in the nursery and initial stage of an endless existence, are very wide apart, — that the latter may find it fitting to do, seek, shun, omit, endure, resign, many things which to the former are very properly matters of indifference. Immortality was, indeed, in a certain sense believed before Christ, but with feeble assurance, and with the utmost vagueness of conception; so that this belief can hardly be said to have existed either as a criterion of duty or as a motive power. How small a part it bore in the ethics of the Stoic school may be seen, when we remember that Epictetus, than whom there was no better man, denied the life beyond death; and in Marcus Antoninus immortality was rather a devout aspiration than a fixed belief. In the Christian revelation, on the other hand, the eternal life is so placed in the most intimate connection with the life and character in this world as to cast its reflex lights and shadows on all earthly scenes and experiences.

Christianity, in the next place, makes to us an ethical revelation in the person and character of its Founder, exhibiting in him the very fitnesses which it prescribes, showing us, as it could not by mere precepts, the proportions and harmonies of the virtues, and manifesting the unapproached beauty, nay, majesty, of the gentler virtues, — *virtutes leniores,* as Cicero calls them, — which in pre-Christian ages were sometimes made secondary, sometimes repudiated with contempt and derision.

It is, I know, among the commonplaces of the rationalism and secularism of our time, that the moral precepts of the Gospel were not original, but had all been anticipated by Greek or Eastern sages. This is not literally and wholly true; for in some of the most striking of the alleged instances there is precisely the same difference between the heathen and the Christian precept that there is between the Old Testament and the New. The former says, "Thou shalt not;" the latter, "Thou shalt." The former forbids; the latter commands. The former prescribes abstinence from overt evil; the latter has for its sum of duty, "Be thou perfect, as thy Father in heaven is perfect." But the statement which I have quoted has more of truth in it than has been usually conceded by zealous champions of the Christian faith; and I would gladly admit its full and entire truth, could I see sufficient evidence of it. The unqualified admission does not in the least detract from the pre-eminent worth of Him who alone has been the Living Law. So far is this anticipation of his precepts by wise and good men before him from casting doubts on the divinity of his mission upon earth, that it only confirms his claims upon our confidence. For the great laws of morality are, as we have seen, as old as the throne of God; and strange indeed were it, had there been no intimation of them till the era of their perfect embodiment and full promulgation. The Divine Spirit, breathing always and everywhere, could not have remained, without witness of right, duty, and obligation in the outward universe and in the human conscience. So, struggling through the mists of weltering chaos, were many errant light-beams; yet none the less glorious and benignant was the sun, when in the clear firmament he first shone, all-illumining and all-guiding.

But in practical ethics a revelation of duty is but a small part of man's need. According to a Chinese legend, the founders of the three principal religious sects in the Celestial Empire, lamenting in the spirit-land the imperfect success which had attended the promulgation of their doctrines, agreed to return to the earth, and see if they could not find some right-minded person by whose agency they might convert mankind to the integrity and purity which they had taught. They came in their wanderings to an old man, sitting by a fountain as its guardian. He recalled to them the high moral tone of their several systems, and reproached them for the unworthy lives of their adherents. They agreed that he was the very apostle they sought. But when they made the proposal to him, he replied, "It is the upper part of me only that is flesh and blood: the lower part is stone. I can talk about virtue, but cannot follow its teachings." The sages saw in this man, half of stone, the type of their race, and returned in despair to the spirit-land.

There is profound truth in this legend. It indicates at once the mental receptivity and the moral inability of man, as to mere precepts of virtue. It is not enough that we know the right. We know much better than we do. The words which Ovid puts into the mouth of Medea, *Video meliora, proboque, deteriora sequor* ("I see and approve the better, I pursue the worse"), are the formula of universal experience. We, most of all, need enabling power. This we have through Christianity alone. We have it: 1. In the Divine fatherhood, as exhibited in those genial, winning traits, in which Jesus verifies his saying, "He that hath seen me hath seen the Father," — a fatherhood to feel which is to render glad and loving obedience to the Father's will and word; 2. In the adaptation of the love, sacrifice, and death of Christ to awaken the whole power of loving in the heart, and thus by the most cogent of motives to urge man to live no longer for himself, but for him who died for him; 3. In the assurance of forgiveness for past wrongs and omissions, without which there could be little courage for future well-doing; 4. In the promise and realization of Divine aid in every right purpose and worthy endeavor; 5. In institutions and observances designed and adapted to perpetuate the memory of the salient facts, and to renew at frequent intervals the recognition of the essential truths, which give to our religion its name, character, and efficacy.

Thus, while right and obligation exist independently of revelation, and even of natural religion, Christianity alone enables us to discern the right in its entireness and its due proportions; and it alone supplies the strength which we need, to make and keep us true to our obligations, under the stress of appetite and passion, cupidity and selfishness, human fear and favor.

Morality and religion, potentially separable, are yet inseparable in the will of God, under the culture of Christ. It used to be common to place the legal and the evangelical element in mutual antagonism. Nothing can be more profane or absurd than this. That which is not legal is evangelical only in name and pretence. That which is not evangelical is legal to no purpose. The religious belief or teaching, which lays not supreme stress on the whole moral law, is an outrage on the Gospel and the Saviour. The morality, which rests on any other foundation than Jesus Christ and his religion, is built on the sand, the prey of the first onrush or inrush of wind or wave. "What therefore God hath joined together, let not man put asunder."

CHRISTIANITY:

WHAT IT IS NOT, AND WHAT IT IS.

By G. VANCE SMITH.

CHRISTIANITY:

WHAT IT IS NOT, AND WHAT IT IS.

I.

IN looking back upon the past history of Christianity, it is easy to trace the existence of two very different ideas of the nature of that religion. Their influence is discernible in what may be termed its incipient form, in perhaps the earliest period to which we can ascend, while it has been especially felt during the last three hundred years, as also it materially affects the position and relations of churches and sects at the present moment. From obvious characteristics of each, these ideas may be respectively designated as the *ritualistic*, or sacerdotal, and the *dogmatic*, or doctrinal. It is scarcely necessary to add, that the two have been constantly intermingled and blended together, acting and reacting upon each other, and either supporting or else thwarting each other with singular pertinacity. Neither of them is found, in any instance of importance, existing wholly apart from the other, so as to be the sole animating principle of a great religious organization. The nature of the case renders this impossible. Ritualistic observances cannot be rationally followed without dogmatic beliefs. The former are the natural exponents of the latter, which indeed they are supposed to represent and to symbolize. Nor can doctrinal creeds, again, wholly dispense with outward rites and forms. Even the most spiritual religion requires some outward medium of expression, if it is to influence strongly either communities or individuals. It must, therefore, tacitly or avowedly adopt something of the dogmatic, if not of the ritualistic, idea, although this may not be put into express words, much less formed into a definite creed or test of orthodoxy.

A common factor of the greatest importance enters into the two conceptions of Christianity just referred to, though not perhaps in equal measure. I allude to the moral element, which may also be denoted as the sense of duty,—duty towards God and towards man. It may, indeed, be said to be a distinguishing glory of Christianity, that it can hardly exist at all, under whatever outward form, without being more or less strongly pervaded by the moral spirit of which the ministry of Christ affords so rich and varied an expression. It is true, however, that the ritualistic idea has constantly a tendency to degenerate into a mere care for church observances, devoid of any high tone of uprightness and purity in the practical concerns of ordinary life. It is a common thing, in that great religious communion of Western and Southern Europe which is so strongly animated by this idea, to see people in the churches ceremoniously kneeling in the act of prayer, while all the time they are busy, with eager eyes, to follow every movement in the crowd around them. In certain countries, many of the ritualistically devout, it is well known, have no scruple in practising the grossest impositions upon strangers; a statement which is especially true of those lands that in modern times have been governed and demoralized beyond others by the influence of the priestly class, with their religion of material externalities. A Greek or an Italian brigand, it is said, will rob and murder his captive with a peaceful conscience, provided only that he duly confesses to the priest, and obtains his absolution. This last is a gross and, happily, a rare case. But, equally with the more innocent acts, it illustrates the natural tendencies of ritualistic Christianity among various classes of persons. In ordinary civilized society, such tendencies are kept powerfully in check by other influences. Hence it is not to be denied that, throughout the Christian world, devotional feeling and the sense of duty are usually deep and active in their influence, and that the practical teachings of Christ, directly or indirectly, exercise a potent control, whatever may be the ritualistic or the dogmatic idea with which they are associated.

The ritualistic conception now spoken of offers us a Christianity which secures "salvation," by the intervention of a priest, — a man who, though, to all outward appearance, but a human being among human beings, yet alleges, and finds people to believe, that he can exercise supernatural functions, and has the power of opening or closing the gates of heaven to his fellow-men. It is needless to say how large a portion of Christendom is still under the influence of this kind of superstition, or how pertinaciously the same unspiritual form of religion is, at this moment, struggling to establish itself, even in the midst of the most enlightened modern nations.

Nor is it necessary here to argue, with any detail, against the notion of its being either inculcated upon us within the pages of the New Testament, or enforced by any legitimate authority whatever. Probably no one who cares to hear or to read these words would seriously maintain that the Gospel of Christ consists, in any essential way, in submission to a priesthood, fallible or infallible, in the observance of rites and ceremonies or times and seasons, or in a particular mode or form of church government, whatever doctrines these may be supposed to embody or to symbolize. Such things have, indeed, variously prevailed among the Christian communities from the beginning. Generation after generation has seen priests, and Popes, and patriarchs, and presbyters, without number. These personages have decked themselves out in sacred garments, assumed ecclesiastical dignities and powers, and sought, many of them, to heighten the charm and the efficacy of their worship by the aid of altars and sacrifices, so called, of prostrations, incense, lamps and candles, and many other such outward accessories. But are such things to be reckoned among the essentials of Christian faith or Christian righteousness? Does the presence or the blessing of the Spirit of God, to the humble, penitent, waiting soul of man, depend upon any thing which one calling himself a priest can do or say for us? Will any one, whose opinion is worth listening to, say that it does?

The teaching of Christ and his Apostles is, in truth, remarkably devoid of every idea of this kind. So much is this the case, that it may well be matter of astonishment to find men who profess to follow and to speak for them holding that in such matters there can be only one just and adequate Christian course,—that, namely, which commends itself to *their* judgment! It is evident, on the contrary,—too evident to be in need of serious argument, —that the very diversities of opinion and practice which prevail in the world — as expressed by such names as Catholic and Protestant, Greek Church and Latin Church, Church of England and Church of Scotland, Episcopalian, Presbyterian, Congregational — prove conclusively that nothing imperative has been transmitted to us. The great Christian brotherhood, in its various sections and diverse conditions, has manifestly been left, in these things, to its own sense of what it is good and right to follow. Thus, too, if we will not close our eyes to the plainest lessons of His Providence, the Almighty Father gives us to understand that He only asks from us the service of heart and life that is "in spirit and in truth;" and, consequently, that we may each give utterance to our thoughts of praise and thanksgiving, to penitence for sin, to our prayer for the divine help and blessing, in whatever form of words, through whatever personal agency, and with whatever accompaniment of outward rite and ceremony we may ourselves deem it most becoming to employ.

The second, or dogmatic, conception of the Gospel has been less generally prevalent than that of which I have been speaking. Yet, ever since the days of Luther, not to recall the older times of Nicene or Athanasian controversy, it has been possessed of great influence in some of the most important Christian nations. Protestant Christianity is predominantly dogmatic. Under various forms of expression, it makes the Gospel to consist in a very definite system of *doctrines* to be believed; or, if not actually to consist in this, at least to include it, as its most prominent and indispensable element. We are informed, accordingly, that a man is not a Christian, cannot be a Christian, and perhaps it will be added, cannot be "saved," unless he receives certain long established doctrines, or reputed doctrines, of Christian faith.

What these are, it is not necessary here minutely to inquire. It is well, however, to note with care that there would be considerable differences of opinion in regard to them, among those who would yet be agreed as to the necessity of holding firmly to the dogmatic idea referred to. A Roman Catholic, of competent intelligence, would not by any means agree with an ordinary member of the Anglican church equally qualified. Both of these would differ in essential points from a member of the Greek church; and the three would be almost equally at variance with an average representative of Scotch Presbyterian Calvinism, as also with one whose standard of orthodoxy is contained in the Sermons, and the notes on the New Testament, of the founder of Methodism. Nay, it is well known, even within the limits of the same ecclesiastical communion, differences so serious may be found as are denoted, in common phrase, by the terms *ritualistic* and *evangelical*, and by other familiar words of kindred import.

Among the great Protestant sects the want of harmony under notice is, doubtless, confined within comparatively narrow limits. But there is diversity, not to say discord, even here. No one will dispute the fact who has any knowledge of the history of Protestant theology, or who is even acquainted with certain discussions, a few years ago, among well-known members of the English Episcopal Church, or with others, of more recent date, among English Independents, — in both cases on so weighty a subject as the nature of the Atonement.[1] Moreover, in the same

[1] Between Archbishop Thomson, in *Aids to Faith*, and some of the writers of *Tracts for Priests and People;* also between several eminent Independent Ministers, in the *English Independent* newspaper (August, 1871).

quarters, varieties of opinion are notorious on such topics as Baptismal regeneration, the authority of the Priesthood, the inspiration of Scripture, eternal punishment,— all of them questions of the most vital importance, in one or other of the popular schemes of the doctrine.

Now the indisputable fact referred to — the existence of this most serious diversity and opposition of opinion and statement — affords the strongest reason for considering it an error of the first magnitude to regard Christianity as essentially consisting in a definite system of theological dogmas. For is it possible to believe that a divine revelation of doctrine, such as the Gospel has been so commonly supposed to be, would have been left to be a matter of doubt and debate to its recipients? Admitting, for a moment, the idea that the Almighty Providence had designed to offer to men a scheme of Faith, the right reception of which should, in some way, be necessary for their "salvation," must we not also hold that this would have been clearly made known to them? so clearly, plainly stated as to preclude the differences just alluded to, as to what it *is* that has been revealed? It is impossible, in short, on such an assumption, to conceive of Christianity, as having been left in so doubtful a position that its disciples should have found occasion, from age to age, in councils and assemblies and conferences, in books and in newspapers, to discuss and dispute among themselves, often amidst anger and bitterness of spirit, upon the question of the nature or the number of its most essential doctrines. Of all possible suppositions, surely this is the least admissible, the most extravagantly inconsistent with the nature of the case.

To this consideration must be added another, of even

greater weight. We gain our knowledge of Christianity, and of the Author of Christianity, from the New Testament. And, in this collection of Gospels and Epistles, it nowhere appears that it was the intention of Christ or of the early disciples, to offer to the acceptance of the future ages of the world a new and peculiar Creed, a Confession of faith, a series of Articles of belief in facts or in dogmas, such as the speculative theologian of ancient and of modern times has usually delighted to deal with. This is nowhere to be seen in the New Testament, although it speedily made its appearance when the Gospel had passed from the keeping of the primitive church into that of Greek and Hellenistic converts.

The only thing that can be supposed to approach this character, within the sacred books themselves, occurs in such phrases as speak of faith in Jesus Christ, or also of "believing" in the abstract, without any expressed object. But in none of these instances can a dogmatic creed be reasonably held to be the object implied or intended. What is meant, is simply belief in Jesus as the Christ,[1] as may be at once understood from the circumstances of the case, and may easily be gathered from a comparison of passages. In the early days of the Gospel, the great question between the Christians and their opponents was simply this, whether Jesus of Nazareth was the Christ or not. One who admitted this, and received him in this character, had *faith* in him, and might be an accepted disciple. One who denied and rejected him, as the multitudes did, was not, and could not be, so accepted. A man could not, in a word, be a Christian disciple, without recognizing and believing in the Founder of Christianity.

[1] Comp. Matt. xvi. 14-16; Acts ix. 22, xvi. 31; Rom. iii. 22, viii. 6, 9.

This explanation of the nature of the Faith of the Gospel will be found to apply throughout the New Testament books. An illustration may be seen in one of the most remarkable passages, the last twelve verses of St. Mark's Gospel, — a passage, it should be noted, usually admitted to be of later origin than the rest of the book. Here (v. 16) we read, "He that believeth and is baptized shall be saved, but he that believeth not shall be damned" (condemned). The meaning is explained by a reference to the related passage, in chapter xxv. of the first Gospel. Here we learn that at the second Advent, shortly to come to pass, those who, having received Jesus as Lord, had approved themselves by their works obedient and faithful disciples, would by him be recognized as his, and admitted to share in the blessings of the promised kingdom of heaven: those who had not done so should be rejected and driven from his presence. It is clear that there is, in such ideas, no sufficient ground for supposing faith or belief in a creed or a dogma to have been intended by the writer of either Gospel.

Let me further illustrate my meaning by a brief reference to an ancient and, by many persons, still accepted formula of orthodox doctrine. This professes to tell us very precisely what is the true Christian faith. In plain terms it says, Believe this, and this, and this: believe it and keep it "whole and undefiled;" unless you do so, "without doubt" you shall "perish everlastingly."

Now my proposition is, that this kind of statement, or any thing like it, is not to be met with in the teaching of Christ, or in any other part of the New Testament. Had it been otherwise, — had he plainly said that the form of doctrine now referred to, or any other, was so essential, there could have been no room for hesitation among those who acknowledged him as Teacher and Lord. But he has manifestly not done this, or any thing like this. Hence, as before, we are not justified in thinking that the religion which takes its name from him, and professes to represent his teaching, consists, in any essential degree, in the acceptance, or the profession, of any such creed or system of doctrine, exactly defined in words, after the manner of the churches, — whether it may have come down to us from the remotest times of ante-Nicene speculation, or only from the days of Protestant dictators like Calvin or Wesley; whether it may have been sanctioned by the authority of an œcumenical council, so called, or by that of an imperial Parliament, or only by some little body of nonconformist chapel-builders, who, by putting their creed into a schedule at the foot of a trust-deed, show their distrust of the Spirit of Truth, and their readiness to bind their own personal belief, if possible, upon their successors and descendants of future generations.

We may then be very sure that, if the Christian Master had intended to make the "salvation" of his followers dependent upon the reception of dogmas, whether about himself or about Him who is "to us invisible or dimly seen" in His "lower works," he would not have left it to be a question for debate, a fertile source of angry contention or of heartless persecutions, as it has often virtually been, *what* the true creed, the distinctive element of his religion, really is. The very fact that this *has* been so much disputed, that such differences do now so largely exist before our eyes, forms the strongest possible testimony to the non-dogmatic character of the primitive or genuine Christianity. The same fact ought to rebuke and warn us against the narrow sectarian spirit in which existing divisions originate, and which is so manifestly out of harmony with "the spirit of Christ."

II.

This absence from the Christian records of all express instruction, on the subjects above noticed, clearly warrants us in turning away from any merely dogmatic or ecclesiastical system, if it be urged upon us as constituting the substance, or the distinctive element of Christianity. We are thus of necessity led to look for this in something else. But to what else shall we turn ? In what shall we find an answer to our inquiry, as to the true idea of the Christian Gospel ?

The reply to this question is not difficult. The true idea of Christ's religion can only be found in the life and words of the Master himself. And these it may well be believed, in their simple, rational, spiritual, practical form, are destined to assume a commanding position among Christian men which they have never yet held, and, in short, to suppress and supersede the extravagancies alike of ritualism and its related dogmatism, whatever the form in which these may now prevail among the churches and sects of Christendom.

This conclusion is readily suggested, or it is imperatively dictated, by various expressions in the New Testament itself. "Lord, to whom shall we go ? Thou hast the words of eternal life : " — such is the sentiment attributed to the Apostle Peter by the fourth Evangelist. Paul has more than one instance in which he is equally explicit: "Other foundation can no man lay than that is laid, which is Jesus Christ;" while in another place he writes, "If any man have not the spirit of Christ, he is none of his." Jesus himself speaks in terms which are even more decided, when he declares, "*I* am the Way, the Truth, and the Life."[1]

In such expressions as these we may, at the least, plainly see the surpassing importance, to the judgment of the earliest Christian authorities, of the personal Christ, of his teaching and example. We are thus emphatically taught, in effect, that we must look to CHRIST, and take HIM, in his life, his words, his devout and holy spirit, as the impersonation of his religion. When it is asked, then, What is the true idea of Christianity, no better answer can be given than by saying, it is Christ himself; that it is *in* Christ himself, in what he was and says and does, in all that made him well pleasing in the sight of God, as the beloved Son of the Almighty Father.

What Jesus was, in his visible life among men, we learn from the Gospel records. We learn it from them alone; for nowhere else have we information respecting him that deserves to be compared with theirs in originality or fulness of detail. It is not necessary to our present purpose to enter at length into the particulars which they have preserved for us, or into the differences between the three synoptical Gospels and the Fourth, in regard to the idea which they respectively convey of the ministry of Christ. The latter Gospel, it may, however, be observed, is usually admitted to be the last of the four in order of time. It is also, without doubt, the production of a single mind; and cannot be supposed, like the others,

---

[1] John vi. 68; 1 Cor. iii. 11; Rom. viii. 9; John xiv. 6.

simply to incorporate, with little change, the traditions handed down among the disciples, for perhaps a long series of years before being committed to writing. But whatever accidental characteristics of this kind may be thought to belong to the respective Gospels, they all agree in the resulting impression which they convey, as to the high character of Jesus. And, it will be observed, they do this very artlessly, without any thing of the nature of intentional effort or elaborate description. They state facts, and report words, in the most simple manner, often with extreme vagueness and want of detail. It thus, however, results, that the image of Christ which the Evangelists, and especially the first three, unite to give us is, above all things, a moral image only; in other words, it has been providentially ordered that the impression left upon the reader is almost entirely one of moral qualities and of character.

It may even be true, as some will tell us, that we have in each of the first three Gospels, not simply the productions of as many individual writers, but rather a growth or a compilation of incidents, discourses and sayings from various sources, and drawn especially from the oral accounts which had long circulated among the people, before they were put together in their present form. But even so, the result is all the more striking. The identity and self-consistency of the central object, the person of Christ, is the more remarkable. Such qualities lead us safely to the conclusion that one and the same Original, one great and commanding personality, was the true source from which all were more or less remotely derived. Hence, even the imperfect or fragmentary character of the Gospel history becomes of itself a positive evidence for the reality of the life, and the peculiar nature of the influence, of him whose career it so rapidly, and it may be inadequately, places before us.

It is, however, to be distinctly remembered that we reach the mind of Christ only through the medium of other minds. So far as can now be known, no words of his writing have been transmitted to our time, or were ever in the possession of his disciples. To some extent, therefore, it would appear, the thoughts of the Teacher[1] may have been affected, colored and modified, by the peculiar medium through which they have come down to us. Under all the circumstances of the case, this inference is natural and justifiable. It is one too of some importance, inasmuch as it directly suggests that, in all probability, the actual Person whose portraiture is preserved for us by the Evangelists must have surpassed, in his characteristic excellences, the impression which the narratives in fact convey. The first generation of disciples were evidently men who were by no means exempt from the influence of the national feelings of their people, or of the peculiar modes of thought belonging to their class. In the same degree in which this is true, they would be unable rightly to understand, and worthily to appreciate the teaching and the mind of Christ. This remark applies perhaps more especially to the first three Gospels, but it is not wholly inapplicable to the Fourth. Indeed, the fact referred to comes prominently out to view at several points in the Evangelical narrative, — as in the case of Peter rebuking his Master for saying that he must suffer

---

[1] The term *Teacher* is constantly used of Christ in the Gospels, though usually disguised in our English version under the rendering "Master." Comp. e.g. Mark ix. 17, 38; Luke x. 25.

and die at Jerusalem; in that of the request made by the mother of Zebedee's children; and in the anticipations ascribed by the first three Evangelists to Jesus himself, of his own speedy return to the earth, — anticipations which are recorded very simply, and without any corrective observation on the part of the writer.[1]

But, whatever the hindrances of this kind in the way of a perfectly just estimation by the modern disciple, the portrait of Christ preserved for us by the Evangelists is, in a remarkable degree, that of a great Religious Character. The Christ of the Gospels is, before all things, a Spiritual Being, unpossessed, it may even be said, of the personal qualities which might mark him off as the product of a particular age or people. He is, in large measure, the opposite of what the disciples were themselves, free from the feelings and prejudices of his Jewish birth and religion. This he evidently is, without any express design of theirs, and by the mere force of his own individuality. He is thus, in effect, the Christ[2] not merely of his immediate adherents, or his own nation, but of all devout men for all ages. He stands before us, in short, so wise, and just, and elevated in his teaching, so upright and pure in the spirit of his life, so engaging in his own more positive example of submission to the overruling will, and touching forbearance towards sinful men, that innumerable generations of disciples, since his death, have been drawn to him and led to look up to him even as their best and highest human representative of the Invisible God Himself.

[1] Matt. xvi. 22, .xx. 20, xxiv. 24–36; Mark viii. 31–33, x. 35–45, xiii. 24–30; Luke xviii. 31–34.
[2] That is to say, "anointed," or *King*, — in other words, Leader, Teacher, Saviour from sin, as the Gospels also expressly term him.

It is very probable, however, that all this was not so fully seen by those who stood nearest to Jesus during his brief and rapid career, as it has been since. At least many, even the vast majority of his day, failed to perceive it. And yet, to a Hebrew reader of the Gospels, the greatness of his character could be summed up in no more expressive terms than by claiming for him that he was the Christ; that he embodied in himself the moral and intellectual pre-eminence associated with that office. In this light he is especially represented in the first three Gospels. In John, too, we have substantially the same thing, though very differently expressed. In that Gospel, he is also the Christ, but he is so by the indwelling of the divine Word. "The Word became flesh and dwelt among us," and the glory which had been seen among men, "full of grace and truth," was the glory even "as of the only-begotten of the Father." Probably no language could have been used that would have conveyed to a reader of the time a higher idea of the moral and spiritual qualities of any human being. And this corresponds entirely with the impression given by other writers of the New Testament, to some of whom Jesus was personally known, — by Peter, for example, by James, by Paul, and by the writer to the Hebrews. They evidently looked back to their departed Master, and up to the risen Christ, as a person of commanding dignity and spiritual power, and this not merely on account of the official title of Messiah which, rightly or wrongly, they applied to him, but for the lofty moral virtues with which his name was to them synonymous.[1] He "who did no sin, neither was

[1] 1 Pet. ii. 21, seq.; iv. 1–5, 13–16; James ii. 1, seq.; Gal. vi. 22–24; Eph. iv. 13–15 and *passim;* Phil. i. 27, seq.; ii. 1–11; Rom. xiii. 14; 2 Cor. iv.

guile found in his mouth," was, without doubt, the most perfect example which they could cite of all that was acceptable in the sight of God. "The spirit of Christ," without which we are "none of his," could be nothing else, and nothing less, than a participation in Christ-like goodness; nor can it therefore possibly be wrong, if we too lay the main emphasis of the Christian profession precisely *here*, where it is laid by the apostles; if, in other words, we pass over, or leave out of sight, as altogether of secondary importance, or of none, those various and often conflicting dogmas and forms and "diversities of administration," about which the Christian world is so sorely, and for the present, so irreparably divided.

The character of Christ stands in very intimate relations with the miraculous powers attributed to him by the Gospels. Those powers, it is needless to say, have been seriously called in question, as actual facts of history, by the critical investigations of recent times. Many persons, it may be, cannot see, and will not admit, that their value has been affected by the inquiries alluded to. To such persons the miracles will naturally retain whatever efficacy they may be conceived to possess as evidence of the divine, that is, supernatural, claims of him who is recorded to have wrought them. They are entitled to their own judgment in the case, as well as to whatever support to Christian faith they think they can derive from such a quarter. At the same time other inquirers may be permitted to think differently. If the lapse of time and the increasing grasp and penetration of critical knowledge necessarily tend to lessen the certainty of the miraculous element of the Evangelical history, may not this too be a part of the providential plan — contemplated and brought about for great and wise ends? May it not be that now the spiritual man shall be left more entirely free to discern for himself the simple excellence of the Christian teaching and example? left increasingly without that support from the witness of outward miracle which has usually been deemed so important, and which is unquestionably found to be the more commonly thus estimated, in proportion as we descend into the lower grades of intelligence and moral sensibility.[1]

But, on the other hand, if this be true, one who may thus think need not of necessity also hold that the miracles of the Gospels did not take place, but that the history relating to them is the mere product of weak and credulous exaggeration. For, in truth, the ends which might be subserved by such manifestations are easily understood. Occurrences so unwonted and remarkable could not fail both to secure the attention of the spectator, and make him ponder well upon the words of the miracle-worker, and also to awaken in him new feelings of reverence towards the mysterious Being who had given such power to men. Thus it is readily conceivable, that a miracle might be a thing of the highest utility to those who witnessed it and to their generation. But then, on the other hand, it is not to be alleged that such occurrences are needed now to show us that God is a living Spirit in the world; or, consequently, that religious love and veneration are in any way dependent upon them, either as facts beheld by ourselves, or as incidents recorded to have been seen by others who lived many centuries ago. And, if this be so, surely we may look with indifference upon

---

[1] In illustration of this remark, it is scarcely necessary to mention the "miracles" of the Roman Catholic Church in all ages.

the most destructive operations of literary or scientific criticism, being anxious only, and above all things, for the simple truth, whatever it may be.

Again, however, it is not to be denied that the possession of miraculous power may have been for Christ himself, not less than for those who saw his works, of the deepest spiritual import. The formation of a character like his would seem peculiarly to require the training that would be afforded by such an endowment. We know how, with ordinary men, the command of unlimited power is, in fact, a test of rectitude, self-government, unselfishness, of the most trying and, it may be, most elevating, kind. The temptations which necessarily accompany it are proverbial. Was Christ exempt from that kind of moral discipline, that supreme proof of fidelity to God? Allowing, for a moment, what the narratives directly intimate, that he felt within himself the force of miraculous gifts, and the capacity to use them, if he had so willed, for purposes either of personal safety or of political ambition;[1] in this, we may see at once, there would be an end to be served of the greatest moment both to himself and to the future instruction of his disciples. By such an experience, the moral greatness of his example might be doubly assured. It would be made possible to him to deny and humble himself, — even, in apostolical phrase, to "empty" himself of his Messianic prerogatives, in order the better to do the Heavenly Father's will, and, preferring even the cross to a disobedient refusal of the cup which could not pass from him, to be "made perfect through suffering," thus showing himself worthy to be raised up at last to be, as he has been, the spiritual Lord of the Church.

[1] Matt. iv. 1, seq.

This idea was, in fact, a familiar one to Paul, as to others of the Christian writers.[1] Its literal truth is enforced by the consideration of the strange improbability that one by birth a Galilean peasant, without any special gifts or powers to recommend him to the notice of his people, should yet be acknowledged by many of them as the promised Messiah; should, in spite of an ignominious death, be accepted in that character by multitudes; and finally, in the same or a still higher character, should acquire the love and reverential homage of half the world.

And yet it may remain true that, as time passes, this consideration shall lose much of its weight, in the judgment of increasing numbers of earnest inquirers. They, accordingly, will cease to place reliance on the outward material sign. Jesus, nevertheless, may still be to them as an honored Master and Friend, whose name they would gladly cherish, for what he is in himself. To those who thus think his character and words will appeal by their own intrinsic worth. He will be Teacher, Saviour, Spiritual Lord, simply by the inherent grace and truth spoken of by the Evangelist of old.

If this be the destined end, we may gladly acknowledge the providential guiding even in this; and we shall certainly guard ourselves against judging harsh or uncharitable judgment in reference to those who on this subject may not see as we see, or feel as we feel; — who, nevertheless, in thought and deed and aspiration, may not be less faithful to Truth and Right, or less loyally obedient to all that is seen to be highest and best in Christ himself.

[1] 2 Cor viii. 9; Eph. i. 20-23; Phil. ii. 5-11; Heb. ii. 9, 10, 18; 1 Pet. ii. 21.

III.

Christ, then, I repeat, thus standing before us in the Evangelical records of his ministry, is the impersonation of his religion. What we see in Him is Christianity. Or, if it be not so, where else shall we look with the hope to find it? Who else has ever had a true *authority* to place before us a more perfect idea, or to tell us more exactly what the Gospel is? The *Church*, indeed, some will interpose, has such authority! But examine this statement, and its untenable character speedily appears. The Church at any given moment is, and has been, simply a body of fallible mortals, like ourselves. If the Christian men of this present day cannot suppose themselves to be preserved from intellectual error in matters of religion, neither can we think the Christian men of the past to have been more highly privileged. In fact, it must be added, as we ascend into the darker periods of Church history, we come upon the most undeniable traces of ignorance, misunderstanding, worldliness and folly, on the part of the ecclesiastics of the early and the middle ages, such as deprive their judgments on the subject before us of all right or claim to unquestioned acceptance. Let any one read, for example, the accounts given by trustworthy historians[1] of that great assembly of the Church which produced the Nicene Creed. Will any one allege that in the passion and prejudice, the smallness of knowledge, the subtlety of speculation, and narrowness of heart, pervading the majority of that assembly, the Divine Spirit was peculiarly present to dictate or guide the decision arrived at, and make it

[1] E.g., in Dean Stanley's *History of the Eastern Church.*

worthy of the blind adhesion of future Christian generations? And, if we cannot thus admit the peculiar idea of Christianity *there* approved, it will surely be in vain to look to any similar quarter, either of the past or of the present, for what shall supersede the living "grace and truth," seen in Christ himself.

This conclusion is greatly strengthened by the briefest reference to the negative results of unbelief and irreligion, so prevalent in those countries which have been the longest under the influence of the old ritualistic idea of the Church and the priesthood. Positively speaking, this idea, it is needless to add, has largely failed in almost every thing except the encouragement among the people of the grossest superstitions[1] — superstitions of which there is no trace whatever in immediate connection with the Christian Master. Not, however, to dwell in detail on this unpromising theme, let us rather turn to the considerations by which our leading position may be confirmed; from which too we may learn that a better future is yet in store for us.

The experience of past ages, the existing sectarian divisions of Christendom, the errors and superstitions involved in the grosser assumptions of Church authority, all unite to compel us to the conclusion of the essentially erroneous character of the old ritualistic and dogmatic conceptions of the nature of the Gospel. They show us not only that dogmas and rites about which the most

[1] A good authority has recently observed, "Catholicism, substituted for Christ, has turned the thought of Southern Europe to simple Infidelity, if not to Atheism: let us take heed that Protestantism does not bring about the same thing in another way in the North." — Bishop Ewing, in a *Letter* to the Spectator newspaper, April 8, 1870. The remark here quoted is of much wider application than the Bishop himself would probably admit!

earnest men are so utterly at variance cannot possibly be of the essence of Christianity, but further that the latter is nowhere to be found except in Him whom in spite of diversities all alike agree to hold in honor. And, in truth, his life, brief and fleeting as it was, may well be said to constitute the Christian revelation. That it does so, and was intended to do so, may, as already observed, be seen better in our day, than it was by the earliest disciples. Their thoughts were preoccupied, their vision obscured, by various influences which prevented them from clearly discerning the one thing needful. The temporal kingdom of their Master for which they were, many of them, so eagerly looking; his speedy return to judge the world, — an expectation of which there are so many traces in Gospels and Epistles alike ; the great and urgent question of the Law and its claims, with that of the admission of the Gentiles to the faith of Christ without the previous adoption of Judaism ; — such thoughts and such cares as these largely engaged and filled the minds of the disciples, within the limits of the period to which the origin of the principal New Testament books must be assigned. After the close of that period, fresh subjects of controversial interest continually arose, until these were gradually overshadowed by the rising authority of the Church and the later growth of sacerdotal power, followed in due course of time by the grosser corruptions of the primitive Gospel which marked the Christianity of the darker ages, and which have by no means as yet spent their power. Thus has it pleased the Great Disposer that men should be led forward to truth and light through error and darkness. Even as the Hebrews of old were gradually brought by many centuries of experience, and in the midst of imperfections and backslidings innumerable, to their final recognition of the One Jehovah, so have the Christian generations been slowly learning and unlearning according as their own condition and capacities allowed. Thus the great development has been running its destined course, and will doubtless conduct us eventually to yet better and truer ideas of what the Almighty purposes had, in Christ, really designed to give to the world.

To vary the form of expression, the life of Christ itself constitutes the revelation of His will which the Almighty Father has given to man by His Son. And that life does constitute a revelation, in the most full and various import of this term. It shows us, in a clear and engaging light, the One God and Father of all, the Just and Holy One, who will render to every man according to his deeds. It shows us the high powers and capacities of man himself; for, while and because it tells him to be perfect even as the Father in Heaven is perfect, it not only recognizes in him the capability to be so, but also abundantly affords the spiritual nutriment by which the higher faculties of his nature may be nurtured and strengthened within him. It shows us how to live a life of religious trust and obedience to the commands of duty, and, amidst many sorrows and trials, still to preserve a soul unstained by guilt. It shows us that this high devotion to the sacred law of Truth and Right is that which is well pleasing to God; and that His will is that man should thus, by the discipline of his spirit, join the moral strength and sensibility in this world which shall fit him, if he will, to enter upon the higher life of the world to come. All this we see plainly expressed and announced in Christ, constituting him the

Revealer in the best sense of this term. All this we do see, even though it may be very hard to find any doctrinal creed laid down in definite words, or any system of rites and ceremonies of worship, of Church government, or of priestly functions and dignities, placed before us as constituting an indispensable part of our common Christianity.

And it is here an obvious remark that, while Christian men have so often questioned and disputed with one another about the essentials of their religion; while they have sometimes, again, been forgetful of its spirit, in their controversies as to its verbal and written forms, — all this time they have been substantially agreed as to the matters which are the greatest and weightiest of all. About the Gospel as embodying and expressing man's faith in God and in heaven, and as setting forth the highest moral law with its exemplification in an actual human life; about the Gospel in these, which are surely its most serious and interesting aspects, there has been no dispute. The great spiritual principles taught by Christ, and the power of his practical exhibition of human duty, have been constantly admitted and — may it not be added? — constantly felt in the world, among all the sects and parties of Christendom, in spite of the differences of forms and creeds which have separated men from each other.

This fact suggests a further consideration of obvious interest. Regarded as a dogmatic or an ecclesiastical system, the Gospel is one of the greatest failures which the world has seen, no two sects or churches, scarcely any two congregations, being agreed as to some one or other of what are deemed its most essential elements. Regarded as a moral and spiritual energy and instructor among men, it is and always has been a quickening power, — tending directly, in its genuine influences, to support and to guide aright, and, even amidst the worst distractions or perversions of human passion and error, whispering thoughts of hope, comfort, and peace, to many troubled hearts. This should not be forgotten in our estimates of the part played by Christianity in past times, or in the judgments sometimes so lightly uttered by a certain class of its critics, who show themselves so ready to confound the religion with its corruptions, and to include it and them in one indiscriminate condemnation. It should help to call us back to juster views of the nature and the function of Christ's religion, and lead us the better to see that these consist, not in its capacity or its success as an imposer of dogmas or of ceremonial acts to be received and carefully performed by either priests or people, but in its power to strengthen with moral strength, to guide in the path of duty, to save us from our sins, to breathe into us the spirit of Christ, and so to bring us nearer to God. Such is the true function and the real power of the Gospel, even though it may constantly have had to act in the midst of gross ignorance, or of false and exaggerated dogmatic conception; nor is it too much to say that this its highest character has not been altogether wanting to it, even in the darkest periods of man's intellectual experience, during the last eighteen centuries.

And not only is this so; but, further, it is evidently not through the *peculiar* doctrines of his church or sect that a man is most truly entitled to the name of Christian, but rather by his participation in what is *common* to all the churches and sects which are themselves worthy of that name. For let us call to mind, for a moment, some of the more eminent Christian men and women of modern times, to whatever sectarian fold they may have owned themselves to belong. Recall the names of a Fénelon, an Oberlin, a Vincent de Paul, a Xavier, a Melancthon, a Milton, a Locke, a Chalmers, a Clarkson, a Wilberforce, a Mrs. Fry, a Keble, a Heber, a Wesley, a Lardner, a Priestley, a Channing, a Tuckerman, with innumerable other truehearted followers of him who both bear witness to the truth, and "went about doing good." In such persons we have representatives of nearly all the churches, with their various peculiarities of doctrinal confession. And must we not believe that such men and women were true Christians? If so, will it not follow that in every one of their differing communions true Christians are to be found? Probably no man, unless it be one of the most bigoted adherents of Evangelical or high Anglican orthodoxy, would venture to deny this. There are, then, good Christians, let us gladly admit, in all the various sects and parties of Christendom; men whom Christ himself, if he were here, would acknowledge and welcome as true disciples. But what is it that entitles such persons all alike to the Christian character and name? It cannot be any thing in which each *differs* from the rest, but rather something which they all have in common. It cannot be any thing that is peculiar to the Roman Catholic alone, for then the Protestant would not have it; nor any thing that is peculiar to the Protestant alone, for then the Roman Catholic would not have it; nor any thing that is peculiar to the Trinitarian alone, for then the Unitarian would not have it. It must be something apart from the distinctive creed of each. It is then something which all must possess, otherwise they would not be truly Christian; which they must have in *addition* to their several distinguishing doctrines, — in company with which the latter may indeed be held, but which is not the exclusive property of any single church, or sect, or individual, whatever.

What then do all the Christian sects and parties, of every name, hold in common, and never differ about? Is it not simply in this, that they receive and reverence Jesus as the beloved Son in whom God was well pleased? that they hold the Christian faith in the Father in Heaven, with all that this involves of love to God and love to man? that they accept the law of righteousness, placed before us in the "living characters" of Christ's own deeds and words, and strive to obey it in their conduct? that they hold the same common faith as to the presence and the providence of God, the future life and the judgment to come? This Christian allegiance, it is true, is expressed under the most different forms of statement, and in many a case it may hardly be definitely expressed at all; but yet even this, and such as this, is, by belief and practice, the common property of every Christian man; and so far as he lives in the spirit of this high faith is he truly a disciple and no further whatever may be the church or sect, or forms of doctrine and worship, to which he may attach himself. And all this, I repeat, is most plainly revealed to us in the spirit and the life of Christ, — insomuch that we feel the statement to be incontrovertibly sure, that he is the truest Christian of all whose practical daily spirit and conduct are the most closely and constantly animated and governed by the spirit and precepts and example of the Master Christ.

It seems strange, when we think about it, that men should have gone so far astray, in times past, from the more simple and obvious idea of Christianity thus laid before us. We may have difficulty in explaining how this has come to pass; how it is that so much of the weight and stress, as it were, of the Christian religion should have been laid upon obscure metaphysical creeds and dogmas, the obvious tendency of which is, and always has been, to divide men from each other, to degenerate into gross superstition, and destroy the liberty " wherewith Christ has made us free," and which, moreover, are nowhere contained in the Scriptures, and cannot even be stated in the language of the Scriptures; how it is, again, that so little emphasis should be laid in these dogmatic formulas upon that obedience which is better than sacrifice, even that doing the Heavenly Father's will, which — strange to tell! — is the only condition prescribed by Christ for entering into the kingdom.

Truly this question is not without its perplexities. But some explanation may be found. It is the obvious law of Divine Providence, it is and has been a great law of human progress, that Truth shall not be flashed upon the mind at once, either in religion or in any other of the great fields of interest and occupation to man; but that it shall be conquered and won through the medium of slow and gradual approach, even in the midst and by the help of misunderstanding and error. It is thus, doubtless, that men are trained to appreciate rightly the value of the truths and principles which they ultimately gain. In other words, past experience goes far to show us that moral excellence and the apprehension of truth, by such a being as man, can only be acquired by means of previous conflict with evil and untruth, in some one or other of their manifold forms; or, if not by an actual personal conflict for each of us individually, at least by means of the observed or recorded experience of others, more severely tried than ourselves.

Thus it has doubtless been with the reception and gradual prevalence of Christian truths and principles. Men have had slowly, by a varied and sometimes painful experience, to learn that it is not by saying, Lord, Lord, by confessing some formal creed, or being included within the limits of some visible church; not by forms and ceremonies of any kind, such as baptism at the hands of a priest, or the confession of sin into his ear, that we may become truly recipients of the light and strength of the Gospel of Christ; but much rather by personal communion with the Spirit of God, by doing the things which the Lord hath said, by striving to be like Christ, in heart and in life, active in goodness, submissive to the Heavenly Father's will, and ready to the work of duty which He has given us to do.

In proportion as this conception of Christianity comes forward into view, and assumes the pre-eminence to which it is entitled, and which is either implied or expressly declared in the principal writings of the New Testament, in the same degree must the merely dogmatic and sacerdotal idea sink into insignificance. It will be seen that moral and spiritual likeness to the Christian Head is what is all-important; and, consequently, that within the limits of the same communion, bound together by the common principle of Christian faith, — the principle of love and reverence for the one Master, Christ, — there may exist the most complete mental freedom, and even, to a very large extent, the most diverse theological beliefs.

IV.

But here I may be met by certain objections which will hardly fail to occur to different classes of readers.

In the first place, it may be said, the idea of the Gospel above presented is itself dogmatic; and indeed that the conception of Christianity as involving definite forms of doctrine is not to be got rid of. This remark I am by no means concerned wholly to escape. Doubtless the Gospel, as it is given in the words of Christ, includes various clearly stated truths respecting the Divine Providence and Will, and the retributions of this world and the next,— truths, I may add, which are not only level to the apprehension of the human faculties, but also in harmony with the highest dictates of the natural conscience and reason of man. But these great truths are not dogmatically laid before us in the Gospel. The mind of each reader is left free to gather them for itself. They are so stated as to quicken and elevate, not to stupefy or render useless, the religious and moral sense of the disciple. They serve thus, in the result, to arouse in him the strength of deep individual conviction, without which they could have little practical value. The teaching function of the Gospel is of *this* kind, rather than dogmatic and denunciatory, in the manner of the creeds. It does not attempt to put before us a ready-made body of doctrine, in such a way as to save the disciple the trouble of inquiry and reflection for himself, as though it would make him the mere recipient of what is imposed upon him from without. Not in this mechanical way, either in the world of outward nature, or in the Gospel of His Son, does the Great Parent speak to the hearts of His children; but chiefly by awakening their higher, devouter sensibilities, and letting them feel the force of truth and right within their own secret spirits. No imposition from without could fitly accomplish this divine work; and we may be well assured that no man living, and no church or sect on earth, has a legitimate authority to define exactly the limits within which Christian belief shall confine itself, or beyond which belief shall not extend, without ceasing to be Christian. Obviously and unquestionably Christ himself has nowhere attempted to dictate his religion in such a way; neither has any of his apostles, not even the ardent and impetuous Paul. On the contrary, the latter, like his Master, constantly attaches the greatest importance to the practical virtues, and to a devout spirit,—in no case making his appeal to a dogmatic statement, or giving us to understand that he had the least idea of any dogmatic system whatever, similar, in spirit or in form, to the creeds of modern orthodoxy.

A second objection may be urged by a defender of the prevailing forms and dogmas of the churches. Such a person may say that, in taking Christ as the measure and representative of his own religion, we leave out of sight all that may have been contributed to its development by the Apostles, to say nothing of their successors, and that the Epistles of the New Testament contain much that is not met with in connection with him. In reply, let it be observed in what terms the Apostles speak of their Master, and of the obedience, the faith, and veneration due to him. Paul, for example, in various forms, tells them to "put on the Lord Jesus Christ;" to let his mind be in them, his word dwell in them richly, to acquire his spirit, to follow him in love and self-sacrifice. He will know nothing, he says, "save Jesus Christ, and him crucified;" and we know how closely he treads in his Master's steps, in the absolute preference which he gives to the Love which, he declares, is greater than faith, and the very fulfilling of the law itself. The same strain is held by others of the Apostles; and there can be no doubt that Christ, under God, was constantly looked up to by them as the great object of the faith, the love, and the imitation of every disciple. It is true, indeed, that there are many things in the Apostolical writings other than we find in connection with Christ's personal life; but these will be found to belong, almost exclusively, to the peculiar circumstances and controversies of the times succeeding his death. In truth, they belong so entirely to them as to have little of practical reference, or utility, beyond. Paul's Epistles, for instance, are full of the long debated question as to the claims of the law upon Gentiles, and the mystery which, he says, had been hidden "from the foundation of the world," that the Messiah should be preached even to those who were not of the fold of Israel. But these are only temporary incidents of the early career of Christianity. They have no intimate connection with the permanent influence of Christ; and we of modern times have little concern with them, except only to be on our guard against letting them unduly sway our judgment and turn us away from subjects of greater consequence, — as too often has happened to the ingenious framers of theological systems. Christianity, in a word, has been only perplexed and impeded in its course, by those thoughtless or over-zealous expounders who have insisted upon constructing schemes of orthodoxy out of the antiquated disputes of Jews and Gentiles.[1]

[1] See, e.g., the Essay on the Death of Christ, in *Aids to Faith*.

In all his Epistles St. Paul, in the true spirit of his Master, gives us clearly to know what is of chief importance. After treating, as he usually does, of the local and passing concerns and disputes which engaged many of his correspondents, he never fails to turn at last to speak of the practical goodness, the purity of heart and life, the kindly affections towards one another, the reasonable service of love and duty, by which the Christian disciple may be known, by which alone he can present himself as a "living sacrifice, holy, acceptable unto God." In such qualities as these, the attainment or the practice of which he so earnestly urges upon his friends, we have precisely what constitute the most marked features in the life and the teachings of Christ. Thus we are brought once more to the old conclusion that in faithful loyalty to Christ, to the highest ideal presented to us of his spirit and character, are to be found the true light and joy and peace of the Christian Gospel.

A third objection is of a different character. There are some things, it will be said, in immediate connection with him whom we term Teacher and Lord, some things in his words and ideas, if not in his actions, which are far from being in perfect harmony with the highest truth, as known to men in these later times. For example, when he speaks as though he believed diseases and insanity to be caused by the presence of a devil, or demon, in the afflicted person, are we to attach importance to this, so as ourselves to think that such disorders are (or were) so produced? — or shall we not rather follow the guidance of modern science, and believe that the various infirmities which, in ancient times, were attributed to evil spirits arose from natural causes, and that the manner in which such things are spoken of in the New Testament is a product simply of the imperfect knowledge of those days?

In reply, there need be no hesitation in saying that we are bound, as beings of thought and reason, to follow the best guidance which God has given us, in these and all other subjects; and by the term *best* can only be understood that which commends itself most forcibly to our rational intelligence. It can in no way be claimed for Christ that he was intellectually perfect; that he did not share in the prevailing beliefs of his countrymen, and partake even of their ignorance. Such a claim as this is certainly nowhere advanced in the New Testament, but the *contrary;* and those who, in our time, would bring it forward should ask themselves whether, by so doing, they are most likely to benefit, or to injure, the cause which doubtless they would desire to support. Jesus himself makes no pretension to intellectual infallibility, but lets us see, in no uncertain way, that he was not unconscious of the limitation of his own knowledge.[1]

In general terms it may be added, the Gospel, when first preached in the world, was necessarily adapted to the people to whom it was addressed. It conformed, in many respects, to their ideas and modes of expression, and also made use of these for its own ends. Had it not done so, how could it have touched and moved them as it did, and as, through them, it has touched and moved the world ever since? Jesus, therefore, himself, and those who took up his work after him, were, in a large degree, men of their own day, imbued with prevailing ideas and feelings, and employing these in their speaking and

[1] Mark xiii. 32.

preaching in the most natural manner. Is it not even so with ourselves at the present moment? For how, indeed, can it be otherwise? And if many of the primitive Christian ideas were more or less erroneous and ill-founded, it is easy to understand that, while the overruling Providence made them its instruments for leading men on by degrees to something better, still it can have been no part of the great design of God that misunderstanding and ignorance should be removed by any other process than by the natural growth of knowledge among men. They were not to be supernaturally refuted, but left to be corrected in due course of time; and the needed correction was and is to come even as men grow wiser and more thoughtful and able to bear it.

Hence, it is not to be questioned, many errors, chiefly of the intellectual kind, attached to the early preaching of the Gospel, and some certainly did to the words of Christ himself; just as very much of human ignorance and prejudice has since and continually been involved in the ideas prevailing as to the character and purposes of his religion. As before observed, man has been made by his Creator to find his way up to light and truth from the most imperfect beginnings, and by a prolonged conflict against and amidst darkness and manifold error. Such is our human nature, and the position which the Divine Will has assigned to us. And so in the early ages after Christ there sprung up the idolatrous worship of the Virgin Mary and of innumerable saints; nor is the world yet free, though it is slowly freeing itself, from the influence of these superstitions and their related errors of thought. Successive generations inherit much of the evil as well as the good, the ignorance as well as the knowledge, of those who have been before them. Thus does the Almighty Father exercise and discipline his human family in patience, in self-control, in the search after truth, even by letting us suffer and work for the good fruits of knowledge and righteousness, instead of giving them to the world at once without thought or effort of our own. This is eminently true in connection with the whole course of Christian development. In Christ's own teachings and those of the Apostles, as time has amply shown, erroneous ideas were not wanting. Peter denied his Master, and thought at first that only Jews could be disciples. Both he and Paul, as well as James, with probably all the early Christians, long cherished the hope of their Master's return to the earth within that generation; a belief which is to be traced also, equally with that in demoniacal possessions, in the recorded words of Jesus himself. Other instances of a similar kind might easily be mentioned.

But, while all this seems perfectly undeniable, has not Divine Providence so ordered that what is really wrong and false in men's ideas of Christian truth shall sooner or later be seen in its real character, in the advancing progress of human knowledge?—and therefore, if we are ourselves only patient and faithful, each of us, to what we see, or think we see, to be right and good, that the untrue in our ideas shall be eventually separated from the true, however close may be the connection which at any time may subsist between them? Such is, doubtless, the Almighty purpose, such the all-sufficient process provided in His wisdom for securing the training and growth of the races and generations of men in the knowledge of Divine things. It follows, again, that whatever in the Christian teaching, as in other teaching, shall stand the test of advancing knowledge, and still approve itself as true and honest and just and pure and lovely and of good report[1] to the purified conscience and practised intellect of man, that shall be God's everlasting Truth; that too He must have designed not only by the word of Christ, but through the living souls of His rational children, to proclaim to the world with the mark of His Divine approval.

It is not necessary here to ask in detail what it is in existing schemes of Christian theology, or in the outward forms and arrangements of priesthoods and of churches, that will bear this test of advancing knowledge, and this scrutiny of the educated intellect and conscience. Doubtless much in the popular creeds of our day will do so; but much more will only be as chaff before the wind, or stubble before the devouring flame. Among the perishable things will surely be the ecclesiastical systems which vary with every different country and church, and along with these the claims to priestly and papal authority and infallibility, about which we again hear such angry contention. Truly, none of these will bear the test and strain of time and knowledge; but only those great and unchangeable principles of spiritual truth, and those deep-lying sentiments of moral right, which are *common* to *all* the different sects and parties of Christendom. These will retain their place among the great motive forces of the world, even because their roots are firmly planted by the Divine hand itself in the very nature of man, and made to be a part of the constitution of his mind; while, also, it is true, and the Christian disciple will ever gratefully acknowledge, they owe their best and highest expression and exemplification to Jesus the Christ, the " beloved Son," in whom God was " well pleased."

[1] Philip iv. 8.

We may conclude then, as before, that in the mind and life of Christ, — in his unshaken trust in the Heavenly Father, and in the heaven to be revealed hereafter, — in his readiness to obey the call of Duty, wherever it might lead him, even though it might be to the shame and the agony of the cross, — in his faithful adherence to the right, and earnest denunciation of falsehood, hypocrisy, and wrong-doing, — in his gentle spirit of forgiveness and filial submission even unto death, — we have the lessons of Christian truth and virtue which it most of all concerns us to receive and to obey. In this high "faith of Christ" we have the true revelation of God's will for man; the Gospel speaking to us in its most touching and impressive tones, — either reproaching us for our indifference and calling us to repentance, or else aiding and encouraging us onward in the good path of righteousness.

So long as Christianity shall be thus capable of speaking to the world, so long will it, amidst all the varieties of outward profession, be a living power for good; and vain will be the representation which would tell us that it is now only a thing of the past, unfitted for the better knowledge and higher philosophy of these modern times. Surely not so! — but, rather, until we have each individually attained the moral elevation even of Christ himself, and can say that we too, in character and conduct, in motive and aspiration, are well pleasing in the sight of Heaven, until we *are* this, and can feel and say this with truth, the religion of Christ will be no antiquated thing of the past to *us;* but from its teaching and its spirit — the teaching and the spirit of Christ — we shall still have wisdom and truth to learn.

May the time speedily come, which shall see Christ's

spirit ruling the individual lives of all around us, — more truly inspiring the thoughts and efforts of our lawgivers, — teaching men everywhere to be just and merciful towards each other; and thus making Christianity, in deed and in truth, the "established religion," the guiding and triumphant power of this and all other lands! Then, indeed, will the daily prayer of all Christian hearts be answered, and the "kingdom of heaven" on earth be truly come.

THE AIM AND HOPE OF JESUS.

By OLIVER STEARNS.

THE AIM AND HOPE OF JESUS.

A LEARNED Historian of the Christian Theology of the Apostolic age observes that what most distinguishes the Jewish religion, at least in its last centuries, is not so much monotheism as faith in the future. While elsewhere we see the imagination of men complacently retracing the picture of a golden age irrecoverably lost, Israel, guided by its prophets, persisted in turning its eyes towards the future, and attached itself the more firmly to a felicity yet to come, the more the actual situation seemed to give the lie to its hopes.[1]

What these hopes were in relation to the future of that people and of the world, what the Messianic ideas and expectations were, we learn from the New Testament, particularly from the Gospels. And we find our impressions from this source made more clear in some points, and in all confirmed, by a study of the Apocalyptic literature, —of those writings of which it was the object to give both shape and expression to the Hebrew thought of the kingdom of heaven, and of the brilliant and miraculous events which would introduce and establish it.

[1] Reuss, History of the Christian Theology of the Apostolic Age.

Jewish Theology in the age of Jesus Christ divided the whole course of time into two grand periods; one, comprehending the past and the present, was that of suffering and sin; the other, embracing the future, a period of virtue and happiness. The last years of the former period formed the most important epoch in the History of Humanity, the transition to a new order of things, and was designated by a peculiar phrase,— the consummation of the age and the last days. It would be introduced by the appearance of the great Restorer or Deliverer of the people of God, and of the world, whom the prophets predicted; and who was called the Messiah, the Anointed of the Lord, — *i.e.*, the King by eminence, the King of Israel. He was to be the successor and the son of David. The precise moment of his appearance was not known. The Jewish theologians tried to determine the precursive signs of the near approach of his advent. The first of these was the period of great wickedness and suffering, marked by a particular name, the anguish, and compared to the pangs of child-birth. Immediately preceding the advent of the King, a prophet of the Old Covenant would be restored to life to announce it, — a part in the miraculous drama commonly assigned to Elijah. The Messiah himself would come on the clouds of heaven, with a retinue of angels, and with a pomp and splendor which would leave no doubt of the fact of his advent. He would come to found the kingdom of God. This implied the political, moral, and religious regeneration of the people. A series of most imposing scenes would follow the advent. At the sound of a trumpet, the dead would arise and appear for the judgment of the last day. The just would take part in the judgment of the reprobate, who would be thrown into the lake of fire, prepared for the devil and his angels to suffer eternal torture. And the kingdom of God or of the Messiah would be established immediately on the earth, which, with the whole of the universe of which it was the centre, would be gloriously transformed to fit it to be the abode of the elect of God.

Into the circle of these ideas and expectations Jesus was born. In it he passed his life, acted and suffered; and claimed to found the kingdom of God. He claimed in some sense to be the Messiah; and, though rejected by his people and put to death, he has borne the name in history, and now bears it. He is Jesus, the Christ. How did he regard these ideas and expectations? Did he adopt them? And, if at all, how far? Did he claim to be such a Messiah as the Jews expected? If so, then Christianity may be what it has been called, "a natural development of Judaism." It is not essentially a new religion. It is not an evolution of a perfect universal, from an imperfect and partial, religion. It is essentially Judaism still; and "the kingdom of God, which Jesus preached in both a temporal and spiritual sense, developed naturally and logically into the Popedom, which is the nearest approximation to the fulfilment of the claim of Jesus. Judaism is germinal Christianity, and Christianity is fructified Judaism." Christianity is only what is weakest and most fantastic in Judaism gone to seed. *The fruit* is the Roman Hierarchy and Ritual. That which is alone characteristic of it is limited and perishable. Jesus himself, though his ambition was a lofty one, was mistaken in an essential point of his self-assertion; and the gospel is not destined to be an universal religion, but only to make some moderate contributions thereto.

It is an important question, then, — one which concerns his worth and position as a man, as well as his wisdom as a founder of a religion, — What did Jesus aim at? and what did he expect as the result of his movement? The answers that have been given may be reduced to three principal forms: 1. He expected to found a political Empire; 2. He expected to introduce a vast Theocracy, to which believers of other nations should be admitted, and which was to be established on the renovated earth, after his death, at his return to take possession of it as King, to reward his followers, and to put all opposition under his feet; 3. He expected to found a purely spiritual communion or society in which he should continue to exercise for ages, by his spirit, word, and life, a power of truth and love over the minds and hearts of men, filling them with the most exalted sense of God.

The first view has been presented by some able adversaries of Christianity, among whom Reimarus led the way in a fragment "On the Aim of Jesus," published with others anonymously in 1778. He charged Jesus with using religious motives as merely a means to a political end; but supposed that, after he found death impending, he renounced the political aim, and pretended that his purpose was only a moral one. A few able scholars have been disposed to blend the last view with the others. They suppose an original Theocratic purpose to have been entertained by Jesus, in which the moral and religious principle predominated, but which was not at first exclusive of the political element. They suppose, however, a progress in his aim; that after his rejection by the people, "which he regarded as God's rejection of any national limitation of his work," he inferred that his mission was to found a spiritual kingdom. Though the direct imputation of a political aim has not been a favorite expedient with ultra-rationalist critics since Reimarus was answered by Reinhard and others, it ought not to be passed without consideration. It is continually reappearing in modified forms. And this happens, because it is impossible to present the hypothesis that Jesus intended to be a Jewish Messiah without involving the supposition of something political in his object, and in his means of accomplishing it. Accordingly a very recent critic[1] of Christianity, writing in the interest of "Free Religion," and representing Jesus as claiming to be a Jewish Messiah, after saying very truly that "the popular hope of a Priest-king transformed itself in the soul of Jesus into the sublime idea of a spiritual Christ ruling by love," is constrained to say, inconsistently, in another place, that, if Jesus had assumed the office, he would not have hesitated to discharge its political duties, and to exercise political sway. Here, then, is a revival of the imputation to Jesus of a political aim. But I am not aware that it is anywhere in recent criticism enforced with any new strength of argument. It is obviously contradicted by the general bearing of his actions, and by the whole tone of his teachings when rightly apprehended. It is contradicted by his utter neglect of political measures. He could not be induced or forced to take the position of a political ruler. Admirers wished to proclaim him King: he sent them away, tore his disciples from them, and went himself into the mountain to commune with God. Asked to settle a dispute about property, he says he has never been constituted an administrator of civil justice. When shown the tribute-money, and inquired

[1] See "The Index," Toledo, Jan. 1 and Jan. 8, 1870.

278 THE AIM AND HOPE OF JESUS.

of if it were lawful to pay tribute unto Cæsar, he makes the memorable reply in which he at once acknowledges the rights of the government *de facto;* and the rights of conscience and religion, which to deny would be usurpation. He was the first to distinguish the spheres of the church and of the state so intimately related, but never to be blended. And this is just what the political Messiah, the Priest-king, could not have conceived. The outlines of his church may serve as the model of a free church to-day. There was no political motive to enter it. It had no officer who could exercise political power. There was no authority but in the congregation. It was amenable to no political head. Its fundamental truths were the equal relation of all men with God as his children, and the common relation of all men with one another as brethren. The only end of his church was the moral and spiritual development of its members and of all men; the only condition of membership, the recognition of this end; and, with it, of the providential gift of truth and life given in Jesus Christ's consciousness of God, and an appropriating and co-operative sympathy with his character and purpose. Its method was free conference and prayer in the spirit of unity, and in devotion to the regeneration of the human family; a method, the results of which, he assured them, would be the reaching of decisions which would be in essential harmony with his own spirit, the Spirit of God. He drew more from the synagogue than from the temple. Worship might ascend anywhere from the heart. One need not go to Jerusalem. No political Messiah could have thought of any centre of the restored Theocracy but the holy city, to which the tribes should repair with their sacrifices, and the converted heathen bring their votive offerings to Jehovah, the God of Jews; but the temple must be destroyed, and not one stone of it left upon another, according to Jesus, in order to prepare for that worship of the Father by men in spirit and in truth, which he, as the Christ, would inaugurate.

We thus come naturally to another point in the discussion. The theories which recognize the political aim of Jesus commonly suppose that he regarded it as his personal mission to restore Mosaism to its primitive purity. And, if he shared in the hope of the restoration of the Theocracy, he would probably take the most conservative ground in regard to the Levitical institutions and the Mosaic precepts. He would believe the Jewish people must be made independent, in order to give supremacy to those institutions. The Roman yoke must be broken, and the coming kingdom be inaugurated with war. Nothing of this, however, is found in the ministry of Jesus Christ. When he preached "the kingdom of heaven is at hand," it was no summons to war. The characteristic qualities of those who belonged to this kingdom were opposed to the Theocratic spirit. And the Sermon on the Mount taught, as clearly as the formal declaration before Pilate, that it was not of this world. Why should his followers be ready to suffer social persecution, if his aim tended in the direction regarded with social favor? What mean the non-resistant exhortations, instructing his followers to waive their rights for the sake of the higher interests they were living for, if he and his adherents are charged with the political duty of driving the invader from the sacred soil? The rise and progress of this kingdom, Jesus said, on another occasion, could not be observed like those of an empire founded by force: it would not "come with observation." It had already come unobserved. It began to come with John the Baptist, until whose work the law was in the ascendant; but since whom men had been pressing into the kingdom of heaven, which was tending to supplant the law. And, on still another occasion, if he expected his movement to leave the Jewish ritual intact, how could he say, with pregnant significance, that new wine must not be put into old wineskins, lest they break, and the wine be lost. I know great stress is laid upon his saying, "Think not that I have come to destroy the law, or the prophets: I have not come to destroy, but to fulfil. For truly do I say to you, Till heaven and earth pass away, not one jot or one tittle shall pass from the law, till all be fulfilled." But, if taken literally, they prove too much; for, according to other passages, his teaching on some points — as, for instance, divorce, and, as many think, the Sabbath — directly conflicted with that of Moses. He threw doubt directly upon the tradition that God rested on the seventh day. God, he said, had been always working up to that hour, and in his own acts of healing done on the Sabbath he had been co-operating with God. We must therefore interpret freely this language, and understand by it the everlasting law. The smallest requirement of the true law, however overlooked and despised it may have been in the popular exegesis, would have its emphasis in the new teachings; and whoever slighted it would be the least in the kingdom of heaven. There is not a word which can be fairly construed into commendation of the Levitical priesthood. He gives to the Mosaic precepts cited the most spiritual interpretation, or sets them aside when they cannot be wrought into a more profound system of natural morality. He implies his superiority to all preceding teachers, including Moses. "It was said to the ancients, but *I* say unto you." Indeed, his tone in this discourse is any thing but that of a Jewish Rabbi of his period. It is that of the most human and universal teaching. It asserts, when we penetrate beyond the immediate occasion of it to its principle, that which is true in all times and places. Those affirmations with which it opens, what are they but declarations, the substantial verity of which it is possible for every man, if he know not now, yet sometime to know in himself. "Blessed are the poor in spirit: for theirs is the kingdom of heaven." The spirit of those who can set a limit to their wants and curb ambition, who do not live blinded by interests to the demands of a pure soul, — the spirit of such is always blessed. Happy he who imbibes it from the circumstances of his life; and happy he who, amidst the blandishments of riches, is taught it by the discipline of Heaven. These are they to whom has come the kingdom of heaven from Jesus' day until now. Then, "Blessed are the pure in heart: for they shall see God." And is not a pure mind the very moral atmosphere in which man sees God as he is, and rejoices in the sight? A man's moral sentiments are the medium through which comes to him the thought of God. Let those sentiments be perverted, and he imagines either that God is not or that he is different from what he is. His wrong mind either obstructs entirely the beam which darts from the Divine essence, or scatters the spotless white of that Sun, the pure aggregate of Divine perfections, into the particolored tints of the earthly and sensual soul itself. Again, "Blessed are the merciful: for they shall obtain mercy."

It is even so. Those who sympathize with human wants will feel the sympathy of God flowing into their souls, and can never lack assurance of the Divine mercy so long as they keep in themselves that pledge of it, — the merciful spirit. And so it is a grand caution, which every one who has wantonly condemned others knows he ought to keep in memory, — "Condemn not, lest ye be condemned." For the undeserved, heavy sentence of condemnation which a man lifts high to hurl with malignant intent at his brother is arrested by an interposing law of Providence, and falls from his weak hand with its full weight upon his own head. And at length we come to what might be thought a studied satire upon the boasted maxims of human wisdom: "Blessed are ye when men shall speak evil of you falsely for my sake." Is this the sober truth? Is not Christ, so true elsewhere, mistaken here? It is a verity as certain as the laws of God. Do not minds advance unequally in truth, in all the successive phases of a soul's spiritual growth? Whoever goes before others in thought and life will find men laying this to his charge. But, if by following the command of Christian truth to his conscience he has opened upon himself the battery of human censoriousness, he may exult; for every unjust word or groundless suspicion will but remind him of his unbribed devotion, and be changed before it touches his deepest happiness into the benediction of God.

Were we to go through what was spoken on the Mount, we might show its truth commanding unquestionably the assent of our moral natures. It all takes hold of our mind and life. It comes to us to throw light on what we do and suffer, and to borrow confirmation from it in turn. Though we fall so far short of it, and could not have conceived it originally and from ourselves, as Jesus did, it so accords with the laws of our being as to seem to be the suggestion of our experience, some admonition floating to us by intent of God on that ever-heaving sea of life, of ambition, of passion, of mutual misunderstanding, of strong loves and piercing griefs, of various mingling sympathies, on whose shore we do now stand, and whose tide, for our few seconds here in time, laves our feet and dashes upon us its spray.

We might turn over other pages of Jesus' instruction beyond that introductory statement of the principles of the kingdom of God, and evolve its sense in terms presenting an undeniable spiritual fact to all our race. For instance, "To him who hath shall be given, and he shall have abundance; but from him that hath not shall be taken away, even that which he seemeth to have." How true! It is verified in the mental condition of every man at this moment. We only seem to have the faculty we do not use. There is no long, healthy sleep to the mind and the moral will any more than to the body; but the alternative is, live or die. And thus Jesus was ever holding up the law of the spiritual life to the light of that day which dawned with his advent. He dwelt on what is inward. Although you cannot find that once, in his popular teaching, he laid stress upon observances, times without number he studiously distinguished between every thing of the nature of ceremonial and those everlasting obligations of justice and humanity, of inward and outward purity, which ought to be recognized in the home and in the state, in all the intercourse of man with man, and in watching over the secret heart. We may not infer that he was hostile to religious forms. He observed them.

He knew that man needed them, and that souls instinct with life would perpetuate them and adapt them to their own wants. But he saw in the spirit of the Scribes the evil of teaching that any arbitrarily imposed outward act can in itself please God; and, in regard to such, the whole emphasis of his teaching was, "These ought ye to have done, and not to have left the other undone." He quoted from the prophets habitually, "I will have mercy and not sacrifice."

Such is the genius of Christianity, — of Christianity as it came from its Founder, — the religion which is said to have ripened into the mediæval theology and the Roman hierarchy. Too little, indeed, has this genius of Christianity been regarded! The old Judaic spirit which brought Jesus to the cross has, among Protestants as well as Catholics, too often crucified the Christianity of Christ. Human metaphysics have been put into creeds and catechisms. Sects have been founded and built up on the importance attached to the form of a rite as a part of essential Christianity. Disputes have raged which the traditions of the Church and the letter of Scripture have failed to settle, and about which Jesus, if teaching among us, would not waste a minute's breath.

If further proof were wanting of the breadth and spirituality of Jesus' view, it might be found in the fact that he was brought to the cross by the pro-Judaism party. His friends would interpret him differently from his enemies. The universality and spirituality of his aim were not at once apprehended by his followers. Their very trust in him would make them slow to perceive his radical meaning; for, to impute to him what was in his mind, would seem to be distrust. They would put a limited construction upon what he said. It would be otherwise with his enemies, who would be sharp and quick to see the full extent to which his words would carry him.

The movement of Jesus, then, may be called revolutionary, not in the sense of aiming directly at political revolution, but in the sense of his expecting to found a free, spiritual, and universal religion, which would uproot and remove in time the partial religions, Judaism included. Still he designed to connect himself with the Old Dispensation. He recognized the Divine mission of Moses and the Providential office of the prophets in preparing for him. In the expectations which they fostered there was something true as well as something false. When they depicted a glorious and happy political condition of the Jewish nation under the Messiah as an earthly king, Jesus must have regarded them as being in error. We find him pronouncing John the Baptist the greatest of the prophets of the old order, and declaring that the least in the kingdom of heaven was greater than he; and the reason is shown by the context of the words (Matt. xi.) to be that John as a Jewish prophet regarded the kingdom of God in part as a political kingdom. But the fundamental idea of the Theocracy, that other nations would be united with Israel under the dominion of the One True God, was one in harmony with Jesus' thought.[1] This expectation Jesus regarded it as his mission to realize and fulfil. He had only to separate from the Theocratic predictions of the prophets the partial political element, to bring them into unison with his universal aim. Whatever in the hitherto prevailing ideas and hopes was capable of expansion he absorbed into himself, that it might be given out in a

[1] See Noyes's Introduction to his Translation of the Prophets.

wider and higher form, and live for ever. A case somewhat parallel might be found in the changes wrought by our late war. Those who took a radical view of the issue of the contest were exposed to the charge of being revolutionary and destroying the Constitution. They could reply, "Yes: the issue will be revolutionary. There will be a new state of law, and of the relations of the people in important respects, effected by carrying out fundamental principles. But those principles were the essence of the Constitution; and to carry them out is only fully to accomplish its purpose, by annihilating transient provisions at war with liberty and social justice, and giving scope to the principles of the Declaration of Independence. We hold to the Constitution. We have come not to destroy, but to fulfil." So Jesus Christ came not to destroy all that had gone before, but to fulfil whatever in it was fundamental to the Divine purpose in relation to man. In this feeling of a real connection between his movement and the Hebrew ideas and hopes is to be found the principal explanation of his confining his labors, and those of the apostles when first sent forth, chiefly to Judea and Galilee. Not only must his own work be limited in its local scope,— for he could not go everywhere,— but the historical basis of his movement lay in the Hebrew history. Among the Hebrew people only could he find suitably prepared immediate disciples. Salvation was to be from the Jews. And, foreseeing that the nation as such would reject him, he saw that it was essential to the extension among the Gentiles of the truths and hopes he inherited as a Jew, essential to the breaking down of the partition wall which now kept out the true doctrine of God from the heathen world, that he should come to a distinct issue with the Jewish authorities, and make it clear and notorious that it was the narrow spirit of Pharisaism and legal formality which crucified him. (If he were lifted up, he would draw all men to him.) And from the first the ruling sect, with the acute instinct of self-interest, discerned the revolutionary character of his movement, — that it elevated man above the Jew, and struck at the root of the idolized Hebrew pre-eminence.

I pass now to a more subtle hypothesis, that Jesus expected to establish the Theocratic empire by angelic assistance on occasion of his return to earth, which would occur at the same time with the great outward change of the world. It is founded on such passages as this: "For the Son of Man is to come in the glory of his Father, with his angels; and then he will render to every one according to his works." (Matt. xvi. 27. Comp. Matt. xiii. 41, and xxvi. 29–60.) It is thus stated by Strauss:[1] "He waited for a signal from his heavenly Father, who alone knew the time of this catastrophe; and he was not disconcerted when his end approached without his having received the expected intimation." His Messianic hope was not political or even earthly. He referred its fulfilment to a supermundane theatre.

Strauss speaks of Jesus' hope as corresponding with the Messianic ideas of the Jews. It took its form from those ideas. Scherer also represents Jesus' idea of the kingdom as wholly Apocalyptic. The *first* criticism to be made upon this hypothesis is, that a Theocratic idea arising out of the Jewish expectations and conformed to them could not dispense with all thought of earthly conflict.

[1] Life of Jesus, Part II. § 66. The charge of enthusiasm is retained, but not discussed, in his Life of Christ for the German people.

The struggle could not have been altogether upon a supermundane theatre, nor the triumph of the Messiah achieved without common warlike agencies. The common Jewish idea was founded on the language of some Hebrew prophets, and appears in the Apocalyptic writings of Christ's age; and his own mind in cherishing the hope attributed to him must have quite surrendered itself to the popular expectation. This expectation supposed some outward conflict as the occasion of supernatural interference. Nor do I know any ground for thinking that in Christ's time the Jews expected the Messiah to prevail with angelic aid without a conflict of arms. Whoever will read Ezekiel and Daniel will see that those prophets expected a contest on earth with earthly weapons, as the occasion for the intervention of Jehovah. And whoever will read the wars of the Maccabees will see how Jewish courage, fired with the expectation of celestial assistance, never stopped to compare the apparent strength of the respective forces. Nor did the Apocalyptic seers dismiss this thought of earthly battle. The book of Enoch speaks of the unconverted as delivered at the judgment into the hands of the righteous, whose horses shall wade in the blood of sinners, and whom the angels shall come to help.[1] The Apocalypse of the New Testament presents the picture of the Messiah as mounted on a white horse, and riding forth to judge and make war; and the comment of Dr. Noyes on this and similar passages is that, in the mind of the writer, there was to be war in heaven and upon earth, before Christ should reign in final triumph.[2] This theory has no distinctive character without supposing the angels acting

[1] Book of Enoch, Dillman, ch. 100.
[2] Rev. xix. 11; comp. Christian Examiner, May, 1860, p. 382.

THE AIM AND HOPE OF JESUS.   289

on the stage of sense and time, and giving the Hebrews the victory. With this expectation is probably connected the "sign from heaven" demanded of Jesus by the Pharisees, a sign which should stimulate Hebrew faith to irresistible warlike ardor. The unconverted were to be vanquished by some mysterious exercise of Messianic power. Hence many were not satisfied with Christ's miracles; not that they disputed their reality, but as being not decisive of his Messianic character. Now, if this had been the thought of Jesus, he would have been disposed to seek an occasion for such interference from on high. It is true, in saying this, we say he must have given himself up to the enthusiasm which so often fanatically manifested itself in his age, and was always ready to break forth. But the idea supposed, when one's whole being was yielded to it, — as Jesus did yield his whole being to the ideas which possessed him, — could not have stopped short of practical action. He must have been prepared in his thought to act with fanaticism. Strauss says, "He did not try to bring about all this by his own will; but awaited a signal from his heavenly Father." The actual Jesus did undoubtedly as Strauss says; but the supposed Jesus would have at some time believed the signal to be given. The idea, and the sort of faith in supernatural aid which accompanied it, would lead him to think the moment had come for this demonstration. "If such were the ideal of Jesus in fact, why did he not seek to realize it at once? Why did he prefer the way of renunciation and self-sacrifice to the possession of the kingdoms of the world? Why, in the place of the Son of Man, have we not a Mahomet six hundred years in advance." The logical and necessary result of belief in his Messiahship, and of faith in this sort of supernatural aid in realizing it, was that he should bring about an occasion for this demonstration. It was an encounter with the Romans, in the hope that Jehovah and the angels would fight for God's people, and be more than strong enough against all odds. "The Messianic Theocracy could not exist as a Roman province."[1] But Jesus studiously avoids conflict with Rome. Besides, the second part of the temptation of Christ sets aside at once this ideal. His early consciousness of wonderful power had not the effect of disposing his mind favorably toward such Jewish Messianic ideas. That consciousness tended rather to spiritualize his thought: we may say, it subdued him. It made his whole feeling moderate, and his whole thought wise and temperate. This is a very remarkable part of the representation of him by the evangelists.

But, secondly, I will now suppose the expectation of Jesus to have been purified from every notion of warlike action. The regeneration (palingenesia) was to be not a political revolution, but a renovation of the earth and the heavens, attended by a resurrection of the dead, of whom the accepted were to dwell with Christ in the renovated world, — not the present earth, but the earth restored, — and that his presence and return were to be visible. This is his coming with the angels to set up his kingdom and to reign.

I. The very language which this hypothesis is adopted to explain, taken in its proper sense, proves too much. Jesus was to be a king on the renewed earth, yet his kingdom was to be different from those of this world. "It is not," he says, "of this world." It is a real kingdom as much as that of David; but it is not to be a worldly rule

[1] Hase's Life of Jesus.

on the one hand, nor a purely spiritual rule on the other. It is political, and not political. According to the writer of the Apocalypse, whose views are supposed to have been sanctioned by Jesus, this king must reign until he has put all enemies under his feet. When the kingdom is consummated, he is to surrender it to his Father. The hypothesis under consideration represents the kingdom as to be consummated at the time of the world-catastrophe which, with the second or real coming of Jesus as Messiah, will occur, according to the alleged words of Christ himself, immediately after the destruction of the city. Why shall not the kingdom be given up immediately to the Father? This king in "the proper sense," and in no purely spiritual sense, who comes visibly, will have no occasion for a reign in the proper sense of the word. Strauss says, "Jesus expected to restore the throne of David, and with his disciples to govern a liberated people. But in no degree did he rest his hopes on the sword of his adherents, but on the legions of angels which the Father would send him. He was not disconcerted when his end approached without the kingdom having come. It would come with his return." But how when he returned was the throne of David to be restored, and a proper, literal reign to exist, and not a mere spiritual reign? This king has no business to perform: his work is all accomplished immediately by a stupendous miracle. And he and his apostles have nothing to do but to sit on idle thrones, or to feast at tables loaded with luxuries which are at the same time mundane and supermundane; to enjoy a sensual paradise, which differs from a Mohammedan paradise only in that it does not consist of the coarsest forms of sensual life. They are to partake of an actual wine, a fruit of the vine, — a new kind of wine; to observe the passover with supermundane food, but food pleasurable to the taste. This Jesus is thought to have expected and promised.[1] I sometimes think this attempt to find a half-way doctrine of Jesus' expectation concerning the future ascribes to him an apocalypticism more inept and fatuous than that of the Jews themselves. It attempts to unite the contradictory. It cannot be stated by Strauss in any thing like the literal sense of the passages on which it is founded, without supposing something of that political element which it is designed to exclude; or else entirely dropping that relation to Jewish hopes to which it is believed to owe its origin, and thus leaving it unexplained. For, if Jesus gave up all expectation whatever of a kingdom of this world, we have no occasion for a visible return.

II. The second objection to this view is that it is incompatible with the most important expressions and opinions of Jesus.

1. The kingdom is to come with the world-catastrophe; and the King is then to come in some mysterious manner on the clouds of heaven. How, then, could Jesus say the kingdom of God cometh not with *observation?* Could any political kingdom arise in a more outwardly striking manner? How does that saying of Christ comport with his promising a literal miraculous light in the heaven (Matt. xxiv. 30) which shall betoken his own coming and the great world-change? That form of coming with a precursive sign in the heaven is just what he contradicted. Such a kingdom would come with a sign which could be watched for, — a sign very different from

[1] See Renan's Life of Jesus, first edition.

those signs of the time, the moral indications, which a spiritual insight might discern. How could he say the kingdom of God was among them *already*, if it were yet to come at the time of the great world-change? How could he say to Caiaphas: "Yes, I am the Messiah; and moreover *from this moment* you shall see the Son of Man sitting on the right hand of power and coming on the clouds of heaven"? It was equivalent to saying, "You have arrested me, you have already doomed me to death. But I am the Anointed of God to introduce the new spiritual kingdom of Humanity; and, from this moment in which you decree my death, my cause takes a Divine impulse, and my purpose strides on to the triumph God has destined for it."

2. This expectation is incompatible with what he says on other topics related to the kingdom, the resurrection, and the future life. This expectation implies the Apocalyptic view of the resurrection. The Messiah was to come to raise the dead. (The Christian world has generally entertained the same view.) The visible return and the resurrection coexisted, probably, in Jesus' mind. If he held the one, he held the other. The two opinions were Siamese twins, connected by a vital bond; separate them and you would kill them both. But Jesus gave a view of the resurrection and the future life totally different from the Apocalyptic one. He taught the *continuance* of life. His argument with the Sadducees proves that doctrine, or it amounts to nothing. God is the God not of the dead, but of the living. The Rich Man and Lazarus, of the parable, are already in a future state of retribution. He who believes on him has "already passed from death unto life." Jesus could not suppose that one who had

received from him the quickening of spiritual life could pass into the under-world, and grope as a shade in the intermediate state. "Whosoever liveth and believeth in him shall never die." Now, to one who is satisfied that Jesus was emancipated from the doctrine of an intermediate state, it must be evident that he could not have held the Apocalyptic notion resting on it of a raising of the dead at the coming of the Messiah, and could not have held to the visible coming of the Messiah who was to come to do that very thing.

The same observation is to be made of the judgment. Jesus shows himself emancipated from the common notion of the judgment, and of a future simultaneous judgment-day. He that believeth on him is not judged. He that believeth not is judged already, in that he has not believed in the only-begotten Son of God. God sent him not to judge or to punish the world, but to save it. The judgment of the world is not to be exclusively at a remote day. It has begun. It is *now*. Christ says, Now is the judgment of this world; now is the Prince of this world to be cast out; now, when Jesus is about to consummate by dying the moral means of that result. Jesus is not to be a personal Judge of men at a remote time. His principles are for ever to judge men, to judge them finally. Not himself as the personal Logos, or as the reappearing Messiah, is to judge men, but "the word he has spoken." These thoughts in the fourth Gospel must have come from Jesus, not from the writer, who shows himself in places not emancipated from the view of his time.

3. The doctrine of Christ's expectation which I am considering is not congruous with the means which he contemplates for accomplishing his work, and with the

view he took of the progress of his kingdom, and of the moral duties and retributions of Humanity. Nothing is clearer than that his kingdom of God was to be a communion of men on earth bound together by the same consciousness of the heavenly Father. It was to extend into another life. But it was to spread more and more widely, and subdue the world to his spiritual dominion. By moral influence he is to be King. This communion is to be the salt of the earth, the light of the world. It is to extend its influence by holy example, by good works. He will be in spirit with the apostles and with his church. He trains them to carry on his work, and tells them to preach the good news to all nations. He does this as if founding a work which shall go on indefinitely. He declares early, in a discourse designed to explain his kingdom, that the law shall not pass away; that it shall in its moral requirements be all realized. Heaven and earth shall not pass away until all shall *be*. And he directs his disciples to pray as much as for daily bread that God's kingdom may come, and that God's will may be done *on earth* as it is done in heaven. Is it possible that this teacher expects all this to be closed in thirty or forty years, by a violent catastrophe, and by the substituting of a universal miracle for this moral instrumentality? He says it is not the Father's will that one of the lowliest shall perish. Did he mean to limit the opportunity of salvation for the race to forty years, and to consign to the torment of Gehenna all who did not accept the new truth in that time? And all this impossibility is heightened by the nature of some of those parables in which he treated of his kingdom. "If the kingdom of God were to be established by an irresistible miracle, on a fixed day, in a manner so splendid, what signify those admirable parables of the mustard-seed, of the leaven, of the net, of the grain growing from itself, which suppose a development, slow, regular, organic, proceeding from an imperceptible point, but endowed with a Divine vitality, and displaying successively its latent energies?"[1] Besides, no one ever more strictly enjoined the duties of life, the everlasting obligations. He contemplates such duties as are to be done in such a world as ours was then and is now, as the essential sphere in which the heavenly spirit must be formed in man. His principle of final judgment is, "Inasmuch as ye have done the duties of Humanity unto your fellow-men, ye have done them unto me. Come, ye blessed of my Father." Could that teacher suppose that the opportunity for performing such duties would cease for ever before the last of his apostles should have died? Could he think that within that time the destinies of Humanity as he knew it would be closed?

These are the principal reasons which determine me to believe that Jesus did not expect to return visibly to raise the dead, judge the world, and be the head of an external Theocratic kingdom on the renewed earth. What, then, shall be said of the language which appears to express that opinion? "Ye shall drink the wine new with me in my Father's kingdom." "Ye shall sit on thrones judging the twelve tribes of Israel," &c. Two considerations are to be kept in sight in establishing the views and expectations of Jesus: first, that he used this language — so far as he used it — in a figurative sense, to represent spiritual and providential facts as he conceived

[1] Réville, Review of Renan's Life of Jesus.

them; second, that the evangelists may have sometimes given to his language a precision and a connection which did not belong to it, as delivered. That he could not have employed this language as it is reported to us, in its literal and proper sense, is to my mind a necessary conviction in the premises. This would suppose that he entertained two orders of conceptions, which were opposed to one another, with a clear profound conviction, and gave them as revelations of God: one his spiritual and rational beliefs; the other his Apocalyptic beliefs. This supposition is the vice of Renan's seventeenth chapter. The language of the Apocalyptic beliefs Jesus might use to some extent as a vehicle for conveying the spiritual and rational to others; and the most explicit language in which he conveyed his spiritual beliefs, so far as it was retained in their feebler minds, might be forced into harmony with their traditional opinions. But that in Jesus' mind, so original, so manifestly filled with fresh thought on every theme of Providence and man, these spiritual apprehensions of a kingdom or communion of God which should act under and within the state, renovating human life and society; of a Messiah who by such a kingdom should fulfil the missionary function of Israel to the race of man; of a resurrection which should be the uninterrupted continuance of the blessed life, or an immediate renewal of the sense of wasted opportunity and law violated on earth; of a judgment both immediate and continual of every soul despising the truth revealed to it; of a retribution to civil societies according to Divine law, — should arise as original conceptions, be held with firm decisive grasp, be of the essence of his instruction, and so pronounced in him that our most advanced modern thought is but the distant echo of his profound and distinct enunciations; and that at the same time he should hold those Apocalyptic traditions, of a visible coming, of a Theocratic throne before whose splendor that of Cæsar would fade away, of a simultaneous resurrection and judgment, — hold them in unimpaired conviction, as truths to be solemnly insisted upon as a part of his revelation, — this, it seems to me, comes as near a psychological contradiction as we can well conceive. And besides, if Jesus had clung to those beliefs as Divine convictions, the language ascribed to him would have had the unity of that of the Epistles and the Apocalypse on this subject. We should not be perplexed with apparent contradictions. As it is, we are obliged to use those words which inculcate his spiritual thought for explaining that part of his language which is conformed to Jewish conceptions.

But, it is said, this language would naturally create misunderstanding, and that it is too bold to be taken in a figurative sense. In regard to the misunderstanding of it, let it be said, if we suppose a mind inspired by God to see far deeper and further than its contemporaries, it must be liable to be misunderstood in proportion to the poverty of the vernacular language. Jesus' inspiration and insight gave his speech a character such as the highest poetic endowment always gives, and made it bold. It is not to be forgotten that he belonged to the east and to the people who have given us the Old Testament prophecies. The boldest tropes were natural to him. In moments of strong moral excitement, they fly from him as sparks from the flint or lightning from the charged cloud It exposes him to the charge of mysticism. We forget that he was not a lecturer, a systematic teacher; but a prophet, a converser in the streets, a popular teacher, a poet sent from God to re-create humanity. Necessity concurred with inspiration to make his speech tropical and often liable to be misapprehended. He was obliged to use images and terms which the people and the schools applied to the Messiah in order to claim, as he meant to claim, a predetermined, providential connection with Hebrew history and hope. When he said to Pilate, "I am a king," it was a truth; but it was a trope. "I am the bread of life," — a truth, but a trope. "I am come to send a sword on the earth, not peace;" "This cup of wine is my blood sealing the new covenant," — truths, but compact with the boldest tropes. When he said, "I am the Messiah," it was a truth, but a trope. It was liable to be misunderstood; but, without it, it was impossible that he should be understood. He saw Satan, after the seventy returned from their mission and related their success, "falling like lightning from heaven." If he foresaw political revolutions which would occur within a generation, and believed they would be employed by Providence to further the establishment of his principles or kingdom, which would then reach a point from which it would be evident, to a sympathizing mind quick to catch the glimpses of a new day, that they would become dominant in humanity, would it be too bold a figure for him to say, "The coming of the Son of Man will be as the lightning which shoots from horizon to horizon," or too bold a figure to describe those precursive overturns and downfalls of the old in language borrowed from Isaiah and Joel, the prophets whom he loved and knew by heart? Might he not believe, identifying his religion and the Divine spirit which would spread it, that at the time of these changes, conspiring providentially with the labors of apostles and evangelists, his voice would call the chosen, those prepared by mental and moral affinity, to the new life-work, to the new order of things; that his call to his own would be like the supposed call of the last trumpet summoning them to come into a spiritual communion of blessed work, and blessed hope? These figures were naturally, almost inevitably, formed in these circumstances.

He used the language given him in the speech of his time in a figurative sense, partly because of the want of proper terms suited to his purpose, and partly because as a popular teacher, desirous to impress the common mind, he could not sacrifice all the associations connected with that. But we often find in proximity with it words of his own, or something in the occasion, which he might expect to constrain the listeners to reflect that he was speaking figuratively; as John vi., "My words, they are spirit and they are life," and the reply Luke xxii. 38, to the information, here are two swords, "It is enough." Were the accounts more full, it is fair to suppose we might have more such expressions. They would not be so likely to be remembered as the striking, figurative words.

There are words of Christ at the Last Supper which seem to me to have occasioned quite unnecessary perplexity. "I say unto you I will not henceforth drink of the fruit of the vine until that day when I drink it new with you in my Father's kingdom." They were the spontaneous outflow of mingled sadness, affection, and hope. He might expect them to be interpreted to his disciples by his situation, by all he had said of leaving them, and by his habit of conveying spiritual thought under the sensuous images suggested by the moment. They referred to the kingdom he died to establish. They were as natural as to say, "Where two or three are gathered together in my name, there am I in the midst of them." But they have been a stumbling-block to students whom we should have expected to be able better to *orient* themselves in the Master's genius and style.

Colani has spent a page to ridicule it, and show that it is not fit for its place.[1] Yet a similar figure is used by occidental preachers, who would not expect to be reproached for coarseness. A young minister on an occasion not unlike that on which Jesus sat with his disciples — occurring as did that passover in the midst of sacrifice and revolution, the Thanksgiving day celebrated after the close of our great war, in our land at once so afflicted and so blessed — addressed his hearers, some of whom had lost sons or brothers in camp or field, in figurative but very appropriate and touching language, in which we may suppose he felt the inspiration of his Master's words at the last meal. It was to the effect that, although those who had fallen in the strife could no more partake with us in the bounty with which the Thanksgiving table would be spread, they would in all future festivals be with us in spirit, and rejoice in the blessings ever more and more to be realized which had been purchased by their sacrifices for our disinthralled country.

Nor do I see any better cause of the offence which is taken at the language ascribed to Jesus in Matt. xix. 28, in the offer of thrones: "In the regeneration, when the Son of Man shall sit on the throne of his glory, ye also

[1] Jesus Christ and the Messianic Beliefs of his Time.

shall sit on twelve thrones judging the twelve tribes of Israel." Let us think how Jesus must have longed to communicate his thought and his hope to those chosen ones; how he would not be willing to drive them away by his very greatness as he sometimes drove away the careless and cavilling; how his mind, if he were a human being and not an automaton, would alternate between the sternest truth-speaking and the necessity of coming closer to them, and giving them hope, and lifting them a little nearer to himself; how like the mother bird, enticing her brood to their first flight, and finding he had at one moment gone beyond them, he would come back, and alight on a point nearer to their apprehension, that he might tempt them to use the untried pinions of their thought, — and we need have no difficulty in seeing that he meant thrones of moral power. I do not know how those men received it; but I do not believe they thought then of political power. If, after Jesus left them, they recalled this and every other such expression as a means of nourishing the hope of an Apocalyptic return and kingdom, the great Teacher and Comforter was not accountable for that perversion.

Jesus' language, then, can be explained without supposing him to have expected visibly to return after death to erect a kingdom of God of which he should be the visible head.

The result of our inquiries is, that Jesus did not aim at any political sovereignty, that he rose by the force of the special endowment of his nature above the Apocalyptic superstition of his age, and that he looked and labored immediately for the moral and spiritual renovation of humanity on this earth. He claimed to be a Messiah;

not a Messiah after the Jewish conceptions, but a man anointed and endowed of God, to perfect by the manifestation of the Divine in the human, the means of this moral renovation of humanity. He regarded the spiritual Messiahship as a divinely appointed means to this end. He aspired to spiritual rule for no end but this, and his aspiration was disinterested, godlike. It has been said that he was ambitious, though it is allowed that his ambition was the most elevated. And he has been compared with disadvantage to Socrates, whose ambition, it is said, was "*to serve without reigning,*" while that of Jesus was "*to reign by serving,*" and the former is justly thought to be the nobler purpose. It is no time to institute a comparison between Jesus and Socrates. I have no wish to disparage the great Pagan. I will allow Grote's estimate, that the Apology as given by Plato is the speech of one who deliberately foregoes the immediate purpose of a defence, the persuasion of his judges; who speaks for posterity without regard to his own life. The aim of Socrates was disinterested, but not so elevated as that of Jesus. The aim of Socrates belonged to the realm of the understanding; the aim of Jesus, to the realm of the Spirit. They both took delight in the exercise of their gift: this is innocent, when not an exclusive motive; but Socrates more consciously sought this delight than Jesus. No self-abnegation can be conceived more entire than that of the Christ as represented by the evangelists with every mark of truth. He sought to reign only as all seek to reign who put forth their powers to assist the development of other minds. He would reign only so, and so far, as this might be to serve his race. He had no ambition. His purpose was not *to reign by serving,* but *to reign that he might serve.* He respected the freedom of the mind. He appealed to reason and conscience. He claimed authority in the name of reason and conscience, and believed that he thus claimed it in the name of God. And if his reign has been more extensive, more durable, and more beneficent than that of others, it is because he has acted by the highest kind and with the largest measure of truth and life, on the highest powers and tendencies of man.

Cambridge: Press of John Wilson and Son.

www.ingramcontent.com/pod-product-compliance
Lightning Source LLC
Chambersburg PA
CBHW031903220426
43663CB00006B/748